D0898938

LIVING DANGEROUSLY

living
DANGEROUSLY

ON THE MARGINS IN MEDIEVAL
AND EARLY MODERN EUROPE

edited by

Barbara A. Hanawalt

and

Anna Grotans

University of Notre Dame Press
Notre Dame, Indiana

HN11
.L58
2007

Copyright © 2007 by University of Notre Dame
Notre Dame, Indiana 46556
www.undpress.nd.edu
All Rights Reserved

0129956006

Designed by Wendy McMillen
Set in 10.4/13.5 Adobe Minion by BookComp, Inc.
Printed on 55# Nature's Recycle Paper in the U.S.A. by Versa Press, Inc.

Manufactured in the United States of America

Library of Congress Cataloging-in-Publication Data

Living dangerously : on the margins in Medieval and early modern
Europe / edited by Barbara A. Hanawalt and Anna Grotans.
  p.   cm.
Includes index.
ISBN-13: 978-0-268-03082-7 (pbk. : alk. paper)
ISBN-10: 0-268-03082-0 (pbk. : alk. paper)
1. Social history—Medieval, 500–1500.   2. Marginality, Social—Europe—
History.   3. Crime—Europe—History.   4. Middle Ages.   5. Civilization,
Medieval.   6. Europe—History—476–1492.   I. Hanawalt, Barbara.
II. Grotans, Anna A., 1961–
  HN11.L58   2007
  305.5'609409024—dc22   2007020096

♻ *This book printed on recycled paper.*

Contents

CHAPTER 5

IAN FREDERICK MOULTON

CHAPTER 6

MARY LINDEMANN

Acknowledgments

In the course of preparing this volume for publication, we have had the invaluable assistance of James Bennett, Susanne Childs, Valerie Emanoil, Henry Griffy, and Elizabeth Zimmerman of the Center for Medieval and Renaissance Studies at The Ohio State University. We thank them for their meticulous work and efficiency in seeing this project to its end. We also owe our gratitude to Barbara Hanrahan and her staff at the University of Notre Dame Press. The Center for Medieval and Renaissance Studies at The Ohio State University initiated the series under the leadership of Nicholas Howe. We dedicate this volume to him.

Introduction

BARBARA A. HANAWALT

Living dangerously, or living on the margins, in medieval and early modern Europe holds considerable fascination. Marginals have been identified as including the poor, people of low status, and lawbreakers. Bronislaw Geremek, in his study of the low life of Paris, lumped all marginals into one class. They were not only people and groups who fell outside the social and economic mainstream, but they also formed an underclass that rendezvoused in taverns and other gathering places.[1] While some of the essays in this book look at the poor or at a criminal underclass, this definition of marginality is far too narrow. It has a structural limitation in that it presumes that only social outcasts will be on the margins of society. The essays in this book portray people living dangerously and on the edges, but they are marginal for many reasons. Poverty and crime may put people into the margins, but not all of the people considered in these essays are poor or criminal. Indeed, medieval and early modern society could express some sympathy for those who fell into want and need. Some marginals were from religious groups persecuted by the dominant state- and church-supported religion. Here one thinks of the Beguines, Moriscos, and Jews. Others were wealthy traders of the seventeenth century who took advantage of the burgeoning speculative markets and fraud. Women could fall into the class of marginal because of their knowledge of the occult or even their sexual or spiritual independence.

Simply because these people or groups were marginal in medieval and early modern society does not mean that they were of no social use, as Geremek would argue. Indeed, a symbiotic relationship often existed between marginals and the social establishment. The dominant culture needed the services of marginals for their own purposes. The mainstream found the margins a place for thrills and titillation—a place to live dangerously—to have sex, to engage in petty crime, or to commit major fraud. The authors show that the exemplars of bad behavior were very useful for setting off good behavior. A German author of romance forgives his hero for his confessed seduction of the king's daughter and lets him win a trial by ordeal so that this social climber can marry the princess. The author praises his hero's otherwise excellent moral character by letting him achieve his upwardly mobile aspirations. The seventeenth- and eighteenth-century moralists who criticized those who traded in false bills of exchange developed a language for praising honest mercantilism. Critics of princes and popes used satire, heavily laden with the imagery of sodomy, to attack their victims. Some marginals (cunning women mostly) sold love potions, herbal cures, spells for getting rid of evil, concoctions to encourage marriage, and so on to respectable people willing to pay. The beggar also had his or her value in the spiritual economy, given the Gospels' message that those who gave alms to the poor would find their passage to heaven made smoother. The very act of giving charity might enhance the social status of the wealthy and bring public recognition and acclaim to the donor. Spiritual comfort was also available on the margins of society, if one thinks of heresies or the many spiritual services that the Beguines practiced, including washing the dead.

The margins in many ways functioned as a safety valve for society. Even the respectable might move into this ambiguous space and place when necessity demanded. Medieval and early modern society was tolerant of those outside the mainstream until they came to the attention of authorities or until the public became frightened of personal violence or began to feel that their space was somehow polluted by the presence of marginals. The local, neighborhood beggar was a figure of pity and charity, but when the population of Europe began to move around in the fifteenth century and to flood the cities, urban and royal authorities began to promulgate laws against "sturdy beggars," who were disruptive and unproductive. The Beguines were marginalized by the Fourth Lateran Council of 1215, which barred the creation of new religious orders. When Marguerite Porete, a Beguine, refused to bow to official censure, she came to the attention of the Inquisition. When two Parisian prostitutes moved from being involved in the sex trade to being accused of murder, they were burned at the stake. Satirists who made accusations of sodomy against powerful political figures ended up in prison or exile.

Another theme that runs through the essays in this book is that a traditional tolerance for those living dangerously and outside the normal constraints of society began to change in the later Middle Ages as the power of the central state grew stronger. Misbehavior, deviance, and escape into the world of marginals was more acceptable when it was a matter of local control, but as the state began to extend its laws into the hinterland and local officials began to lose power to state bureaucrats and law enforcers, the degree of tolerance decreased. When it was unified under Ferdinand and Isabella, Spain moved from being the religiously tolerant society that it had been in the Middle Ages to being a persecuting society. The centralized tools of the state and the army in conjunction with the Church were employed in the persecution of Jews and Muslims and ultimately drove them out of Spain.

Not only changes in the state, but also changes in religion, made a difference in toleration in the sixteenth and seventeenth centuries. Lutheranism, Calvinism, and the newly reformed Catholic Church imposed stricter moral standards on members and on society as a whole. Again, the latitude allowed to those living on the margins was curtailed. Sodomy, seldom mentioned in the Middle Ages, became illegal, risky, and more publicized. Gypsies were harassed, and even Muslims and Jews in Spain who had converted to Catholicism were held in suspicion. Seventeenth-century speculators were condemned as being unfit for the sober and serious business of governing the new Protestant republics.

Richard Firth Green, in "'Nede ne hath no lawe': The Plea of Necessity in Medieval Literature and Law," explores a famous proverb that appears in *Piers Plowman*. The character of Need explains that when clothing and sustenance are lacking, then it is all right to take what is necessary. In the countryside, where food could be in short supply and devastating famines were not uncommon, need was often looked upon by Langland's contemporaries as an excuse for begging and petty theft. Need was also an excuse for a messenger to take a shortcut across a field of standing grain. The maxim *necessitas non habet legem* appeared in at least the thirteenth century to defend acts that were either excusable or justifiable. Green traces the various cases and legal tracts in medieval law in which the dictum moves beyond literature and is explicitly applied. Extreme poverty was an excuse for petty theft. By the seventeenth and eighteenth centuries, criminal acts committed out of private need disappear almost entirely, but the plea of public necessity became more frequent. The first reference to this that Green identifies dates from the early seventeenth century, when James I argued for the crown's need to mine saltpeter on private land. The shift away from *nede ne hath no lawe* also appears in handbooks for justices of the peace in the eighteenth century. The move toward state enforcement of law privileged the state and left behind the charitable interpretation of "need" that one finds in Langland. The niche for petty theft in order to survive disappears.

Medieval society was one of social change, with some people rising through the ranks and others falling into poverty. Vickie Ziegler in "Upward Mobility in the German High Middle Ages: The Ascent of a Faithful Liar" talks about the ordeal in Konrad von Würzburg's *Engelhard*, a late thirteenth-century poem. The poem, perhaps addressed to a socially ambitious urban audience in Basel, shows that the upwardly mobile were also a marginal group who desired to move into the ranks of nobility but found their way blocked by tradition and inherited titles. Engelhard, offspring of poor nobility, has very good qualities but lacks possessions to advance himself sufficiently to marry the king's daughter. But he moves into the position of the king's most trusted servant. He is a brilliant knight, has solid judgment, and above all is faithful to the king's service. Engelhard not only wins over the king, but also succeeds in seducing the princess. Found in a compromising position with her by the king's nephew, he must fight a duel. Although Engelhard acknowledges the truth of his seduction, Konrad has him win the duel, thus allowing the aspiring Engelhard to increase his social standing and marry the princess. The faithful service Engelhard rendered the king is rewarded. Social margins and laws were permeable in romance by the thirteenth century.

Dyan Elliott's "Women in Love: Carnal and Spiritual Transgressions in Late Medieval France" moves us to marginalization based on gender, occupation, social groups, sorcery, and sexuality. She gives a background to living dangerously by exploring what we mean by the canny (known, normal) and the uncanny (unknown, occult). It is the uncanny that gets marginalized. The Fourth Lateran Council of 1215 attempted to regulate both the formation of marriages and to forestall the creation of new religious orders. Nonprocreative sex (including prostitution), though always forbidden, was newly stigmatized, as was the pursuit of a religious life outside an approved order (i.e., the Beguines). To explore these two marginal groups in more detail,

Elliott has looked at the case of Margot de la Barre, a prostitute, who ended up in the Châtelet, the Parisian prison, in 1390 for practicing sorcery to help a fellow prostitute, Marion La Droiturière, to secure a man's love. Reading the case closely, she shows how the accused prostitutes, eventually burned for sorcery, tried to understand their interrogators' wishes and make their testimony conform to their expectations. Equally alien to the spirit of regulation that directed the Fourth Lateran Council was the Beguine mystic, Marguerite Porete. The three women—two sinners and one religious woman—were single and not under patriarchal protection, a precarious position for a woman to be in throughout the Middle Ages. Further, Marguerite Porete's book, *The Mirror of Simple Souls,* was burned by the Church. The book was an erotic invocation to love of the divine, perhaps even with lesbian overtones. Marginal women, even single women and prostitutes, could be tolerated in the society, but when they became too obvious to authorities, they were penalized.

Anne J. Cruz's essay, "Gendering the Disenfranchised: Down, Out, and Female in Early Modern Spain," continues the story that Elliott has begun of suspicion of women but adds the categories of Gypsy and Morisca to make the marginalization even greater. Renaissance Spain, of course, used the Inquisition to eliminate Moriscos and harass Gypsies, but these marginal groups, as Cruz shows, also performed useful functions for the society. Cruz explores the heroine of Miguel de Cervantes's novella *La gitanella* (*The Little Gipsy Girl*) as having a contradictory, double role: she is both a chaste Gypsy and a vagabond virgin. As such, Cervantes can use her as a foil to investigate and expose aristocratic Spanish society compared to Gypsies. While Cervantes regards Gypsies as past masters in the art of thieving, his heroine, who turns out to be a noble girl stolen and raised by Gypsies, demonstrates that they also have some virtues. Cruz places the novella in the historical context of sixteenth-century Spain. Inquisition records show that, like Parisian prostitutes, Gypsy women were accused of sorcery for making love potions. They and other marginalized women were a threat to society. Moriscas suffered from similar accusations, in addition to those related to their adherence to Islam. Sexuality and irreverence toward Christianity alone did not lead these women into conflicts with the law—they too were skilled at healing and at potions. She concludes that these marginal women were not only victims of patriarchy, but they also subverted it to their own ends.

Gender and sexuality played a large role in the early modern period. As Ian Frederick Moulton points out in "Sodomy and the Lash: Sexualized

Satire in the Renaissance," sex and sexual subjects, particularly sodomy, became a way of satirizing and talking about taboo subjects, such as politics and religion. Sodomy, Moulton observes, was punishable by law, but it was not regarded as effeminate, as it would be in the modern world. Indeed, courting women was viewed as more feminizing than buggery. References to sodomy were common in John Donne, Ben Jonson, and Thomas Nashe when they wished to make fun of political figures and personal enemies. The English satirists, however, were not nearly as explicit in their invocation of sex in general and sodomy in particular as were the Italian models that they admired. Popes and the papal court were ripe for the sexual innuendos of these Italians. But, as Moulton shows, Antonio Vignali's *La Cazzaria* (*The Book of the Prick*), written in the mid-1520s, went further than any other text in linking sexual aggression with criticism of politics. Vignali's works, however, were too explicit even for the Renaissance acceptance of raunchy humor. The use of sodomy for satire could be dangerous for authors. Nicolò Franco was tortured and executed; Pietro Aretino was stabbed and driven from Rome; Nashe fled London after his satirical play, *The Isle of Dogs,* was performed; and Jonson, Nashe's collaborator, was imprisoned.

Leaving the free use of sexual humor to the social and political critics of the Italian and English Renaissance, we move into the world of northern European republics and serious social and economic commentary in Mary Lindemann's "The Wind Traders: Speculators and Frauds in Northern Europe, 1650–1720." The new capitalist economy had given rise to instruments such as stocks and bills of exchange that could be stolen and forged. Many speculators lived very much on the economic edge, and their inflation of the market hurt the more honest dealers. These marginals were certainly not the lower classes, but rather were people who lived dangerously, either at the center of trade or on its peripheries. The boundaries between the honest trader and the scoundrel blurred, as critics were quick to point out. Rather than talking about sodomy, the playwrights and pamphleteers of the eighteenth century spoke of men going "mad," of "playing," of being "wind traders." Between 1650 and 1720 the discourse that developed around speculation was used to criticize political, moral, and mercantile faults alike. The case of the South Sea Company in England, which was universally called "hokus-bokus," was particularly egregious, leading to the South Sea Bubble. The underlying problem, however, was a deeper one, because it commented upon the ability of these traders/speculators to be citizens and to govern soberly the wealthy republics of northern Europe.

The authors in this volume have explored a number of different texts and contexts that show us how various people in the medieval and early modern periods lived dangerously and on the margins of society. We have traversed considerable territory in these essays, moving from the concept of "need" permitting theft when a person faces starvation to the condemnation of scoundrels of the mercantile economy who used false bills of exchange to defraud honest people. Sometimes the marginals were victims of forces larger than themselves, as were the Beguines, Gypsies, and Moriscos. At other times the actors, such as the Renaissance satirist, sought out dangerous adventures for the excitement and challenges they provided. Marguerite Porete felt that she had a greater truth than the Church in her embracing of divine love and went out of her way to preach her views. The essays show us two sides of the coin. People at large found those on the outskirts of respectable and honest society useful at times, but at other times they found this demiworld threatening and too dangerous to tolerate. The volume offers a rich and diverse picture of marginals seeking regulation of their lives in order to avoid danger; flirting with the possibility of death to express their ideas and beliefs; offering their skills for a price; and looking for wrongful gain, but not out of need.

NOTE

1. Bronislaw Geremek, *The Margins of Society in Late Medieval Paris,* trans. Jean Birrell (Polish ed., 1971; French ed., 1976; Cambridge: Cambridge University Press, 1987).

"Nede ne hath no lawe"

The Plea of Necessity in Medieval Literature and Law

RICHARD FIRTH GREEN

The opening scene of the final apocalyptic passus of *Piers Plowman* (in both the B and C versions) finds Will heavy-cheered, ailing of heart, and, above all, hungry: "for y ne wiste where to ete ne at what place."[1] Shortly before noon, he encounters a character called Need, who berates him for not simply helping himself to the necessities of life:

> Couthest thow nat excuse the, as dede the kyng and oþere,
> That thow toke to lyue by, to clothes and to sustinaunce,
> Was bi techyng and bi tellyng of *Spiritus temperancie*
> And þat thow nome no more then nede the tauhte?
> > (*PPl.* C.22:6–9)

The odd reference to the king is explained by a cynical comment at the end of the previous passus:

> And yf me lakketh to lyue by, þe lawe wol þat y take hit
> Ther y may hastilokest hit haue, for y am heed of lawe.
> > (*PPl.* C.21:468–69)

The next few lines of his speech are introduced by a proverb and seem intended to rehearse received wisdom.

> And nede ne hath no lawe nor neuere shal falle in dette
> For thre thynges þat he taketh his lyf for to saue:
> That is mete, when men hym werneth for he no money weldeth,
> Ne wyght þat now wol be his borwe ne no wed hath to legge;
> And he cacche in þat caes and com therto by sleithe
> He synegeth nat sothlich þat so wynneth hys fode.
> And thow he come so to a cloth, and can no bettere cheuesaunce,
> Nede anoen-riht nymeth hym vnder maynprise.
> And yf hym lust for to lape the lawe of kynde wolde
> That he dronke at vch a dysch ar he deye for furste.
> So nede at greet nede may nyme as for his owne
> Withouten consail of Conscience or cardinale vertues,
> So that he sewe and saue *Spiritus Temperancie.*
>
> (*PPl.* C.22:10–22)

Need spends twelve lines extolling Temperance as the greatest of the four cardinal virtues (23–34) and concludes his speech with sixteen lines praising need in terms normally applied to the life of patient poverty, lived as an *imitatio Christi.*

The character of Need and the sentiments he expresses have been the subject of much critical debate over the past half century. Robert Frank and Morton Bloomfield laid out the battle lines. "Need's speech," wrote Frank, "is really a warning against the life of need. Need puts man outside the laws of property and morality, outside the guidance of conscience and the cardinal virtues. It makes man lawless."[2] "Need," retorted Bloomfield, "is the determinant of superfluity, the crucial issue in man's humanity to man.... Need attempts to bring to the stumbling hero of the poem a sense of order which can be determined only by need."[3] Over the years, Frank's position has won considerably more converts than Bloomfield's,[4] and probably the most frequently cited supporter of it has been Robert Adams, who adduces two medieval biblical glosses (Gregory's on Job 41:13 and Bernard's on Psalm 90:5–6) to argue that Langland's Need should be read as both the Psalmist's "noonday demon" and Job's harbinger of the Antichrist.[5] What all Need's detractors seem to be agreed on is that Langland used him as a vehicle for satirizing the friars and their hypocritical creed of voluntary poverty. At least two critics, Pamela Gradon and Lawrence M. Clopper, have even gone so far as to argue that need *is* a friar, though the text offers no explicit support for such a view.[6] As a result, begging, which is barely mentioned in the passage—indeed, if we take the word *byde* in the phrase "to byde and to be nedy" (at line 48) as meaning "to endure" rather than "to beg," it is not mentioned at all[7]—has been discussed at length, whereas the more prominent question of justifiable theft has been very little explored.

By and large, those for whom Langland's Need is a pejorative quality have had trouble with this aspect of the maxim *nede ne hath no lawe*. Though they concede that churchmen, friars and antimendicants alike, preached that it was lawful for those in extreme destitution to take what they needed in order to keep themselves alive, these critics cannot quite bring themselves to believe that Langland himself can really have been endorsing such a position. As we have seen, Robert Frank thought that Need "makes man lawless." For Mary Carruthers, "Need's argument, baldly stated, is a justification for stealing,"[8] while for Robert Adams, Need advocates "the casual acceptance of theft."[9] Plainly, such readers are disturbed by Need's advice, but even those, like Penn Szittya, who adopt a more level tone are clearly surprised by it. Need's "most startling claim," according to Szittya, is "that the needy man is entitled to take what he needs."[10] Very few of these critics seem prepared to lend much weight to the fact that the narrator, Will, encounters this figure outside his dreams, that he meets him at a time when he is hungry, and thus, in a quite literal sense, that the need he is confronting is his own.

What I wish to argue here is that Need's claim would not have seemed at all startling to Langland's own audience, that the issue was not restricted to the abstruse realms of theological speculation, and that it would have had immediate and practical implications in his day. Though "nede ne hath no lawe" has been variously described as a proverb and as a legal maxim, Langland certainly seems to be treating it as a basic legal tenet here. Moreover his references to the "borwe" and "wed" that were a standard feature of traditional contract procedure and to the "maynprise" of the king's courts suggest that he is thinking primarily of everyday secular justice, not some abstract ideal of natural law. Though it is true that Need does at one point turn to the "lawe of kynde" for justification, this should not be taken to imply that he is invoking the academic jurisprudence of natural law. As Jill Mann has recently shown, he is simply invoking the principle of economic fairness, by which everyone is entitled to a share in the gifts of nature bestowed on us by God.[11] Customary law readily acknowledged the primacy of such a "lawe of kynde": a fifteenth-century custumal from Winchelsea, for instance, renders *iura naturalia* as "the laws of natural reason, upon the which and of the which do proceed and are founded all the laws and customs according unto the laws of England,"[12] and a French custumal (from Bordeaux) gives *rason naturau* precedence over civil law within the town's jurisdiction.[13]

The impression that Langland is concerned with everyday secular law is confirmed by a second appearance of the same maxim in a passage from the C text, which has no equivalent in B. Here, Rechelesse, a figure of questionable authority, compares the legal liability of a messenger who trespasses on a wheat field with that of a merchant:

> Thogh the messager make his way amydde the fayre whete
> Wol no wys man be wroth ne his wed take—
> > *necessitas non habet legem*—
> Ne non haiward is hote his wed for to taken.
> Ac if the marchaunt make his way ouer menne corne
> And þe hayward happe with hym for to mete,
> Oþer his hatt or his hoed or ellis his gloues
> The marchaunt mote forgo or moneye of his porse,
> And ȝut be ylette, as y leue, for the lawe asketh
> Marchauntz for here marchaundyse in many place to tolle.
> > (*PPl.* C.13:42–50)

Whether the suggestion is, as Derek Pearsall claims in his edition, "that the messenger, because he has no money to pay the fine, commits no offense in breaking the law," or whether, as Walter W. Skeat (correctly, I believe) has it, that "messengers were sometimes privileged, and might take a short cut without trespass" (i.e., the necessity to make good time exempted them from some forms of legal liability),[14] it is evident that we are again dealing here with the nuts and bolts of customary process (in this case the jurisdiction of the village hayward).

Langland's claim that necessity of some kind (either hunger, or poverty, or urgent business) puts one beyond the reach of the law is expressed with particular starkness a few lines later:

> The messager aren this mendenantz þat lyuen by menne almesse,
> Beth nat ybounde as beth ȝe ryche to bowe to þe lawes.
> > (*PPl.* C.13:78–79)

Unfortunately this reading is not entirely secure. In his 1978 edition of the C text Pearsall apparently supplied the word *bowe* to fill a blank left in his copy text (MS X). If so, he must have rejected the variant readings of the four other MSS he consulted: "boþ þe two lawes" (P), "boþe two lawes" (U), "boþe þe lawes" (J), "boþe to þe lawes" (T). Skeat had adopted the first of these four readings in 1873,[15] while George Russell and George Kane were to adopt the second in their 1997 edition of the C text.[16] What must have looked like an ingenious but unattested conjecture when Pearsall made it in 1978, however, can now be shown to have manuscript support (it is the reading of MS N), and on the grounds of sense, syntax (the next line continues with a series of three infinitives: "to lene . . . to lerne . . . to faste"), and as the *durior lectio* that explains the form "to bothe two the lawes," which appears in a total of eight MSS (not to mention the X scribe's uncertainty), it seems to me superior. Moreover, as we have seen, Langland is quite prepared to argue elsewhere that there *are* circumstances under which those in need are not bound to bow to the laws, so that there is a strong prima facie case for accepting N's unique reading here. Yet so foreign to modern notions of justice is the idea that anyone, let alone the poor, should be exempt from the operations of the law that Russell and Kane have chosen to reject Pearsall's reading, without even according it the dignity of a counterargument.

In order to understand why readers of Langland have been so reluctant to accept his claim that extreme need justifies theft (or trespass), it might be instructive to consider briefly the later history of the plea of necessity at common law, a history that has both been shaped by and helped to shape changing social attitudes to poverty.

The two branches of the necessity defense at common law, public and private, have two quite distinct histories. In some respects each appears as a mirror image of the other, the plea of public necessity growing in proportion to the diminishing importance of the plea of private necessity and offering a striking, if somewhat disturbing, insight into the growth of the modern state. Excluding the vexed question of taxation, and leaving aside civil and canon law jurisprudence,[17] we can trace the plea of public necessity back to only the early seventeenth century, when James I employed it to argue for the crown's need to mine saltpeter on private land[18]—though, if Langland's account of the messenger that we have just looked at really means that such officers were exempt from local prosecution, its shadow history may be far older.[19] It has, however, gone from strength to strength, and with the tremendous explosion of administrative law in the second half of the twentieth century it has become a routine justification for state intrusion into the affairs of the individual: the petty bureaucrat who wants to build a four-lane highway through your backyard knows that he can always rely on a defense of public necessity should you feel inclined to object.

Private necessity, on the other hand, from promising beginnings has dwindled to almost nothing—occasionally cropping up in such recherché areas of maritime law as whether you have a right to harborage for your vessel in a storm, even against the wishes of the dock owner and at risk of damage to his private property (*Ploof v. Putnam* [1908]).[20] Its presence on the criminal side is somewhat easier to trace, however, and, as it happens, the leading cases in this area, *U.S. v. Holmes* (1842) and *Regina v. Dudley and Stephens* (1884), are also maritime cases—no doubt because seafarers, then as now, are particularly vulnerable to acts of God.[21] The authority of such cases has meant that under the criminal law necessity is now no longer admitted as a generally available defense. Only in very exceptional circumstances (one imagines, for instance that it might have been available to Peter Sellers in the film *Doctor Strangelove,* when he is forced to damage the property of the Coca-Cola Company of America in order to try to avert a nuclear war) can necessity be used to excuse a criminal act. Able seaman Alexander Holmes found himself in an overcrowded longboat when his ship, the *William Brown,* foundered after striking an iceberg while sailing from Liverpool to Philadelphia. Along with three or four other sailors, he appears to have thrown some fifteen passengers overboard in order, as he later claimed, to prevent the longboat from being swamped; he was eventually to find himself on trial for manslaughter in Philadelphia on the evidence of some of the surviving passengers (his fellow sailors, presumably equally culpable, having managed to avoid arrest). Despite an ably argued defense of necessity, the jury found him guilty (though with a recommendation of mercy), and he served six months of hard labor.[22]

The more famous *Dudley and Stephens Case* also involved survival in an open boat, but here the charge was murder. When the pleasure yacht the *Mignonette* foundered in the south Atlantic, her four-man crew managed to survive for nineteen days without food or water before the ship's boy, William Parker, was killed and eaten by the others. Such maritime cannibalism appears to have been fairly common in the nineteenth century, and Captain Tom Dudley, by all accounts a respectable and godfearing man, made no secret of his actions either upon being rescued or on his return to England. Indeed, he seems to have been genuinely surprised to find himself arrested for murder. Popular sentiment was certainly strongly on his side, and when he and his mate, Edwin Stephens, were sent to trial at the Exeter Assizes, it is doubtful that the local jury would have convicted them had it not been shamelessly browbeaten by the judge, Baron Huddleston, who was determined to have his precedent. Though sentenced to hang, they received a conditional pardon and were freed after six months in prison.[23] *Dudley and Stephens* is far from being the only cannibalism case in the nineteenth century. There was, for instance, Alferd Packer, "the Great American Anthropophaginian"—memorably admonished by a Colorado judge in 1883: "There was seven democrats in Hinsdale county, and you've ate five of them."[24] But none of these cases explored the necessity defense more thoroughly, or rejected it more conclusively, than *Dudley and Stephens.*

If *Dudley and Stephens* marked the effective end of the general application of the private necessity defense at common law, its beginnings are shrouded in mystery. No doubt because of the nature of the records, the earliest instances tend to occur on the civil rather that criminal side, and though the first case in which it was employed is sometimes said to be *Mouse's Case* in 1608 (a case in which a ship's passenger sued for the loss of goods jettisoned in a storm),[25] there is a far fuller discussion of it in Edmund Plowden's report of *Fogassa v. Reniger,* heard in the Court of Exchequer Chamber over half a century earlier.[26] It is here, nearly two hundred years after Langland began writing *Piers Plowman,* that we find the first recorded instance of the maxim *necessitas non habet legem* being used in an English courtroom.[27]

Fogassa, like *Mouse,* was a maritime case, and it too involved the jettison of cargo in a storm, though here it is the plaintiff who employs the plea of necessity (ironically, in light of its subsequent history) in an attempt to avoid the abusive application of administrative law. Antonio Fogassa was a Portuguese merchant who was caught in a storm in The Solent while making his way to Southampton with a cargo of green (unprocessed) woad. In order to prevent his ship, the *Sancta Maria de Togma,* from foundering, her master, Manuel Lopez, jettisoned about a third of this cargo, and thus lightened, Fogassa's vessel managed to make port safely. Now, under recent English statute law, merchants were required to declare the nature and quantity of their merchandise and pay full customs duty on it before bringing it ashore, but poor Fogassa could no longer be certain how much of his cargo remained on the ship. Accordingly he received permission, as he claimed, to land the remaining cargo and have it weighed before paying all the outstanding duty on it. No sooner had he done this than the customs officer, Robert Reniger, with the officiousness habitual to his kind, impounded 1,693 quintals (hundredweights) of his green woad on the grounds that it had been landed illegally and declared it forfeit to the king in the Court of Exchequer. Hardly surprisingly, Fogassa appealed. Reniger claimed that there had never been a proper contract between Fogassa and himself and that the strict letter of the law should be upheld. The appellant argued that whether there had been such a contract or not (and naturally he claimed that there had), the necessity forced upon him by a storm at sea should have exempted him from the effects of the law: "[I]f the ship had caught fire," Fogassa's counsel argues, "and he had thrown the woad on shore before arranging for or paying the customs duty he would have been excused because of the necessity of the matter; it happened here that the storm that arose at sea could not be resisted so that when they threw the woad out of the ship into the sea in order to save their lives and as a result could not know the precise amount remaining on board they ought not to be held liable for their lack of precision. . . . It seems to me that he defends himself well and that the rigor of the tempest should excuse the rigor of the law" (fol. 10a).

The hypothetical situations and actual precedents adduced to support this position cover a wide selection of analogous cases, from excusable homicide (as when one is forced to kill in self-defense) to the necessity of putting a benign construction on a statute that might otherwise have a harmful effect, but among those more immediately relevant to the present discussion, we find: innkeepers excused from reimbursing their guests for lost belongings that had been looted by an invading army (fol. 9b); prisoners forced, by their prison catching fire, to ignore a statute forbidding escape; a jury that disbands before reaching a decision "pur feare de vn grande tempest" (fol. 13b); friends and relatives of a madman forced to beat and bind him in order to prevent him doing damage; and a defendant prevented from making a court appearance by a flood (fol. 18b). Moreover, two examples, one from Roman history and the other from the New Testament, are adduced presumably to show that civil and canon law shared a similar view of necessity. Though starving beggars stealing the necessities of life and messengers taking shortcuts through standing corn are not directly mentioned, Fogassa's counsel, as I have said, does cite Langland's maxim *necessitas non habet legem:* "And this way of understanding and expounding laws is not a misreading or a distortion of them, but a way of tempering the rigor of the law. And we also see (as I've said) that necessity provides a good excuse in all laws and that all laws make allowance for necessity, for it is a common proverb that *necessitas non habet legem;* and therefore necessity provides a good excuse in our law and in every other law" (fol. 18b). *Fogassa's Case* was never formally decided (a writ of privy seal was sent to the Court of Exchequer ordering Fogassa's goods to be restored and the proceedings against him stayed). According to Edmund Plowden this writ was merely an expedient for saving the crown embarrassment, for an overwhelming majority of the senior judiciary would have found for the plaintiff had the trial ever come to issue.

When Fogassa's counsel cites the maxim *necessitas non habet legem,* however, he is introducing a significant new argument into his defense. Few people, then or now, would have had much difficulty with his claim that "necessity provides a good excuse in our law and in every other law" or with its implication that the law's primary job is to decide how much weight should be given to such an excuse in any specific case (none in the case of *Dudley and Stephens,* for example; a great deal in *Mouse's Case*). But it should be pointed out that the maxim *necessitas non habet legem* taken by itself does not merely excuse Fogassa's action, it also justifies it, and it is vital that we should appreciate this distinction.

The law has two ways of displacing blame from acts that in the normal course of things might be regarded as blameworthy. It can choose to consider circumstances that might be seen as mitigating or extenuating the actor's guilt in some way, or it can deny the very existence of guilt by arguing that some aspect of the act places it beyond the law's reach. The first of such acts it will label excusable, the second justifiable. Thus, an excusable act is one that, while remaining unquestionably illegal, may go unpunished because punishment would clearly serve no reasonable social or legal purpose. A justifiable act, on the other hand, is one that the law regards as blameless, however illegal in other circumstances. Thus, where homicide committed by the private citizen is always culpable (though, in cases involving, for example, self-defense, or extreme provocation, or mental instability, potentially excusable), that committed by the public executioner, say, or by the soldier on active service, is treated as justifiable, that is to say, lawful. Self-evidently, the law as a formal institution has little to tell us about such justifiable actions: the hangman will not have to defend his homicidal vocation in court, no jury will be asked to determine his guilt or innocence, no judge will be required to pass sentence upon him. Yet in some ways what the law treats as justifiable will tell us as much about the wider judicial and social culture within which it operates as what it is prepared to regard as excusable.

That *necessitas non habet legem* should be taken as justifying, not merely excusing, certain acts is clear from the work of the thirteenth-century common law jurist Henry Bracton. Three times, though each time in a very restricted context, Bracton cites this maxim in the significantly more explicit form, *quod alias non licitum esset necessitas faciat licitum.* One concerns circumstances that justify a sheriff's distraining the lands or chattels of a defendant under a writ of *quare impedit* in order to force him to appear in court within the appointed time: "Now, however, for good reason and of necessity, since what would not otherwise be lawful necessity makes so [quod alias non licitum esset necessitas faciat licitum] we must proceed more speedily because of the shortness of time."[28] The other two concern situations where the intent of the law might otherwise be frustrated by a technical restriction: on a widow's holding in dower a manor that was the head of a barony, in one case (2:269); and on a plaintiff's swearing out a writ of entry beyond a set time limit in the other (4:44). In these last two, the necessity plea almost appears to act as a primitive substitute for an equitable remedy and as such implies that it may once have had a far wider application than its later history might suggest. This impression is confirmed by an even earlier example of the maxim *quod alias non licitum,* one that, directly or indirectly, may well have been Bracton's source: the very last of the decretals of Gregory IX (1227–41).[29] In a slightly variant form, *quod non est licitum lege, necessitas facit licitum,* this maxim forms the fourth in a series of eleven general *regulae iuris* that are evidently meant to be understood as the fundamental tenets of canon law. The text cited in support of this particular one is Mark 2:27, "the sabbath was made for man not man for the sabbath," the rebuke Jesus gives the Pharisees who criticize him for allowing his disciples to pick ears of corn on the sabbath.[30] Clearly this is intended as a warning against the narrow and formalistic application of the law.

Though many Langland scholars seem to associate Need's maxim exclusively with the friars, its very first appearances (in Saint Bernard and in Gratian) actually predate Saint Francis, and both interestingly are used to justify tempering the rigid application of the law. Bernard uses it in the course of a discussion of why a prelate may not override the monk's vows of obedience: "a prelate may not forbid me any of those things I have vowed nor restrict them further than I have vowed. My vow may not be increased without my will nor diminished without absolute necessity. Necessity, indeed, has no law and on this account allows for a dispensation."[31] And Gratian, qualifying the point that the sacraments may be validly performed by simoniac priests, distinguishes between two kinds of sacraments: "alia sunt dignitatis, alia sunt necessitatis." The genuine penitent, he says, may always rely on the latter (those that are vital to salvation), "since necessity has no law but itself makes its own law."[32]

In the course of the thirteenth century, however, *necessitas non habet legem* seems to have become particularly associated with the question of whether those in extreme need were justified in taking the necessities of life. Saint Thomas Aquinas, citing yet a third variant of this maxim, *in casu extremae necessitatis omnia sunt communia,* supplies the classic statement of this position: "in cases of extreme necessity everything becomes common property. . . . Therefore a man in extreme need is entitled to take what belongs to another to keep himself alive."[33] He justifies this doctrine, as does Langland, by appealing to the law of nature.[34] By the fourteenth century this seems to have been standard Church teaching, appearing, as Thomas P. Dunning has pointed out,[35] in Holy Church's sermon at the very beginning of *Piers Plowman:*

> And þerfore he hiȝte þe erþe to helpe yow echone
> Of wollene, of lynnen, of liflode at nede
> In mesurable manere to make yow at ese.
>   (B.1:17–19)[36]

No doubt the friars were particularly effective publicists for such a position, but it could never have gained wide acceptance had it not been in tune with the temper of the times. Janet Coleman has argued that from the mid-twelfth century "a growing population, increasingly conscious of social stratification[,] . . . the transformation of agrarian structures, [and] the development of a money economy and urbanization" all combined to bring about "a new economic poverty" and that the thirteenth century, influenced by Saint Francis, witnessed the beginnings of a reevaluation of "practical attitudes to property and poverty." "Only by the thirteenth century," she writes, "could theft in the case of extreme necessity be morally condoned."[37] Moreover, that others than the friars recognized the validity of the necessity defense is quite clear from a remark in one of the London sermons of virulent antimendicant Richard FitzRalph (1357): "dici potest quia casus necessitatis non venit sub lege, sed intelligitur a lege exceptus" (it can be said that a case of necessity does not come under the law, but is understood as excepted from the law).[38]

FitzRalph here is quite explicit that necessity was to be regarded as the legal justification for certain actions and not merely as an excuse. We should hardly expect, however, that the niceties of such a distinction were always so clearly appreciated, and this was particularly so where the doctrine appears in the vernacular. The early fifteenth-century English tract *Dives and Pauper,* for instance, says first that need excuses theft in dire necessity and then, almost in the same breath, that there is no theft in such a case:

> ʒif ony man or woman for myschef of hungyr or of þrest or of cold or for oþir myschef, whyche myschef he may nout flen to sauyn his lyf but he takyn þingis aʒenys þe lordys [owner's] wil, ʒif he take so onyþing in peryl of deth or in gret myschef, *nede excusith hym from þefte* & fro synne ʒif he do it only for nede & nout for couetyse. And he owyth to enformyn his conscience and þinkyn þat ʒif þe lord of þe þing knewe hys myschef he schulde nout ben mispayd, & *þan doth he no þefte,* for in gret nede alle þing is comoun. Also for þe lord is boundyn to helpyn hym in þat nede. And also for nede hat no lawe. Example ha we in þe gospel, wher we fyndyn þat þe discyplis of Crist for hungyr toke herys in þe feld & gnoddyn [hem] & etyn [þe corne] for hungyr. . . . For it is a general reule in þe lawe þat nede hat no lawe.[39]

Similarly, the penitential manual *Jacob's Well,* written a little later, seems unable completely to accept that necessity exempts one from blame. We find the penitent thief advised to make restitution of the property he has stolen wherever possible, though when his wife and children would otherwise starve, "þanne nede hath no lawe, for þanne in þat nede, wyif and chyld muste lyue be þi good whiche þou hast falsly get."[40]

Secular law was not entirely free from such a confusion of categories (as indeed we have seen from *Fogassa's Case*),[41] but as I hope to show it was in principle no less sympathetic to the plight of the desperately needy than canon law. In England canon law had no jurisdiction over felons (unless they happened also to be clerics), so it is important to try to discover whether such texts as *Dives and Pauper* are expressing a pious, but impractical, ideal, or whether "it is a general reule in þe lawe" should be taken to mean that secular courts in the late fourteenth century would also have entertained a defense of extreme necessity against a charge of petty larceny, for this will have an important bearing on the way we read Langland's portrait of Need.

It is quite clear that in cases of grand larceny (those involving a sum of more than twelve pence) necessity was not a generally available defense. One of the defendants in the late thirteenth-century *Placita Corone* tries to plead necessity in a case of horse theft with a singular lack of success. Tricked into making a confession by the judge ("Keep God before your eyes and tell us the truth of this matter, and we shall be as merciful as we can, according to the law"), the thief says,

> The great poverty and distress, which I have for long undergone, pressed me so hard that I thought to be relieved of my troubles by the value of this horse: and it was for this reason that I took it, by temptation of the Devil, otherwise than I ought to have done.

The judge asks him how long he has been doing things of this sort, and the thief answers,

> Truly, sir, I never acted in this way, no matter what poverty or distress I suffered before this occasion.

Wherein the judge's capacity for mercy lay is unclear, for after this confession the trial is brought to a speedy and mortal conclusion: "et suspendatur."[42] The *Placita Corone* has been justly described as a "handbook for accused felons,"[43] and it may well be that the necessity defense is raised here primarily as a warning to those who might be tempted to use it in inappropriate circumstances.

Petty larceny, by contrast, was so comparatively trivial a matter that it seems rarely to have attracted formal written notice. Unfortunately (since it would greatly strengthen my case), one of the strongest pieces of evidence for the acceptability of the necessity defense in cases of petty theft, cited by both Frederic William Maitland and Theodore F. T. Plucknett, turns out to be founded on a misunderstanding. By the late thirteenth century, says Maitland, "folk are saying that the limit of twelve pence allows a man to keep himself from starvation for eight days without being guilty of a capital crime."[44] Plucknett, no doubt taking his cue from Maitland, repeats the view that medieval common lawyers recognized a rule that "a man can steal enough to keep himself from starvation for a week without committing a major crime."[45] Alas, both these statements are based on the misreading of a gloss in the Cambridge MS of *Britton*. The thrust of this gloss is in fact quite different: twelve pence, the glossator argues, was chosen as the cutoff point for a capital crime because this sum is enough to keep a man alive for eight days—that is, a man deprived of food for such a period may be expected to die on the following day; thus, to rob him of twelve pence is to put his life potentially at risk and may therefore be considered as the legal equivalent of murder.[46]

Elsewhere in *Britton*, however, we do find hints that necessity might form the basis of a defense, and these, in fact, constitute the only direct medieval common law evidence of which I know. In defining the crime of burglary, *Britton* lists certain groups that are exempt from conviction: these include, not only children under age, idiots, madmen, "and others who are incapable of committing a felony [nule felonie faire]," but also "poor people who through hunger enter the house for victuals under the value of twelve pence" (poueres que pur feyn entrent pur ascun vitaille de meindre value de .xii. deners).[47] And in the section on larceny, *Britton* says of "small thefts, as of sheaves of corn in harvest, or of pigeons or poultry" that "if the thieves are not found to be otherwise of bad character, and the thing stolen is under the value of twelve pence, they shall be put in the pillory for an hour in the day, and be not admissible to make oath on any jury or inquest, or as witnesses."[48] They are to be punished by mutilation (or in the case of repeat offenders by death), however, if they should be of ill repute, or if they are found to have acted out of simple wickedness and not out of need: "nient par besoigne." In *Britton*, then, poverty and need are clearly factors in assessing guilt in cases both of burglary and larceny, though whether necessity justifies these acts (the implication of the statement about burglary) or merely excuses them (as in the larceny passage) is less clear.

Though *Britton* remains the one solid piece of evidence available to us, it is possible to glean a few other hints that extreme poverty might justify stealing the necessities of life in the eyes of the law. In another of the sermons of the fourteenth-century Irish archbishop Richard FitzRalph, for instance, the prelate recalls hearing that in Paris when a beggar was caught stealing he had his pockets searched, and if "he was found with money sufficient to buy the bread he had stolen he was promptly hanged. But if he was found to be penniless he went scot free."[49] That such a story is told of Paris might seem to argue that the practice was unknown in fourteenth-century Ireland, but FitzRalph is here discussing charitable test cases, so he is probably drawing his audience's attention to the searching of the thief's pockets rather than the grounds for clemency. It seems possible, indeed, that the French were regarded as being unduly harsh in their punishment of petty larceny—this at least is the view of the Cambridge glossator of *Britton*.[50] Incidentally, this crude objective test solves one of the problems that the necessity defense has always posed for lawyers—that need is a notoriously subjective quality, which makes it hard to draw a firm line.[51] As Lear famously says, "O! reason not the need; our basest beggars / Are in the meanest things superfluous." It also helps us understand why Langland's Need should be so staunch an advocate of the virtue of Temperance, a fact that has puzzled many commentators from Morton Bloomfield onward. The necessity defense, as Need recognizes, is only available to those who steal "in mesurable manere."

It would be particularly gratifying to be able to follow *Britton* further into actual case law, but the trail in this direction becomes very faint. There are two obvious reasons for this: in all situations where necessity was regarded as a justification, the principle would have had no case to answer (as with our earlier example of the hangman) and so there would have been no record of his actions; where, on the other hand, it was treated as an excuse, the sums involved would have been too small to attract much written notice. Clearly, cases like the one FitzRalph describes were rarely of sufficient importance to come before the king's justices, though they must have been common enough in the manorial courts that Langland himself seems to be evoking. At first glance the formula by which defendants were sometimes excused fines in such courts, *condonatur quia pauper,* would seem to confirm my reading of Langland, but in a high proportion of instances those so excused seem to have been guilty of merely failing to pay fines or perform their customary duties to the court rather than of committing acts of petty larceny. One economic historian has even argued that in the thirteenth century "fines condoned *quia pauper* are evidence of peasant illiquidity, rather than destitution,"[52] though this has been questioned by J. B. Post.[53] Nevertheless, it is certainly possible to find uses of this formula that apparently concern both destitution and petty theft. When the court in Wakefield in 1349 condoned a fine of one penny levied against William Broun because he had failed to pay Hugh dele Okes for a bushel of rye worth five pence, for instance, it is difficult to believe that "peasant illiquidity" was really the issue.[54] Similarly, when we encounter thirteen people fined sums between twopence and eight pence in the court roll for the Manor of Downham, Cambridgeshire,

1324, for carrying off "grain in Autumn *contra le Belawe*" (apparently they had been indulging in a little premature gleaning), the reason that only one of them, Ella le Staunge, was "condoned *quia pauper*" is presumably that she alone had been genuinely impoverished.[55] Incidentally, there is some slight evidence that the towns may have shown less forbearance in such matters than the countryside. The late thirteenth-century *Leges Burgorum* at least reads, "If anyone be taken in a borough with bread stolen to the value of ¹/₂d. he ought to be flogged through the middle of the town. And for a theft worth from ¹/₂d. to 4d. he ought to be flogged harder."[56] Of course it remains possible that such punishments were subject, as in Paris, to a necessity test.

The necessity defense in medieval common law has a curious half-life in a handful of sixteenth- and seventeenth-century treatises. Richard Crompton, in his 1583 reissue of Anthony FitzHerbert's book on the office and authority of justices of the peace (ca. 1538), seems to have been the first to notice *Britton*'s passage on burglary with its apparent endorsement of the necessity defense,[57] but his point was taken up in a much more influential work, Michael Dalton's *The Countrey Iustice*. "It is not Burglary in an Infant vnder 14 yeares of age," writes Dalton, "nor in poor persons that vpon hunger shall enter a house for victuall vnder the value of xii."[58] It would be interesting to know whether such seventeenth-century justices of the peace "as [had] not been much conversant in the studie of the Lawes of this Realme" modified their decisions in the light of Dalton's rule, or whether it merely set the seal on what had been common practice anyway. Both Crompton and Dalton interpret *Britton* to mean that burglary prompted by need was justifiable rather than excusable, and this view was to raise the ire of the great seventeenth-century jurist Sir Matthew Hale. In his *History of the Pleas of the Crown* (ca. 1670), Hale vigorously attacked Dalton for claiming that "a poor person in case of necessity for hunger" might be justified in committing burglary; "for tho I do agree that a judge ought to be tender in such cases, and use much discretion and moderation, yet this must not pass for law, for then we shall in little time let loose all the rules of law and government, and burglaries, robberies, yea murders themselves shall be excusable under pretense of necessity." "Where laws are settled," he continues, "there are other remedies appointed for the relief . . . of the poor."[59] No doubt Hale is thinking here of the Elizabethan Poor Law Acts of 1597 and 1601. Hale's editor, Sollom Emlyn, smugly expands the point in his edition of 1735: "the law supposes, that no man can in a well governd [*sic*] commonwealth be driven to such a necessity; this supposition is the more reasonable in *England*, where there are so many laws and such large sums yearly collected for the relief of the poor, as are more than sufficient for that purpose."[60] It is tempting to look forward from Hale and Emlyn to that unfeeling nineteenth-century judge who was unwilling to entertain a plea of necessity even from men who had spent nineteen days in an open boat with no food or water, and to sympathize with Aubrey Gwynn's view of the contrasting attitude of the medieval lawyer: "the justice of those days was rough and ready but it was not lacking in human kindness."[61] But only, I fear, at the risk of senti-mentalizing the Middle Ages. What the existence of the necessity defense in medieval law really tells us, I suspect, was that there were times when the poor experienced such desperate destitution that even the law could not bring itself to add to their misery.

We should certainly feel no surprise that Langland's portrait of Need reflects contemporary legal practice, since he shows himself alert to such obscure points of customary procedure elsewhere,[62] but the main purpose of this extended exploration of the legal background to "nede ne hath no lawe" has been to provide a counterweight to those critics who insist on tak-ing a disparaging view of Langland's personification. I trust it will not seem unduly harsh to imply that by misreading, not only the law of Langland's day, but also the social conditions under which it operated, they are in dan-ger of revealing themselves as the heirs of Hale and Emlyn. It should be obvious by now that my own sympathies are more closely aligned with that small group of, mostly left-wing, critics who see neither Need nor the needy as the objects of Langland's satire, with the position of David Aers, for in-stance, who regards Langland's Need as an affirmation of "the *rights* of those in need, in contrast to the newer ethos which . . . advocated a punitive and discriminatory poor relief as a component of labour discipline,"[63] or even with the dramatic claim made by Geoffrey Shepherd (in a festschrift for the Marxist historian Rodney Hilton) that Need shows Langland "thought-fully embracing a cosmic Fabianism."[64] If nothing else, I hope my explo-ration of the legal implications of the maxim "nede ne hath no lawe" in the late Middle Ages has shown that Will's waking encounter with Need offers a credible context for the narrator's account of his own destitution and that it not only confronts us with what Kathleen M. Hewett-Smith has recently called "an historically immediate material world,"[65] but also offers us a co-herent way of reading that world. This is why I believe that Derek Pearsall's suggestion (in his note to *PPl.* C.22:37) that "perhaps Langland is setting be-fore us the *reality*, not the authority, of Need," presents us with something of a false dichotomy: Need certainly offers us an unvarnished portrait of desperate misery, yet it is from that very misery that he derives his authority.

In some ways, R. W. Frank's quarrel with R. E. Kaske over the meaning of the Hunger episode earlier in the poem (A.7:156–307; B.6:171–331; C.8: 167–352) parallels the critical debate over the Need episode. "The scene tells of real hunger," wrote Frank, "violent gut-griping hunger (B.6.171, 175, 178) that leaves sunken cheeks and rheumy eyes and brings the sufferer close to death (B. 6.176–7, 175, 180). . . . For this reason I cannot accept R. E. Kaske's learned argument that 'a hunger for righteousness' is an issue in the Hunger scene."[66] Frank is not saying that we should invariably privilege what he calls the "experiential significance" of Langland's work over its allegorical meaning, of course, merely that this meaning can be fully appreciated only where the world of experience is taken into account. Jill Mann's recent discussion of the Need episode offers a brilliant illustration of this. Mann in fact reads not only the opening lines of its final passus, but the poem as a whole, in terms of what she calls Langland's "need ethos." For her the *ius necessitatis* in *Piers Plowman* takes on a metaphysical cast—God's need to redeem mankind providing him with his justification of breaking the Old Law.[67] Need as a redemptive principle might be thought to be at odds with Need as an apocalyptic sign, but neither, it seems to me, lies outside the poem's possible experiential significance. Even those who feel compelled to reject the demonization of Need remain free to take him as a harbinger of the Antichrist, in line with Gregory's moralization of Job. As Katherine Kerby-Fulton has pointed out, Need may quite as easily be regarded as "a neutral misfortune."[68] *Sub specie aeternitatis*, Need may well provide a rationalization for the Incarnation, but in the temporal sphere it is perfectly intelligible that the thoughts of a narrator wracked by need should turn to the Apocalypse (just as his vision of the last age of the world should remind him of his own senescence and impotence). If that is indeed the case, we should hardly be surprised that, like Oliver Wendell Holmes's celebrated "bad man," Langland's Will is able to expound this forgotten aspect of the customary law from a particularly privileged perspective.

NOTES

1. Derek Pearsall, ed., *Piers Plowman by William Langland: An Edition of the C-Text* (London: Edward Arnold, 1978), C.22:3. Hereafter *PPl.* in the main text.

2. Robert Frank, *Piers Plowman and the Scheme of Salvation: An Interpretation of Dowel, Dobet, and Dobest* (New Haven, CT: Yale University Press, 1957), 114.

3. Morton Bloomfield, *Piers Plowman as a Fourteenth-Century Apocalypse* (New Brunswick, NJ: Rutgers University Press, 1962), 135.

4. For a recent claim that this debate represents an "ultimately unresolvable" enigma, see Anne Middleton, "Acts of Vagrancy," in *Written Work: Langland, Labor, and Authorship,* ed. Steven Justice and Kathryn Kerby-Fulton (Philadelphia: University of Pennsylvania Press, 1997), 270–72.

5. Robert Adams, "The Nature of Need in *Piers Plowman* XX," *Traditio* 34 (1978): 273–301.

6. Pamela Gradon, "Langland and the Ideology of Dissent," Sir Israel Gollancz Memorial Lecture, *Proceedings of the British Academy* 66 (1980): 203; Lawrence M. Clopper, *Songes of Rechelesnesse: Langland and the Franciscans* (Ann Arbor: University of Michigan Press, 1997), 71n8.

7. See Wendy Scase, *"Piers Plowman" and the New Anticlericalism* (Cambridge: Cambridge University Press, 1989), 68–69.

8. Mary Carruthers, *The Search for St. Truth: A Study of Meaning in Piers Plowman* (Evanston, IL: Northwestern University Press, 1973), 160.

9. Adams, "The Nature of Need," 281.

10. Penn Szittya, *The Antifraternal Tradition in Medieval Literature* (Princeton, NJ: Princeton University Press, 1986), 269.

11. Jill Mann, "The Nature of Need Revisited," *Yearbook of Langland Studies* 18 (2004): 11–13.

12. *Borough Customs,* ed. Mary Bateson, 2 vols., Selden Society 18 and 21 (London: Quaritch, 1904–6), 2:59.

13. Ibid., 2:59n2.

14. Walter W. Skeat, ed., *The Vision of William concerning Piers the Plowman in Three Parallel Texts; Together with Richard the Redeless,* 2 vols. (Oxford: Clarendon Press, 1886), 2:174.

15. Walter W. Skeat, ed., *The Vision of William concerning Piers the Plowman [the C Text],* Early English Text Society OS 54 (London: Oxford University Press, 1873), 235.

16. George Russell and George Kane, eds., *Piers Plowman: The C Version,* (London: Athlone Press; Berkeley: University of California Press, 1997), 458.

17. See, for example, Charles C. Bayley, "Pivotal Concepts in the Political Philosophy of William of Ockham," *Journal of the History of Ideas* 10 (1949): 201–4 and passim.

18. The "King's prerogative in saltpetre" (4 James I) is claimed to rest on "the necessary defence of the realm." *The twelfth part of the Reports of Sir Edward Coke, Kt.* (London: Printed by T.R. for Henry Twyford, and Thomas Dring . . . , 1656) [Wing C4969], 12–15. For the sake of the general reader I have expanded the cryptic form in which legal commentators generally cite such law reports.

19. Wyclif argued that "the crown might legitimately seize the goods of the clergy for the defense of the realm." Scase, *"Piers Plowman" and the New Anticlericalism,* 66.

20. *Vermont. Supreme Court. Vermont Reports, Current Cases,* 81 (St. Albans: J. Spooner, 1908), A.188. I am grateful to Dennis Klimchuck of the University of Western Ontario for drawing this case to my attention.

21. See A.W.B. Simpson, *Cannibalism and the Common Law: The Story of the Tragic Last Voyage of the Mignonette and the Strange Legal Proceedings to Which It Gave Rise* (Chicago: University of Chicago Press, 1984).

22. Ibid., 160–76.

23. Ibid., passim.

24. Ibid., 158.

25. *The twelfth part of the Reports of Sir Edward Coke, Kt.*, 63.

26. *Cy ensuont certeyne cases reportes per Edmunde Plowden un apprentice de le commen ley, puis le premier imprimier de ses Commentaries* . . . (London: Richard Tottell, 1584) [STC 2004]; translated as *The commentaries, or Reports of Edmund Plowden* . . . : *containing divers cases upon matters of law, argued and adjudged in the several reigns of King Edward VI., Queen Mary, King and Queen Philip and Mary, and Queen Elizabeth, 1548–1579* . . . (London: S. Brooke, 1816).

27. I wish to thank David Seipp of Boston University for providing me with this information.

28. *De legibus et consuetudinibus Angliae,* ed. George E. Woodbine and trans. Samuel E. Thorne, 4 vols. (Cambridge: Harvard University Press, 1968–77), 3:269.

29. *Decretales Papae Gregorii IX,* bk. 4, tit. 41, c. 4., in *Corpus Iuris Canonici,* ed. Emil Friedberg, 2 vols. (Leipzig: Tauschnitz, 1879), 2:927.

30. This (in the variant form given in Matthew 12:1–8) is also the biblical authority cited in *Fogassa v. Reniger* (fol. 19a).

31. *Patrologia Cursus Completus: Series Latina,* ed. J.-P. Migne, 217 vols. (Paris, 1844–55), 182:867.

32. *Decretum magistri Gratiani* pt. 2, cause 1, q. 1, c. 39, in *Corpus Iuris Canonici,* ed. Emil Friedberg, 1:374.

33. Saint Thomas Aquinas, *Summa theologiae* 2a 2æ, 32, 8, ed. Thomas Gilby and T.C. O'Brien, 60 vols. (London: Eyre and Spottiswoode; New York: McGraw-Hill, 1964–76), 34:263.

34. Ibid., 2a 2æ, 66, 7, 38:81.

35. Thomas P. Dunning, *Piers Plowman: An Interpretation of the A Text,* 2nd ed. (Oxford: Clarendon Press; New York: Oxford University Press, 1980), 21.

36. George Kane and E. Talbot Donaldson, eds., *Piers Plowman: The B Version,* (London: Athlone Press, 1975).

37. Janet Coleman, "Property and Poverty," in *The Cambridge History of Medieval Political Thought, c. 350–c.1450,* ed. J.H. Burns (Cambridge: Cambridge University Press, 1988), 629.

38. Quoted by Szittya, *The Antifraternal Tradition,* 269–70.

39. Priscilla Heath Barnum, ed., *Dives and Pauper,* 2 vols., Early English Text Society 275 and 280 (London: Oxford University Press, 1976–80), 2:141.

40. Arthur Brandeis, ed., *Jacob's Well* (London: Paul, Trench, Trübner, 1900), 206.

41. The earliest coherent application of this distinction that I have found is in Francis Bacon's *Elements of the common lawes of England* (London: Robert Young, 1630) [STC 1134]. Discussing his fifth rule, "necessitas inducit privilegium quoad iura privata," Bacon distinguishes three kinds of necessity (preservation of life, obedience to a superior, and acts of God). Only the first of these, he argues, justifies otherwise illegal acts, although the other two may excuse them (29–34).

42. J. M. Kaye, ed. and trans., *Placita corone, or La corone pledée devant justices,* Selden Society (London: Quaritch, 1966), 17.

43. Alan Harding, *The Law Courts of Medieval England* (London: Allen and Unwin; New York: Barnes and Noble, 1973), 78.

44. Sir Frederick Pollock and Frederic William Maitland, *The History of English Law before the Time of Edward I,* 2nd ed. (1898; Cambridge: Cambridge University Press, 1968), 2:498.

45. Theodore F. T. Plucknett, *A Concise History of the Common Law* (Boston: Little, Brown, 1956), 447.

46. *Britton,* trans. Francis Morgan Nichols (Washington: Byrne, 1901), 47. For a similar argument see Robert Mannyng of Brunne's *Handlyng Synne,* ed. Idelle Sullens, Medieval and Renaissance Texts and Studies, 14 (Binghamton: State University of New York, 1983), ll. 1325–32.

47. *Britton,* 36.

48. Ibid., 52.

49. Aubrey Gwynn, "Richard FitzRalph, Archbishop of Armagh," *Irish Quarterly Review* 25 (1936): 93.

50. *Britton,* 47.

51. See Claude Gauvard, *"De Grace especial": Crime, état et société à la fin du moyen âge,* 2 vols. (Paris: Publications de la Sorbonne, 1991), 1:400–410.

52. Alfred N. May, "An Index of Thirteenth-Century Peasant Impoverishment? Manor Court Fines," *Economic History Review,* 2nd ser., 26 (1973): 398.

53. J. B. Post, "Manorial Amercements and Peasant Poverty," *Economic History Review,* 2nd ser., 27 (1975): 308–11.

54. Helen M. Jewell, ed., *The Court Rolls of the Manor of Wakefield,* Yorkshire Archaeological Society, 2nd ser., 2 (Leeds, 1981): 129–30.

55. M. Clare Coleman, ed., *Court Roll of the Manor of Downham, 1310–1327* (Cambridge: Cambridge Record Society, 1996), 76.

56. Bateson, *Borough Customs,* 1:55.

57. Richard Crompton, *L'office et auctoritie de iustices de peace* (London: Richarde Tottill, 1583) [STC 10978], fol. 21b.

58. Richard Dalton, *The Countrey Iustice, Containing the Practise of the Iustices of the Peace out of their Sessions, Gathered, for the better helpe of such Iustices of Peace as haue not been much conversant in the studie of the Lawes of this Realme* (London: Societie of Stationers, 1618) [STC 6205], 234.

59. Sir Matthew Hale, *Historia placitorum coronae* (London: E. and R. Nutt, 1736), 565–66.

60. Ibid., 567

61. Ibid., 93.

62. To take one obvious example, his remark that "hit is nat vsed on erthe to hangen eny felones / Oftur then ones" (*PPl.* C.20:421–22) reflects the medieval custom that if a hanged felon revived after being cut down (or if the rope broke) he or she went scot-free. See Baudouin de Gaiffier, *Études critiques d'hagiographie et d'iconologie* (Bruxelles, Société des Bollandistes, 1967), 194–232. For legal reports of such an event see Naomi D. Hurnard, *The King's Pardon for Homicide before A.D. 1307* (Oxford, Clarendon Press, 1969), 44 and 176; responses in *Notes and Queries* 9 (1854), by William Kelly, p. 280 (issue

230), and William Bates pp. 453–54 (issue 237); David Seipp, "Crime in the Year Books," in *Law Reporting in Britain,* ed. Chantal Stebbins (London: Hambledon Press, 1995), 19n26; and Nicole Gonthier, *Le Châtiment du crime au Moyen Âge, XIIe–XVIe siècles* (Rennes: Presses universitaires, 1998), 149. Skeat (*Three Parallel Texts,* 2:263–64) cites an instance from 1363, but there are no grounds for accepting his claim that Langland had this specific case in mind.

63. David Aers, *Community, Gender, and Individual Identity: English Writing, 1360–1430* (New York: Routledge, 1988), 63.

64. Geoffrey Shepherd, "Poverty in *Piers Plowman,*" in *Social Relations and Ideas: Essays in Honour of R. H. Hilton,* ed. T. H. Aston et al. (Cambridge and New York: Cambridge University Press, 1983), 189.

65. Kathleen M. Hewett-Smith, "'Nede Ne Hath No Lawe': Poverty and the De-Stabilization of Allegory in the Final Visions of Piers Plowman," *William Langland's Piers Plowman: A Book of Essays* (New York: Routledge, 2001), 233.

66. R. W. Frank, "The 'Hungry Gap,' Crop Failure and Famine: The Fourteenth-Century Agricultural Crisis and *Piers Plowman,*" *Yearbook of Langland Studies* 4 (1990): 97–98.

67. Mann, "The Nature of Need Revisited," 24–28.

68. Kathryn Kerby-Fulton, *Reformist Apocalypticism and "Piers Plowman"* (Cambridge: Cambridge University Press, 1990), 148.

Chapter 2

Upward Mobility in the German High Middle Ages

The Ascent of a Faithful Liar

VICKIE ZIEGLER

As Professor Hanawalt indicates in her introduction, those living on the margins of society did not merely include the poor, criminals, and lower classes, but could also include individuals from upper classes, such as those rising through the ranks on merit or noblewomen who exercised sexual independence, as the heroine in our story does. Konrad von Würzburg's (1230?–1287) *Engelhard,* written in the second half of the thirteenth century, not only contains such "marginals" in the persons of the two main characters, Engelhard and Engeltrud, but also presents one of the most vivid accounts of upward mobility and apparent tolerance of criminal behavior in medieval German literature.

Konrad knew firsthand about social mobility in his time: he himself was of non-noble origins but became one of the best-known authors of his time. Born in Würzburg, he probably left there around 1257–58 for the lower Rhine area, where he spent several years. The remainder of his life was spent primarily, if not exclusively, in Basel, where he was a prominent citizen at the time of his death.[1] A versatile and productive author in several genres, he wrote a number of extensive narratives, as well as shorter tales, legends, and various types of poetry including love songs and social commentary.[2] He remains an important German literary figure just behind major writers such as Gottfried von Straβburg, Wolfram von Eschenbach, and Hartmann von Aue.

Konrad's short romance *Engelhard* provides a fascinating fictional aperçu into the meteoric rise of an impoverished Burgundian son of the lower nobility to the throne of Denmark through an unlikely career path that consisted, on the one hand, of extraordinarily loyal and meritorious service, and, on the other, of seducing the king's only child and rigging an ordeal to convince others of his innocence. Such a career pattern implies both the possibility of upward mobility as well as a disposition toward tolerance among the upper levels of the aristocracy. The story of Engelhard's trajectory into the highest reaches of medieval society reveals the value of both character and great talents in social mobility, because it is these qualities that provide the basis for his good reputation in the Danish court. These assets guarantee as well the invaluable assistance of his powerful friend, Dietrich, and the expected tolerance on the part of Konrad's readers, who are enjoined by his prologue to see Engelhard's story as a positive example of fidelity, even though he is guilty of fornication, treason, perjury, and fraud in an ordeal by battle.[3] (See the appendix to this chapter for a plot summary of the passages relevant to my argument.)

Since Engelhard's character and talents seem to be the driving force that ensures both upward mobility and tolerance, it is to these that we must look for the quality or qualities that made for his spectacular success. That achievement, according to Konrad's prologue, is his devotion to the virtue of fidelity, a quality that has distinguished Engelhard's family for generations.[4] Konrad tells us that Engelhard's story gives us many wonderful examples of this virtue, which is so lacking in his own age. He offers this tale as a motivating force for those who hear it (ll. 190–215).

The treatment of upward mobility in this work could also have been affected by the needs and aspirations of Konrad's probable audience, since their expectations may well play a crucial role in the portrayal of social mobility in the work.[5] Writing in the second half of the thirteenth century, Konrad was well positioned to see the preoccupation with upward mobility among ambitious noble families as well as among members of the lower nobility and urban ruling classes. Though it is not possible to date this work—and therefore its probable audience—with any degree of certainty, the two likely scenarios, involving patronage from either the House of Kleve in the north or the Habsburgs and Basel patricians in the south, are the likely options. Both groups would have contained ambitious individuals who would have seen in the meteoric rise of Engelhard a character who mirrored many of their own hopes. Consequently, the impossibility of ascertaining which of these two audiences was Konrad's intended one does not affect the basic outlines of this analysis.[6]

Whether he wrote for the aristocrats of Kleve or the wealthy upper class of late thirteenth-century Basel, Konrad hopes in his prologue to motivate his readers to practice *triuwe* (fidelity) through the example of Engelhard's incredible ascent from impoverished minor foreign aristocrat to reigning monarch of Denmark. Engelhard goes through three main stages in the attainment of his goals: the lengthy period of time he spends in the service of the monarchy in Denmark, where he attracts the favorably disposed attention of the king and his chief retainers; the love story between himself and the princess; and the ordeal. Each of these stages arises out of the other. Engelhard's extraordinary service and his merits lead the king to choose him as a companion to his daughter after the death of the queen. Engelhard's knightly prowess on the tournament field is the prerequisite for Engeltrud's allowing Engelhard to be her lover. The ordeal, of course, arises from Ritschier's accusation against Engelhard, but the fact that he is even allowed to clear himself through a judicial ordeal against a much more highly placed nobleman than himself is indicative of how far he has risen in standing and reputation. Indeed, Konrad uses the ordeal by battle to fix the positive characterization of Engelhard as well as the negative one of the king's nephew, Ritschier. The dramatic context of the ordeal in which this occurs reflects changing social values.

In order to understand how Konrad shaped his presentation of social mobility as outlined above, we must first look at how he changed and fashioned his material. The Amicus/Amelius legend, a major source for Konrad, was well-known in medieval Europe as an extraordinary example of the fidelity between two look-alike friends, who help each other in two times of crisis: one involving the replacement of the accused in the judicial duel by his look-alike friend; and the other involving a miraculous cure for leprosy that involves the slaughter of one's own children. Konrad changed much of the essence of this legend by an extensive increase in the amount of space given over to the love story, making fidelity between the two lovers a much more important motif. Because of the centrality of the love story for Konrad, he lengthens this section of the work through the addition of a trial scene, in which he deepens the legal and psychological preparation for the ordeal. Neither the trial scene nor the extensive love story were part of his sources, yet, together with the duel itself, they make up almost 80 percent of his version, with the love story consisting of more than half of the total.[7] This change enables him to expand on the rewards of fidelity for Engelhard, who gains a trusted friend, a highborn wife, a kingdom, and riches.

Financial security had been a goal of Engelhard since his youth (ll. 285–320); Konrad's emphasis on the monetary benefits of *triuwe* in the prologue strikes a new note, anticipating a knightly protagonist whose value system includes the procurement of wealth as a major goal.[8] In the introduction, Konrad details the economic or financial good to be obtained by the practice of this virtue, including the procurement of a good administrative position (administrator of fortresses [ll. 41–42]) and the protection of assets: "The rich and powerful have more need of fidelity than anyone else, because if no one were trustworthy, the possessions of the mighty would disappear" (ll. 104–7).[9] This concern with financial matters and their role in the achievement of virtue and reputation appears repeatedly in the characterization of Engelhard.[10]

While the narrator laments the fact that material wealth is so important in the practice of virtue (ll. 269–77), he accepts the situation as it is and points out that the modest means of Engelhard's noble parents have an adverse effect on Engelhard's position in the world. Like his forefathers, who have always been devoted to *triuwe,* he is a good person who cannot rise through the social echelons without adequate means. Three passages, the first spoken by the narrator and the second two by Engelhard, address this idea:

He was blessed with all good gifts of fortune, lacking only possessions, which, however, must accompany a "noble heart" if he is to achieve great recognition. Truly, insofar as I can ascertain, a noble man can scarcely be esteemed with meager wealth. (ll. 264–71)

I believe that in my case the name and duties of a knight must suffer damage. (ll. 290–91)

I trust in his [King Fruot of Denmark's] good reputation, that he will receive me in a friendly manner and will give me many large fiefs as a reward. That is certainly better than continuing to live in such a shameful condition. (ll. 314–19)[11]

Repeatedly throughout the work, Engelhard shows that he is well aware of the advantages of money in social advancement, coupled with faithful and superior performance in service to his lord. These ideas would have been at home among an audience in the ambitious House of Kleve or an urban audience. Engelhard's position may have been especially satisfying to many of the latter group, who had wealth but were not of noble birth. He must use his wits to advance and achieve what they already have in the way of material goods and accomplishments.

Coupled with this practical attitude toward wealth and advancement are passages in which external rank seems to be of premier importance. Ritschier lives by his assumed superiority. King Fruot does not see Engelhard as a worthy match for his daughter. Even Engeltrud has attacks of class consciousness in regard to Engelhard's station, which the narrator hastens to tell us are typical of women's tactics when they are really interested in the man in question (ll. 2075–178). Such passages should not be seen as a negation of those in which only personal virtue and talent seem to be the determining factors in reputation; rather both types of comments, those that indicate the importance of rank and those that emphasize personal achievement, reflect a social context characterized by fluidity and a certain ambiguity.[12] Dietrich, the son of a ruler, and Engeltrud both recognize Engelhard's innate superiority, which is underscored by the amount of space given over to a tournament in which Engelhard defeats kings and outshines two thousand other knights (ll. 2463–892).[13] The repeated emphasis on Engelhard's extraordinary gifts in comparison to those more highly born than he justifies his rise on merit, a theme that most probably appealed to aristocrats of a lower station as well as to an urban audience.

Further confirmation that attitudes toward inborn privilege versus merit determined who was rewarded and who was punished comes in Konrad's characterization of the king's nephew, Ritschier. He is consumed with envy toward the upstart courtier Engelhard, who has become the king's confidant and favorite. The unexpected bonus of discovering Engelhard and Engeltrud in a compromising situation gives him the opportunity for which he has been waiting, since both he and his rival were knighted and he was bested in the tournament. In his description of Ritschier's relation of the defeat to the king, Konrad leaves no doubt as to Ritschier's motives or to his position as the negative counterpoint to Engelhard:

> The only reason he [Ritschier] hated the *faithful* one [Engelhard] was because he was so respected at the court. For that reason he [Ritschier]

had yearned for a long time to be able to destroy Engelhard's reputation completely with a serious blow to it. He really wanted to weaken
his strong standing. His heart bounded with high spirits and was joy-
ful, because he now could make his offense known. Full of *faithless-
ness* and *deception,* he opened his *dishonest* mouth. (ll. 3485–99)[14]

The italicized words framing the above quotation reflect the narrator's consistent moral evaluation of Ritschier. In terms of the work's moral compass,
Ritschier is already guilty of *untriuwe* (infidelity). From the moment of discovery, Ritschier and his motivation appear in the worst possible light. He
reports the incident to the king with the sole motivation of enhancing his
reputation by wrecking Engelhard's.[15]

While Engelhard's rise on his own merits could reflect the aspirations of
Konrad's audience, whether ambitious nobility or Basel patricians, Ritschier,
both on a personal as well as on a class level, as the English king's son, insists
on maintaining the old order. Only Ritschier and the king condemn the relationship with Engeltrud because Engelhard has stepped out of his station
(ll. 3528–40 and 3710–15). By insisting on his own prerogatives, Ritschier dis-
turbs the harmony among different levels of the upper class and is punished
through the loss of the duel.[16] Ritschier's own base behavior reflects his
misunderstanding of *triuwe* and his innate inferiority vis-á-vis Engelhard,
who is the embodiment of fidelity.

Fidelity, then as now, is most vividly put to the test in crisis situations.
In Konrad's romance these involve Engelhard's love affair and the judicial
duel. Because the events leading up to the judicial ordeal and the ordeal itself form the crisis situation in which Engelhard's attempts at upward mobility will either succeed or fail spectacularly, they deserve careful analysis.
Moreover, it is not only Engelhard's marginality that is at center stage, but also
that of Engeltrud. She is a marginal, certainly not on account of birth, but
because of her willingness to endanger her privileged position out of love
for a marginal. The expansion of her role in Konrad's work affords the opportunity to examine not only another type of marginality, but also another
kind of fidelity, that between man and woman. Konrad thereby shifts the
focus in the first part of the work from the Dietrich/Engelhard relationship
of the Amicus/Amelius legend to the love affair. The intensity and depth of
Engelhard and Engeltrud's love for each other adds a great deal of tension
and significance to the rigged ordeal. Their love does not arise out of a mo-
mentary burst of passion but out of a series of tests and crises, including

Engeltrud's rescue of Engelhard when he falls deathly ill due to unrequited love (ll. 2259–401). While there has been some criticial disagreement about how well integrated the scene is and what level of *triuwe* Engeltrud shows, there seems to be textual evidence that she does indeed reflect aspects of Konrad's conception of *triuwe* as outlined in the prologue.[17] Throughout the love section, Engeltrud is described in thoroughly positive terms: she is a perfect love partner. In a secular context, she is as ideal in her role as the saintly queens who underwent the ordeal by fire were in theirs.

Engeltrud, in comparison with other women in literature and legend who stand accused of sexual misconduct, is unique both in that she is single and she does not have to undergo the ordeal herself to clear her reputation. Her father is ready to disinherit her because she is a "tougenliche brût," a clandestine bride (ll. 3716–18). After the late twelfth century, consent was the significant factor in determining whether or not a marriage was valid; the Church recognized such marriages, though it did so without enthusiasm.[18] It is perhaps for this reason that her father will cut her off from the family if Ritschier's accusation is true. He must recognize her new standing, but he can dismiss her from power and influence, saying that he will disinherit her.[19] Engeltrud's one-way ticket to the margins of society can be revoked only through proof of her innocence.

Engelhard and Engeltrud both realize that they will spend the rest of their lives in a marginal position with neither wealth nor status unless Engelhard can prove through trial by battle that he did not do what he in fact did. Since Engelhard ultimately does achieve his goals and demonstrate *triuwe* to Engeltrud through manipulation of the legal system, this section provides important information about Konrad's apparent attitudes toward upward mobility as well as toward fidelity. The social context of this ordeal, with the envious, deficient, yet truthful nephew of the king losing to the lying knight of lower standing, who was otherwise a model of knightly virtues, brings Engelhard triumphantly to the pinnacle of the social structure, reflecting changing social values.

Trial by battle remained in use in the German lands through the late fifteenth century. Recent research has shown that, as an ongoing legal procedure, its appearance in literature reflected in varying ways and degrees the social context in which a given literary account was written.[20] While the ordeal by fire involved an encounter between the accused and the elements, the trial by battle did not demand an immediate response from the natural world, since there was no question as to which party had won. While God was expected to intercede on the side of the honest combatant, no matter how redoubtable his adversary,[21] ordeal by battle still provoked a certain amount of disquietude. Medieval people knew that many factors outside of divine intercession could influence the course of the duel. Because of the possibility of fraud, trial by battle attracted ongoing clerical criticism but still played an important role in certain serious crimes as a legal means of dispute settlement. However, precisely because nature did not need to determine guilt or innocence in the manner expected in other ordeals, there was no need for priests to certify the results of the ordeal. Consequently ordeal by battle remained a valid legal procedure long after 1215, when the Fourth Lateran Council forbade clerical participation, though the ultimate fate of this procedure was sealed.[22]

The trial by battle was often used for capital and heinous crimes, whether clandestine or not. Fornication with the king's only heir in *Engelhard* is repeatedly referred to as a breach of *triuwe*,[23] and consequently, since the monarch is involved and because it interfered with the continuance of the dynasty, it falls into the area of treason.[24] Given the social circumstances of the offense and the status of the offenders, it is not surprising that both the accuser and the accused are knights and would therefore be likely to settle the matter with combat.[25]

The judicial duel appears in *Engelhard* as a serious legal undertaking that assumes that the participants had integrity in their positions.[26] In this regard, the attitude toward the ordeal by battle reflects both the ongoing use of the judicial duel in contemporary courts as a means of dispute settlement and an assumption of equitable, or perhaps rigged, outcomes. The problematic aspect of this late thirteenth-century ordeal has been that the person who does not tell the whole truth and nothing but the truth triumphs. While this situation obtains in Gottfried von Straßburg's famous version of Isolde's trial by fire, Gottfried at least manifests his dissatisfaction with the unilateral ordeal.[27] No such criticism occurs in Konrad's work, though the means used to save Engelhard's life involve major efforts at deception, such as lying to the king about his daughter's romantic entanglement and the substitution of a conveniently look-alike friend, Dietrich, in the duel. The loser of the duel, the king's nephew Ritschier, is the one who told the truth.[28] As in the case of Tristan and Isolde, this ordeal must prove that the lovers were not lovers. However, unlike Isolde, the accused Princess Engeltrud stands outside the process. She and her knightly lover Engelhard are declared innocent in a trial by battle in which neither of them takes part.[29]

The decision by the king to settle the issue through a duel comes about in a trial scene that has similarities to the comparable section of *Tristan* (*Tristan*, ll. 15325–531).[30] Like King Mark, who is despondent about personal betrayal, Fruot is stricken with grief at Ritschier's news. In both cases, the monarch turns to counselors for help. But while Isolde's case, as that of the exemplary queens in the legends, involved bishops, we do not find an episcopal presence in *Engelhard*, perhaps reflecting the post-1215 prohibitions against involvement of the clergy in trials by battle.[31] Fruot's counselors limit themselves to prudent legal advice. The king is of course the judge, and as a judge concerned with a reputation for fairness, he should let Engelhard come to his rights (*Engelhard*, ll. 3654–61). The counselors suggest strongly that an envious man will often slander another and point to Engelhard's excellent record of loyalty to the king, further evidence of the importance of reputation in medieval legal procedure.[32] Engelhard, though a foreigner, has acquitted himself very well in his service to the king. In contrast to the court of King Mark's treatment of Tristan, Fruot's counselors want to give Engelhard every benefit of the doubt (ll. 3648–53).[33]

The trial consists of contradictory statements by Engelhard and Ritschier. In the course of charge and countercharge (fornication versus consuming envy), Konrad includes material that is of interest in his framing of the rigged oath. At the end of one of his impassioned denials of the accusation against him, Engelhard says that he cannot allow himself to say more, since Ritschier, as a nephew of the king and an English prince, stands in a far higher position than he at court (ll. 3880–90). Engelhard, as the son of a Burgundian noble, is far away from family and in a subordinate social position.[34] As in the case of Isolde, who lamented the fact that she, as a foreigner, had no compurgators,[35] Engelhard lacks relatives who can vouch for his character or family standing at the court.

An absence of oath-helpers was one instance that could call forth a trial by battle. Another, as King Fruot says, was the lack of witnesses (ll. 4108–9).[36] A further important factor in justifying the trial by battle was its ability to establish the reputation and honor of those involved.[37] Since Engelhard has no relatives at Fruot's court and because his honor and reputation are severely compromised, Konrad gives added legal justification for the use of the trial by battle. In his accusation of Engelhard to King Fruot, Ritschier refers frequently to Engelhard's family background (ll. 3530, 3540, and 3896–97); the king also mentions it (ll. 3710–15). Engelhard has to fight to defend his reputation as well as Engeltrud's or be seen as the person who broke

knightly codes of behavior. Ritschier must fight to prove he is not a liar
(ll. 4010–13).

While Engelhard intimates that he is prepared to do what is necessary
to clear his name (ll. 3992–4000), the demand that a battle settle the issue
comes from Ritschier:

> If you wish to be judged innocent, that must occur at a site with
> sword against sword. . . . Before I blush with shame and stand here as
> a liar, I would prefer to put my life in the balance voluntarily. One
> should ascertain the whole truth with deadly blows of the sword.
> Even if you were to swear many oaths to us, that would be of little
> use. If you really want to defend yourself and acquit yourself of this
> accusation, then you must be victorious over me in battle. There is
> nothing else on this earth that can help you out of this difficult situ-
> ation. (ll. 4003–5; 4010–23)[38]

Ritschier's speech reflects the three significant points of medieval legal procedure in criminal cases: an accuser must make the complaint, be ready to
prove it, and accept the consequences if he is wrong.[39] No matter how many
oaths Engelhard swears to the contrary, it will not, in his rival's view, help his
case.[40] The call here for a duel looks as if it corresponds to the plaintiff's
anticipatory rejection of an oath.[41] Why does Ritschier reject out of hand an
oath from Engelhard?

There was a growing tendency in the Middle Ages to repudiate the validity of oaths in court cases because of the prevalence of successful perjury.
The punishment called down from God for a false oath could be a long time
in coming. Both the ordeal and compurgation were negative proofs: the accused, in contrast to Roman law, had to prove that he did not commit the
crime in question.[42] As with the ordeal, swearing an oath also submitted
the individual to God's judgment.[43] Undergirding both the ordeal and the
oath was the concept of immanent justice, which assumed divine intercession when necessary in human events. False oaths could elicit both immediate and long-term divine reactions; immediate ones might include the
impossibility of the oath-helpers repeating the oath as demanded.[44] One of
the problems with perjury, however, was that divine retribution for a false
oath might occur well after the verdict and its attendant consequences. Trial
by battle as well as ordeals had the advantage of an immediate judgment.[45]

Since ordeals were used only as a last resort in medieval judicial procedures, the offenses involved were ones in which testimony and the swearing

of oaths were not convincing or applicable and where there was no other means of discovering the truth.[46] These legal realities may be reflected in the just-quoted passage from *Engelhard*. Engelhard, both as a foreigner of lower status and, in Ritschier's eyes, a man whose reputation as a truthful individual was in doubt, could not absolve himself with an oath; he has to fight a duel to clear his name.

Contemporary legal reality is also reflected in the long series of conflicting statements, since a trial by battle was often ordered under these circumstances. In this way the courts could avoid perjury.[47] Engelhard's behavior is indicative of trial proceedings of the time as well: when he finishes his plea before the king and wants to restore his reputation, he makes the implicit offer to accept an ordeal and leaves the choice of his purgation up to others; this bearing is comparable to Isolde's stance in *Tristan*:

> so that I may be acquitted, however one wishes to reach a verdict in my case, that is the desire of my heart. I am prepared to do what is asked with willing effort. (ll. 3995–4000)[48]

The king, as judge of the court, orders the trial by battle that Ritschier demands and to which Engelhard agrees. The trial scene, with its fast-moving sequence of charge and countercharge, has created a legal situation in which trial by battle seems the natural and only course to take. Konrad's care in placing the ordeal in the context of a court-like situation may represent an attempt on his part to give a legal justification for the duel.

That Konrad is not interested in mechanical ritual without meaning is apparent in two other important areas: the binding of Engelhard; and the absence of the oath before the battle, which states what the ordeal was to prove.[49] In the first flush of anger after Ritschier's report, the king declares that Engelhard must die and orders him immediately bound with bands of steel. Binding had a long history in Germanic and medieval German law. In the earliest times, it was considered especially humiliating for a free man, and it constituted a kind of arrest. If he were brought into court bound, it indicated that he was convicted, and the meeting of the court served primarily to carry out the sentence. The council of nobles called to sit in judgment on Engelhard exhort the king to let him tell his story to them (ll. 3640–67). In advance of his appearance before the council, he is unbound (ll. 3671–73). This statement meant more to Konrad's readers than it does to us. Had he been brought bound before the court, it would have indicated that he was guilty and that he might well not have had an opportunity to defend himself.[50]

The manner in which Engelhard is allowed to appear, after Engeltrud's impassioned entreaty to God, sends a clear signal to the reader that Engelhard will be given a chance to make his case without a presumption of guilt. Konrad's attention to the meaning of details such as this one shows us that he was cognizant of contemporary legal practices and their significance.[51] Engelhard's privileged position before the court also indicates what a key role *triuwe* has played in Engelhard's social advancement. Had he not been a model of faithful service to the king, he would not have been given this opportunity.

In order to maintain his fidelity to Engeltrud, Engelhard must now find a way to save his life and protect her reputation. There is never any doubt that if Engelhard steps in that ring and fights to prove what he said was true that he will lose (ll. 4128–33 and 4450–55).[52] Dietrich, however, can win because he is innocent of the charge (ll. 4493–95 and 4742–47). There is a one-sided oath during the course of the battle, in which Ritschier swears that his hand will prove the truth of what he has said (ll. 4914–19).[53] Shortly thereafter, Dietrich chops off his left hand. Ritschier must lose, since Dietrich is innocent; the mutilation is a punishment for his oath.[54] Since the oath originally was a kind of swearing in which one's own body was surety, false oaths traditionally brought some kind of physical impairment, which could be inflicted by man or God. Since it was a permanently visible punishment, it was a lifelong branding. It also brought with it the loss of many legal rights, a state of affairs certainly known to members of Konrad's audience.[55]

Ritschier was punished because he tried to maintain the old order. Indeed, he was punished in the most telling way possible, because he lost many of the legal rights he previously enjoyed.[56] Such maiming was a lifelong stigma and indicated to whomever Ritschier met that he lacked a good reputation. While the loss of Ritschier's hand leads Fruot to stop the fight, the narrator leaves no doubt that we should understand Ritschier's maiming as a result of his character:[57]

> Ritschier must be deprived of a hand for the rest of his life and as a faithless coward endure diminished honor and scorn. His hate has bought him reproach and his envy has procured great disadvantages and loss. (ll. 4962–67)[58]

Ritschier's jealous belief that the destruction of Engelhard's standing was a worthwhile goal destroys his own reputation and makes him an object of scorn. His envy blinds him to merit, leading him to resent Engelhard's social ascent and to retreat into the traditional emphasis on the position that came to him through his birth.

At this point, the resolution of the trial by battle comes quickly. Dietrich/ Engelhard receives Engeltrud as a reward for his service to the king. After his return, Engelhard becomes king of Denmark. His long quest for social and financial security has met with spectacular success, but it is *triuwe* that binds all together. While *triuwe* on some levels involves bonds between and among others, certainly the material advantages it brings involve self-interest. We see these multiple bonds at play in the ordeal scene, which involves *triuwe* in the levels just mentioned: Engelhard toward Engelhard, Engelhard toward Engeltrud, Dietrich toward Engelhard. That Dietrich's *triuwe* gives him strength over Ritschier's envious treachery becomes apparent on several occasions. Konrad's overriding concern with the value of *triuwe* on many levels leads him to change fundamentally the emphasis of the story and, in so doing, crystallize these changes in his concept of the ordeal. The legal function of the ordeal is made to conform to the overall theme of his work, the value of *triuwe,* which leads to social mobility and the means to maintain one's new status.

Konrad did what he set out to do: to encourage the practice of *triuwe* through the telling of Engelhard's story,[59] a highly positive account of the rise of a minor foreign noble to the highest levels, an account that mixes great moral virtue with the realization that wealth aids in general recognition of that virtue. Konrad's accents, his points of emphasis, need to be seen in the context of his patrons' attitudes, whether they were minor nobility or late thirteenth-century Basel patricians. Differences in birth seem not to have been the consistent determining factor: much more important were the struggles for preeminence in politics and society and material wealth. In the early fourteenth-century *Karlmeinet,* written in Aachen, we find similar favorable treatment of the minor nobility in a trial by battle; the challenger to the Genelun figure is no longer a relative of Roland, but the son of a minor noble, whom Roland befriended. This young man receives extraordinary honors from Karl after his victory in the judicial duel, even though he is certainly lower in rank than any of the aristocrats of the court. Karl kisses his champion on the mouth and richly rewards him with lands and possessions. The older blood ties, which obliged relatives to avenge the death of a family member, have fallen away. In their place comes a defender whose worth lies in his character, from which arises a sense of loyalty due to Roland's kindness toward him.[60] In such a social context, Ritschier's insistence in Konrad's romance on the privileges of birth and his refusal to recognize the merits of Engelhard's loyal and superior service put him on the wrong side. His insistence on an inherited position and his refusal to understand Engelhard's true merit lead him to make a court case that turns out to be just as false as his own understanding.

APPENDIX: PLOT SUMMARY OF KONRAD VON WÜRZBURG'S *ENGELHARD*, ll. 1–5075

The work begins with a lengthy description of fidelity (*triuwe*), its value, and its diminished importance in the world in which Konrad finds himself. He presents the story of Engelhard, which he says he has from Latin sources, as an exemplary tale designed to awaken interest in this virtue among those who hear it. This story dates from a time in which fidelity was highly esteemed. Its main character, Engelhard, is one of ten sons born to a poor Burgundian nobleman. Engelhard, the most gifted of all the children, decides to seek his fortune at the court of King Fruot of Denmark, because he realizes he will not have the necessary financial means to gain the reputation to which both birth and desire destine him. His father gives him three apples to use in choosing a worthy companion; only the person who immediately offers him half of the apple will be a reliable friend. Dietrich, the son of the Duke of Brabant, who is traveling incognito, passes the test. He and Engelhard could have been twins, both in physical appearance and in mental attributes. They spend several years in King Fruot's service, during which time both notice and are admired by the king's only child, Engeltrud. Dietrich is called back to Brabant by the death of his father and the wish of his mother and other lords that he assume his inherited position. Unwilling to leave Engelhard, he is finally convinced that he should do his duty but insists that Engelhard must come to visit him and can always have whatever he needs from him. Although Dietrich has promised to make him a knight and keep him handsomely, Engelhard feels that it would be dishonorable to leave King Fruot, who has treated him so well.

After Dietrich's departure, Engelhard is even more admired by everyone except the king's nephew, Ritschier, who is horribly jealous of Engelhard's talents and standing. Meanwhile Engeltrud is consumed with her love for

Engelhard, which she dare not reveal. Her mother dies suddenly, adding the grief over her loss to her secret despair. Her father, thinking to help his beloved daughter with the loss of her mother, suggests that Engelhard be her companion. She pretends to be indifferent to Engelhard, who soon is inflamed with a secret passion for her. In due course, she notices a change in his facial color when they are together and presses him for the reason. When he admits to his secret passion, she tells him that the situation is an impossible one and never to speak of it again.

Engelhard soon lies at death's door due to his unrequited love. Engeltrud visits him, telling him that while a relationship with him would ruin her reputation and perhaps cost him his life, she cannot let him die. She suggests that Engelhard be knighted with Ritschier and take part in a tournament. If he does so, she will reward him for his service.

After his knighting, Engelhard performs in an extraordinary manner in a tournament, returns to Fruot's court, and learns from Engeltrud that he should meet her in the orchard that lies next to her part of the palace. She appears in a dress that apparently leaves little to Engelhard's imagination. In his excitement, he forgets to lock the garden gate. Later on, Ritschier, who is after his hunting hawk, goes through the gate and finds them in flagrante. He runs immediately to the king.

Engelhard and Engeltrud of course realize the gravity of their situation. Engeltrud wants Engelhard to flee to save his life, but he refuses, deciding to lie his way out of the situation. Because of his standing at court, he is allowed to deny that what took place did take place; there are no other witnesses but Ritschier. Engelhard offers to fight to defend his name and a judicial duel is set for a date six weeks in the future.

Engelhard asks permission to spend the time in a monastery to repent of his other sins, so that the ordeal will not render a judgment on him for another misdeed. Instead, he heads straight for Brabant, arriving in the middle of the night so that no one sees him. He asks Dietrich for help. Dietrich installs Engelhard in his marital bed and heads for Denmark, knowing that he can safely fight the duel as a stand-in for Engelhard, since no one can tell them apart. Dietrich is, of course, innocent of Ritschier's charge and can expect to win. Engelhard tells the duchess, Dietrich's wife, that he has put the sword between them for six weeks as an act of penance on his part.

Dietrich arrives in Denmark just before the judicial duel, which he wins, cutting off Ritschier's left hand in the process. He is given to Engeltrud in marriage and returns to Brabant as soon as possible. Engelhard takes his place and becomes king following Fruot's death.

Notes

1. See Rüdiger Brandt, *Konrad von Würzburg: Kleinere epische Werke* (Berlin: Erich Schmidt Verlag, 2000), 15–18; Werner Meyer, "Konrad in Würzburg und am Niederrhein," in *Das ritterliche Basel: Zum 700. Todestag Konrads von Würzburg,* ed. Susanne Bruggmann and Christian Schmid-Cadalbert (Basel: Öffentliche Basler Denkmalpflege, 1987), 20–22; Heinz Rupp, "Konrad von Würzburg," in ibid., 32–35.

2. Joachim Bumke, *Geschichte der deutschen Literatur im hohen Mittelalter* (Munich: Deutscher Taschenbuch Verlag, 2000), 240–41; Brandt, *Konrad von Würzburg* (2000), 9–32; Hartmut Kokott, *Konrad von Würzburg: Ein Autor zwischen Auftrag und Autonomie* (Stuttgart: S. Hirzel Wissenschaftliche Verlagsgesellschaft, 1989), 9–16.

3. The question of tolerance toward such obvious crimes in late thirteenth-century upper-class life is a difficult one, which is connected in some degree with attitudes toward the ordeal at that time. This question will be discussed in more detail later in the analysis.

4. Konrad von Würzburg, *Engelhard,* ed. Ingo Reiffenstein (Max Niemeyer Verlag: Tübingen, 1982), ll. 198–268. Hereafter all text references are taken from this edition. The translations are my own.

5. Bumke, *Geschichte der deutschen Literatur im hohen Mittelalter,* 241, notes that Konrad's patrons, whom he frequently named, were leaders in the Church and in the secular world. See also Tom Scott, *Society and Economy in Germany, 1300–1600* (Basingstoke, Hampshire: Palgrave, 2002), 22, who notes that patricians in late medieval German cities continued to reflect the values and ideals of aristocratic society.

6. The dating of *Engelhard* has aroused a great deal of controversy, since the original manuscript exists only in a sixteenth-century version and does not name a patron. The critical analyses that concern themselves with the probable date and place of composition also use their individual interpretations of Engelhard's origins to prove larger theories with which their discussions deal. Since the place of composition has some relevance to this interpretation in regard to the motif of upward mobility, a brief look at the controversy is in order. The two basic positions concern whether the work was written for the House of Kleve in the north or during Konrad's residency in Basel, in connection with the Habsburgs and Basel patricians. Upward mobility for the House of Kleve at the time in question, as well as for the lower nobility and ruling class of Basel, seems to have been an ongoing preoccupation, so the place in which Konrad composed *Engelhard* will not change the basic outlines of this analysis. At this point, however, there can be no certainty about which specific historical situation provided the context for the work. In his recent book *Konrad von Würzburg* (2000), Brandt discusses the two schools (27–32) as well as the historical background (33–43) and says that the limited degree of certainty in the various studies dealing with this question is a real frustration. At present there is no dispassionate evaluation of the merits of both positions. Each critic who

takes up the matter argues from a certain point of view. Those interested in pursuing this question further can consult the following materials: W. Günther Rohr, "Die niederrheinische Schaffensphase Konrads von Würzburg als germanistische Legende," in *Dialektologie zwischen Tradition und Neuansätzen: Beiträge der Internationalen Dialektologentagung, Göttingen, 19–21. Oktober 1998* (Stuttgart: F. Steiner, 2000), 417–30; Reinhard Bleck, *Überlegungen zur Entstehungssituation der Werke Konrads von Würzburg, in denen kein Auftraggeber genannt wird* (Vienna: K. M. Halosar, 1987), 53–58; Heinz Thomas, "Konrad von Würzburg und die Habsburger," *Deutsches Archiv für Erforschung des Mittelalters* 52 (1996): 345–76; Alfred Ritscher, *Literatur und Politik im Umkreis der ersten Habsburger* (Frankfurt: Peter Lang, 1992), 64–66; Helmut de Boor, "Die Chronologie der Werke Konrads von Würzburg, insbesondere die Stellung des Turniers von Nantes," *Beiträge zur Geschichte der deutschen Sprache und Literatur* 89 (1968): 268.

7. For information on the connection between the Amicus/Amelius legend and *Engelhard,* see Rüdiger Schnell, "Die Wahrheit eines manipulierten Gottesurteils: Eine rechtsgeschichtliche Interpretation von Konrads von Würzburgs 'Engelhard,'" *Poetica* 16 (1984): 24–60; Peter H. Oettli, *Tradition and Creativity: The "Engelhard" of Konrad von Würzburg: Its Structure and Its Sources* (New York: Peter Lang, 1986), 47–76; and Rüdiger Brandt, *Konrad von Würzburg* (Darmstadt: Wissenschaftliche Buchgesellschaft, 1987), 137–38. For information about changes in length and emphasis of various parts, see the above-cited Reiffenstein edition's introduction, xix–xx. While Konrad's sources contained elements suggesting the love story that he developed, none of them treated it in the extensive way that he did. Barbara Könneker also comments that, in contrast to Konrad, the love motif in other versions is only there to motivate the fight and that the woman is not important otherwise in the plot. See her article "Erzähltypus und epische Struktur des *Engelhard:* Ein Beitrag zur literarhistorischen Stellung Konrads von Würzburg," *Euphorion* 62 (1968), 239–77.

8. For comments about this prologue, see Brandt, *Konrad von Würzburg* (2000), 112n68. Brandt also notes that in Konrad's lifetime the older feudal economy was being replaced by a monetary one (35). See also his comments about the special relationship of the financially affluent to *triuwe* (111n65). See also Oettli, *Tradition and Creativity,* 80–84. Financial gain did not appear as a motivating force in the Amicus/Amelius tale; Konrad either invented it or found it in whatever he used as his primary source. In any case, other thirteenth-century German writers such as Thomasin von Zerklaere (1215) and Der Marner noted the advantage that a rich man had over a poor but talented one.

9. "die rîchen die bedürfen doch / triuwen baz dan iemen. / ob triuwe pflaege niemen, / sô würde kranc der rîchen habe."

10. Money, or the lack of it, also figures in Engelhard's decision to leave home, because his parents will have one less mouth to feed (ll. 280–305). See Edith Feistner, "Konrads von Würzburg 'Engelhard', Rudolf von Ems 'Willehalm von Orleans' und Phillipes de Beaumanoir 'Jehan et Blonde': Motive und Strukturen der narrativen Großform im 13. Jhdt.," *Jahrbuch der Oswald von Wolkenstein Gesellschaft* 5 (1988/89): 329–40, esp. 333.

11. "er was gar aller sælde vol, / wan daz im brast an guote, / daz edeles herzen muote / bieten muoz geleite / ze hôher werdekeite./ Wan zwâre, als ich erkennen kan, / sô mac vil kûme ein edel man / wert gesîn in kranker habe"; "ich wæne, an mir *verderben*

muoz / ritters name und ouch sîn amt"; "ich getriuwe sînen êren / daz er mich vazze schône / und er mich noch ze lône / vil rîchiu swertlêhen gebe. / daz ist vil bezzer denne ich lebe / alsô *verdorbenlîche.*" For *verderben,* Lexer lists a variety of meanings, ranging from becoming useless, coming to nothing, coming into difficulties, dying, and getting into a shameful situation (Matthias Lexer, *Mittelhochdeutsches Handwörterbuch,* vol. 3 [Leipzig: S. Hirzel, 1878], cols. 93–94). Most versions of the Amicus/Amelius legend have the two young knights at the court of Charlemagne, but Fruot's court was seen in thirteenth-century medieval German literature as a model of knightly culture in regard to generosity and courtly ideals (Oettli, *Tradition and Creativity,* 85, 108–9).

12. See Timothy Jackson, "Der Adel im Werk Konrads von Würzburg: Idealisierung und Kritik," *Jahrbuch der Oswald von Wolkenstein Gesellschaft* 5 (1988/89): 109–23.

13. Oettli, *Tradition and Creativity,* 86, comments that the Normandy tournament is most probably an addition of Konrad, perhaps inserted to show Engelhard's prowess in battle. Such a public display would have made the victory of Engelhard over Ritschier in the judicial duel less surprising. Fortunately Dietrich was just as capable.

14. "sô truoc er dem *getriuwen* haz, / durch anders niht wan umbe daz / daz er ze hove was sô wert. / dâ von sô hæte er ie gegert, / daz er im al sîn êre / verdrücken möhte sêre / mit ernestlîchen sachen. / er wolte in gerne machen / an sînen starken wirde kranc. / sîn herze in hôhem muote ranc / und hæte freudebæren sin, / durch die schulde daz er in / vermelden möhte bî der stunt. / er tet ûf sînen *falschen* munt / vil *ungetriuwe- clîche* alsô."

15. The following passages, which appear immediately after Ritschier's discovery of the couple, reflect the same ideas: "was truoc Ritschieren dar? / daz in got verdamne!" (What brought Ritschier here? May God condemn him! [ll. 3266–67]); "dô Ritschier über si was komen / und er si ligende alsô vant, / zornes wart sîn herze ermant / und sîn ungetriuwer muot" (When Ritschier had surprised them and saw them lying together, then his heart and his faithless spirit were full of anger [ll. 3276–79]). A further possible expression of the narrator's disapproval of Ritschier could lie in his choice of apparel for the battle: he is dressed completely in black, while Dietrich is in white. The narrator notes in this passage that Dietrich had always been a model of decency and fidelity (ll. 4686–99). The choice of white for Dietrich's costume seems to reflect his virtue, while Ritschier's preference for black could reflect the inner condition of his soul. Behr, in discussing the connections between Gottfried's *Tristan* and *Engelhard,* notes that Ritschier takes over Marjodoc's role of the envious accuser (Hans-Joachim Behr, "Liebe und Freundschaft im *Engelhard* Kondrads von Würzburg," *Jahrbuch der Oswald von Wolkenstein Gesellschaft* 5 [1988/89]: 319–27, esp. 323).

16. Dieter Seitz, "Konrad von Würzburg," in *Einführung in die deutsche Literatur des 12. bis 16. Jahrhunderts,* vol. 2, *Patriziat und Landesherrschaft: 13.–15. Jahrhundert,* ed. Winfried Frey et al. (Opladen: Westdeutscher Verlag, 1982), 135–54 (151). See also Herbert Herzmann, "Die alte Ordnung und der neue Mensch: Zum Engelhard des Konrad von Würzburg," in *Sprache, Text, Geschichte,* ed. Peter K. Stein (Göppingen: Kümmerle, 1980), 385–407, esp. 395.

17. See *Engelhard,* ll. 2269ff. When Engeltrud hears about Engelhard's impending death she did "*als ein friunt dem friunde tuot,* / *der lîhte schamerîchen muot* / *ze rücke wirfet, swenne er siht,* / *daz sîner helfe im nôt geschiht*" (*as one friend does for the other,*

throwing aside all modesty, when he sees that the other needs his help). In order to re-vive him, she promises to return his love if he succeeds in a tournament, adding: "lieze ich nû verderben / dich, *friunt*, wie tæte ich danne? / Man sol getriuwem manne / mit liebe leit vertrîben" (If I let you perish, *my friend*, what would I be doing? For a loyal man, one should drive away sorrow with love [ll. 2374–77]). In another section, Engel-trud uses *friuntschaft* and *minne* interchangeably (ll. 2930–33). Peter Kesting compares Engeltrud's *triuwe* with that of Dietrich and Engelhard ("*Diu rehte wârheit*: Zu Konrads von Würzburg 'Engelhard,'" *Zeitschrift für deutsches Altertum* 99 [1970]: 257). Könneker sees no connection between the *minne* and the *triuwe* themes; however, were there a link, it would weaken her point (Könneker, "Erzähltypus und epische Struktur des *Engel-hard*," 239–77, esp. 260). Reiffenstein complains about a lack of integration (*Engelhard*, xix). Kokott sees *Engelhard* as the story of a young man determined to better his sta-tion in life, a goal that would be very difficult without the connection to the princess (*Konrad von Würzburg*, 44–45 and 48). Peter H. Oettli sees the section on the love be-tween Engelhard and Engeltrud as completely integrated into the major themes of *tri-uwe* ("Verschränkung und Steigerung: Zur Interpretation von Konrads von Würzburg, *Engelhard*," *Zeitschrift für deutsche Philologie* 105 [1986]: 63–77, esp. 73–77).

18. In discussing Alexander III's marriage doctrine on the importance of consent, Brundage notes that it enabled couples to marry when family opposition would have precluded their union (James A. Brundage, *Law, Sex, and Christian Society in Medieval Europe* [Chicago and London: University of Chicago Press, 1987], 335–36; see also 189–90 and 276).

19. See *Engelhard*, ll. 3716–19: "und zwâre sît daz Engeltrût / hât übergangen mîn gebôt, / sô muoz si darben, sam mir got, / des daz si von mir erben sol" (And truly since Engeltrud has not obeyed my commandment, then she must do without her inheritance).

20. See my recent book, *Trial by Fire and Battle in Medieval German Literature* (Rochester, NY: Camden House, 2004), esp. 7–11.

21. Ritschier expresses this belief in ll. 4034–38: "Zewâre, wæret ir ein rise, / ich wolte iu kampfes doch gestân, / ûf den vil sæleclîchen wân / daz got die rehten wârheit / mit sîner helfe nie vermeit" (Truly, even if you were a giant, I would yet be victorious over you in battle, in the blessed belief that God never forsakes the real truth). The phrase "die rehten wârheit" figures in the *Engelhard* interpretation; see Kesting, "*Diu rehte wârheit*," 246–59.

22. Robert Bartlett, *Trial by Fire and Water* (Oxford: Oxford University Press, 1986), 116–22. See also Gerald Buchda, "Der Beweis im sächsischen Recht," in *La Preuve: Recueils de la Société Jean Bodin pour l'histoire comparative des institutions* 17 (1965): 519–46, esp. 531–32. Hermann Nottarp notes that, in the case of a duel, the secular judge, not a priest, decides on guilt or innocence (*Gottesurteile* [Munich: Kösel Verlag, 1956], 265). Misgivings about the trial by battle were of long standing: for example, an eighth-century Langobard king, Liutprand, already expressed doubts about its validity, as did the Salian Franks (270). Analysis of the rigged ordeal in *Engelhard* seems to posit public acceptance and opinions about the ordeal as unvarying throughout the thir-teenth century. The major changes that Innocent III caused in legal practices by his edict in 1215 are not mentioned by Schnell in "Die Wahrheit eines manipulierten Gottesurteils."

23. Ritschier refers to the weakening of the king's honor (ll. 3508, 3518) and his reputation (ll. 3543–44). The king says: "sît daz er nû die triuwe sîn / an mir sô gar zerbrochen hât" (Since he has now broken his fidelity to me so completely [ll. 3582–83]); see also ll. 3572, 3574, and 3708–9. Schnell also notes that Engelhard's behavior constitutes a breach of the *triuwe* relationship ("Die Wahrheit eines manipulierten Gottesurteils," 31).

24. Kokott, *Konrad von Würzburg,* 57, notes that Ritschier's accusation of treason was certainly justified.

25. The link between offenses of a traitorous nature and the judgment of God through battle was so powerful that Frederick II specifically excepted accusations of treason when he abolished trial by battle for southern Italy. See Bartlett, *Trial by Fire and Water,* 107.

26. Konrad's familiarity with legal procedures is well documented in his works. See Brandt, *Konrad von Würzburg* (1987), 100–105; *Der Schwanritter* contains another trial by battle.

27. See Gottfried von Straßburg, *Tristan und Isold,* ed. Friedrich Ranke (Bern: A. Francke, 1946), ll. 15733–55. For a discussion of the critical history as well as Isolde's ordeal itself, see Ziegler, *Trial by Fire and Battle in Medieval German Literature,* 123–32.

28. Because his mother is the king's sister, Ritschier would have been expected to have had a very privileged position with the monarch. The sister's son frequently enjoyed a special bond with her brother among the medieval nobility. Constance Brittain Bouchard discusses this bond in life and in literary texts in *Strong of Body, Brave and Noble: Chivalry and Society in Medieval France* (Ithaca, NY: Cornell University Press, 1998), 77. However, Ritschier certainly does not have the king's attention in the way that Engelhard does. The differences are particularly striking when one compares Ritschier's role at court with that of Tristan. See Kokott, *Konrad von Würzburg,* 49, and the detailed discussion of class difference, 54–57.

29. Women could in unusual instances fight in such duels. See Jean Gaudemet, "Les Ordalies au Moyen Age: Doctrine, législation et pratiques canoniques," *La Preuve: Recueils de la Société Jean Bodin pour l'histoire comparative des institutions* 17 (1965): 99–135, esp. 113.

30. Timothy Jackson's article, "Abraham and Engelhard: Immoral Means and Moral Ends," in *Connections: Essays in Honor of Eda Sagarra on the Occasion of her Sixtieth Birthday,* ed. Peter Skrine, Rosemary E. Wallbank-Turner, and Jonathan West (Stuttgart: Hans-Dieter Heinz, 1993), 117–26, contains a section in which he compares this ordeal scene with that of Isolde.

31. While the bishops are not present during the crucial council session leading up to the trial, they do come to watch the battle (ll. 4608–10).

32. See Bartlett, *Trial by Fire and Water,* 30–31.

33. This attitude reflects Konrad's obvious sympathies with the ambitions of those who wish to break into the highest levels of their social structure. The sympathetic treatment of the court favorite, Engelhard, in this context could reflect values and aspirations of Engelhard's audience and patrons, whether that consisted of the House of Kleve or the patricians of Basel. In their hopes to enjoy the privilege and position of the highest aristocracy, they were forced to depend on their own wits and skills. For comments about Konrad's Basel audience, see Seitz, "Konrad von Würzburg," in *Einführung*

in die deutsche Literatur des 12. bis 16. Jahrhunderts, vol. 2, ed. Frey, 135–54, esp. 148–51. Werner Meyer notes that the ability of the *cives* to ascend into the knightly class in Basel came about in 1227 through a royal privilege. Basel was especially well-known in the thirteenth and fourteenth centuries as a preferred venue for knightly tournaments ("Basel im 13. Jahrhundert," in *Das ritterliche Basel,* ed. Bruggmann and Schmid-Cadalbert [Basel: Öffentliche Basler Denkmalpflege, 1987], 25–26). See also Brandt, *Konrad von Würzburg* (2000), 35, and Ritscher, *Literatur und Politik im Umkreis der ersten Habsburger,* 67.

34. Engelhard refers to his social position at other times, such as in his defense before King Fruot (ll. 3736–43).

35. Gottfried von Straßburg, *Tristan,* ed. Ranke, ll. 15494–95; see also Bartlett, *Trial by Fire and Water,* 32.

36. Nottarp, *Gottesurteile,* 270. Obviously, there was the testimony of Ritschier. The nobles have already remarked on the taint of self-interest that colors his evidence. Another reason that Ritschier's account is not sufficient to convict and that Konrad gives no explanation for that fact may lie in legal usage. Bartlett, in discussing an early thirteenth-century Austrian legal code, notes that somewhere between two and seven eyewitnesses seemed to be sufficient to convict without an ordeal (*Trial by Fire and Water,* 29).

37. Nottarp, *Gottesurteile,* 270.

38. "welt ir unschuldic werden, / daz muoz ergân ûf erden / mit swerte engegen swerte[.] / . . . ê daz ich werde schamerôt / und ich ein lügener bestê, / sô wil ich mîn leben ê / mit willen ûf die wâge legen. / man sol mit grimmen swertes slegen / beherten ganze wârheit. / wan swüeret ir uns manegen eit, / es künde iuch kleine für getragen, / welt ir entreden unde entsagen / iuch benamen des geziges, / seht, sô müezet ir des siges / an mir gewaltic werden. / niht anders kan ûf erden / gehelfen iuch ze dirre nôt."

39. Bartlett, *Trial by Fire and Water,* 29.

40. Bartlett says: "Exculpation by oath alone and exculpation by ordeal were mutually exclusive; hence, where oaths were unacceptable, the ordeal became a natural recourse" (ibid., 30). See also John Baldwin, in his discussion of the *Roman de la violette,* written by Gerbert de Monteuil around 1227–29; in the first ordeal by battle portrayed in this work, both oaths and clergy were absent ("The Crisis of the Ordeal: Literature, Law and Religion around 1200," *Journal of Medieval and Renaissance Studies* 24 [1994]: 327–53).

41. Nottarp, *Gottesurteile,* 270; see also Schnell, "Die Wahrheit eines manipulierten Gottesurteils," 48–59.

42. Henry Charles Lea, *The Duel and the Oath,* ed. Edward Peters (1866; Philadelphia: University of Pennsylvania Press, 1974), 74. Lea adds that Roman law put burden of proof on the accuser, since it held that proof of a negative was not possible morally. See Udo Kornblum, "Gerichtlicher Eid," in *Handwörterbuch der deutschen Rechtsgeschichte* [hereafter *HWBDR*], ed. Adalbert Erler and Ekkehard Kaufmann, vol. 1 (Berlin: E. Schmidt, 1971), col. 863. See also Hans Hattenhauer, "Der gefälschte Eid," in *Fälschungen im Mittelalter,* pt. 1, *Gefälschte Rechtstexte: Der Bestrafte Fälscher* (Hannover: Hahn, 1988), 661–89.

43. Bartlett, *Trial by Fire and Water,* 30. For a discussion of oath-taking in early Germanic law, see Ian Wood, "Disputes in Late Fifth- and Sixth-Century Gaul," in *The*

Settlement of Disputes in Early Medieval Europe, ed. Wendy Davies and Paul Fouracre (Cambridge: Cambridge University Press, 1986), 14–18.

44. Lea, *The Duel and the Oath,* ed. Peters, 7. See also Bartlett, *Trial by Fire and Water,* 30, who says that the oath was more dependent upon future judgment by God than it was upon an immediate reaction.

45. Heinz Holzhauer, "Der gerichtliche Zweikampf," in *Sprache und Recht: Beiträge zur Kulturgeschichte des Mittelalters. Festschrift für Ruth Schmidt-Wiegand zum 60. Geburtstag* (Berlin and New York: De Gruyter, 1986), 263–83, esp. 276.

46. Bartlett, *Trial by Fire and Water,* 24–27.

47. Nottarp, *Gottesurteile,* 270.

48. "alsô daz ich ûf erden / unschuldic müeze werden, / swie manz erteilen künne mir. / also stât mînes herzen gir / und ist mîn lîp dar zuo bereit / mit willeclîcher arebeit." For Isolde's offer, see Gottfried von Straßburg, *Tristan,* ed. Ranke, ll. 15511–17.

49. See Ekkehard Kaufmann, "Binden," in *HWBDR,* vol. 1, cols. 437–39.

50. See Dieter Werkmüller, "Handhafte Tat," in *HWBDR,* vol. 1, cols. 1968–69, and Kaufmann, "Binden," in ibid., cols. 437–38. Werkmüller states that the bound individual caught in the act and brought before the court was not only incapable of defending himself physically but also incapable of mounting a legal defense (col. 1969).

51. At this point, Engelhard requests permission to spend six weeks in a monastery repenting of his sins and making spiritual preparation for his trial (ll. 4155ff.). Although he plans to use this time to travel to Dietrich, the request was not at all unusual. Kokott implies that the six-week period of time Engelhard receives from the court before the duel is due to his own eloquent efforts (*Konrad von Würzburg,* 50). In actual fact, it was common to allow a period of time to get one's affairs in order, should one lose the ordeal.

52. Brandt, *Konrad von Würzburg* (2000), 124n101, says that this passage shows that Engelhard believes in the function of trial by battle. The text shows that Engelhard is convinced that he will lose if he does battle, a belief that still reflects the ordeal's origins in magical thinking, a strict formulaic approach that forced supernatural powers to render a just verdict. Since trial by battle was still a viable legal procedure in the German lands at this time, Engelhard's attitude is not anachronistic. See Bartlett, *Trial by Fire and Water,* 103–26. Engelhard knows if he fights, he will lose through God's direct intervention, because Ritschier represents the factual truth, which Engelhard has been hiding (see ll. 4122–37). If Dietrich fights, he has not had an intimate relationship with Engeltrud, and he represents an objective truth, which, however, on a factual level, is not the real truth. In this regard, both Isolde's ordeal and Engelhard/Dietrich's are comparable. Both Engelhard and Ritschier agree that God, through the ordeal, will establish "just truth" (ll. 4035–43). In his carefully documented discussion of the meaning of this term, Kesting does not mention the possibility that in the context of the trial by battle, which is the subject of discussion, where God will make the truth known, part of this meaning is a legal one ("*Diu rehte wârheit,*" 246–59, esp. 247ff.). Lexer, *Mittelhochdeutsches Handwörterbuch,* vol. 2, cols. 376–77, indicates (col. 376) that the adjective *rehte* can have such a meaning. Konrad notes that both men who step into the circle, the legal space, are innocent (l. 4748), but since *triuwe* will help "wider valschem muote" (against a dishonorable attitude) (l. 4751), Dietrich can afford to be relatively unconcerned about Ritschier's threats (ll. 4752–55).

53. Kokott, *Konrad von Würzburg*, 58, notes that Dietrich does not reply.

54. Klaus Jörg Schmitz, *Konrad von Würzburg: "Stellenkommentar"* (Göppingen: Kümmerle, 1989), 68, notes that in the Latin version of the saga, Ardericus (Ritschier) is killed. Konrad is the first to use the loss of a left hand. Schnell believes that Konrad tried to muddy the waters with his decision to cut off the left instead of the right hand, which is usually the hand used to swear with ("Die Wahrheit eines manipulierten Gottesurteils," 55–57). However, that may not have been Konrad's intent. M. Kobler's article, "Hand," notes that while perjury normally demanded the loss of the right hand, as a special act of clemency, the left could substitute (*HWBDR*, vol. 1, col. 1928). Heinz Holzhauer, "Meineid," in the *HWBDR* notes that the loss of a hand is the usual punishment for perjury in the capitularies (vol. 3, col. 450). Konrad's audience would of course have thought of this frequent punishment for perjury. See *Handwörterbuch des deutschen Aberglaubens*, ed. H. Bächtold-Stäubli and E. Hoffmann-Krayer, vol. 3, cols. 1379ff., esp. 1385–87; *Deutsches Rechtswörterbuch*, ed. Adalbert Erler and Ekkehard Kaufmann, vol. 4, cols. 1560ff., and Karl-Heinz Göttert, *Tugendbegriff und epische Struktur in höfischen Dichtungen* (Köln: Böhlau, 1971), 161, who notes that the left hand's negative meaning played a role. See also Kokott, *Konrad von Würzburg*, 58, Schmitz, *Konrad von Würzburg*, 68, and Janet L. Nelson, "Dispute Settlement in Carolingian West Francia," in *The Settlement of Disputes in Early Medieval Europe*, ed. Davies and Fouracre, 47, who notes a reference to loss of hand for the perjurer in trial by battle in a Carolingian capitulary of 816.

55. Holzhauer, "Meineid," in *HWBDR*, vol. 3, col. 448.

56. Such punishment received mention during the council scene, when the nobles made the following statement about corporal punishment for false oaths: "sîn zunge müeze im noch erlamen, / swer in ziu verlogen habe" (ll. 3666–67). Hans Hattenhauer notes that legends contain frequent mention of punishment after perjury (*Das Recht der Heiligen* [Berlin: Duncker and Humblot, 1976], 75). See also Hattenhauer, "Der gefälschte Eid," in *Fälschungen im Mittelalter*, pt. 1, 662. See also Ruth Schmidt-Wiegand, "Eid und Gelöbnis, Formel und Formular im mittelalterlichen Recht," in *Recht und Schrift im Mittelalter: Vorträge und Forschungen*, vol. 8, ed. Peter Classen (Sigmaringen: Thorbecke, 1977), 55–90, esp. 55; Ruth Schmidt-Wiegand, "Gebärdensprache im mittelalterlichen Recht," *Frühmittelalterliche Studien* 16 (1981): 363–79, esp. 377.

57. Brandt notes that Ritschier's motivation is false, since it arises out of envy toward Engelhard, while Dietrich's is good, since he wants only to help his friend (*Konrad von Würzburg* [2000], 125n104). Kokott apparently does not take this passage into account when he maintains that it remains an open question whether or not this mutilation should be considered as a punishment (*Konrad von Würzburg*, 58–59).

58. "Ritschier muost einer hende / darben alle sîne tage / und als ein ungetriuwer zage / enpfâhen laster unde schimpf. / mit hazze koufte er ungelimpf / und schaden grôz mit nîde."

59. Brandt notes that the long-established tradition of didactic intent in medieval literature frequently combined with a lamentation about the collapse of the virtue advocated (*Konrad von Würburg* [2000], 55). The relating of the story was considered to be the remedy, an approach Konrad certainly advocates.

60. See *Karl Meinet*, ed. Adalbert von Keller (Stuttgart, 1858; Amsterdam: Rodopi, 1971), A 530, ll. 12–17.

Chapter 3

Women in Love

Carnal and Spiritual Transgressions in Late Medieval France

DYAN ELLIOTT

The interplay between structure and antistructure invariably gives rise to a shadow world simultaneously fostered by, and festering within, this generating matrix. This world is confected from detritus that was shed en route to the establishment of new forms. Thus while individuals are, from a certain perspective, in training to inhabit the new structures that society has ordained for them, many of the shadow world's characteristic features reach out to them as strangely familiar, filling them with nostalgia for a past they cannot quite remember. Sigmund Freud sees this kind of potentiality in the generation of the uncanny double, which he describes as a repository for "all the unfulfilled but possible futures to which we still like to cling in phantasy, all the strivings of the ego which adverse external circumstances have crushed, and all our suppressed acts of volition which nourish in us the illusion of free will."[1] And, as Freud is at pains to remind us, the category of the uncanny (in German *unheimlich*—literally the "unhomely" or "unfamiliar") is a species of the *heimlich*—the "homely" or the "familiar." In other words, the German language simultaneously entertains two entirely opposite definitions of *heimlich*—one betokening homely comfort; the other signifying varying shades of concealed or supernatural malice.[2] Similarly, the English word for "canny" has the same bifurcated capacity, accommodating occult and supernatural meanings that would normally be regarded as the preserve of the "uncanny."[3] In short, the uncanny or unfamiliar is what we choose to exile, suggesting that at some distant time it was intensely familiar. We recognize it as alien and menacing only when it attempts to come home.

The process of estranging what was once familiar happens not just developmentally as we progress from childhood to adulthood, but also sociohistorically, as groups of individuals are psychically inducted, or even pummeled, into new emotional and institutional standards. But, as in the case of a dream, the shadow world can put these elements together in a manner that is both unpredictable and terrifying while at the same time strangely appealing. In such cases, the powers of attraction and repulsion to these forms are felt equally.

The creative powers of regulation are especially apparent in the high Middle Ages at the Fourth Lateran Council of 1215—surely one of the "ur" moments of structuration for Latin Christendom. In an effort to tighten the ecclesiastical hold on both secular and religious life, Lateran IV sought both to regulate more closely the formation of a marriage and to defend the essential worthiness of the institution, in keeping with the gradual sacramentalization of marriage that had been occurring over the course of the twelfth century. This same council also expressly prohibited the formation of new religious orders.[4] But such prohibitions gave rise to two rather predictable groups of outcasts. One was epitomized by the demimonde of the prostitute, in which illicit nonprocreative sex defied the new emphasis on the divine procreative purposes of matrimony. A second group contained individuals who wished to pursue a religious life but were nevertheless unwilling or unable to comply with Lateran IV's mandate that they join a preexisting religious order—a condition exemplified by the Beguine movement. What was, perhaps, less predictable was the sheer virtuosity with which these expelled groups retained and mirrored what society sought to jettison from its own understandings of love. Moreover, the very existence of these groups, who were essentially serving the function of a social unconscious, challenged certain sanctioned divisions and prohibited forms between spiritual and carnal love. Authors such as R. I. Moore have indicated the extent to which the rhetoric of persecution can unite groups as disparate as heretics, Jews, and lepers into an undifferentiated Other.[5] The two groups I will be considering clearly begin with more in common than this triune set of outcasts. Moreover, expulsion from society's corporate body is possessed of a magnetism all its own, which ultimately draws the two groups closer still.

A Woman Scorned

My point of entry into illicit sexuality is through the criminal prosecution of a certain Margot de la Barre that appears in the register of the Parisian prison the Châtelet toward the end of July 1390.[6] Margot had been a free-lance prostitute, although by the time of the trial, when she must have been somewhere in the vicinity of sixty years of age, she was no longer practicing her trade.[7] She was accused of poisoning the recently married Hainsselin Planiete and his wife Agnesot by the application of suspect charms. Margot did admit that she had administered certain wreaths made out of herbs in an effort to cure the headaches of the wife, whose condition, Margot claimed, improved. By her own account, she gently approached Agnesot's sickbed, saying: "Agnesot, my friend, I didn't give you a wreath at your wedding, and for this reason I am giving you this wreath, which I hold in my hand; and I promise you that it's a long time since you wore a better wreath for recovering your health."[8] Margot also acknowledged that she subsequently treated the husband, Hainsselin, for a fever, although she did not know with what result.[9] The various counselors deliberating on the case, however, were suspicious of the aging prostitute's way of life and purported remedies and decided to put Margot to the "question," the age-old euphemism for torture, to see if they could learn anything more.[10] This application of torture, the first of three, did not elicit any further information. But the apprehension and subsequent questioning of Margot's friend, a young prostitute named Marion La Droiturière, led to further revelations. Eventually breaking under the pressures of torture, Marion admitted that she had enlisted Margot's knowledge of magic in order to retain the affection of Hainsselin, her lover, and to undermine his recent marriage.[11] Eventually, Margot's confession, extracted by the repeated use of torture, would substantially corroborate Marion's claims.[12] Both women were, accordingly, burned for sorcery in early August of the same year at the swine market located beyond the Porte Saint-Honoré. Neither had goods worth confiscating for the crown.[13]

As emerged in the course of the two women's testimony, Marion was desperately in love with Hainsselin and was prepared to take any measures to retain his love. She had already followed the advice of a drinking companion, "another daughter of sin" from Flanders, who had volunteered that the way to increase the mutual love between Marion and Hainsselin was for Marion to mix her menstrual blood in wine that she would then share with her lover.[14] Marion took her advice, but the spell did not procure the desired effect, since she later learned of Hainsselin's engagement to Agnesot. It was at this point that Marion appealed to Margot, who, after making her swear secrecy "by her faith and the oath of her body," an oath she made her repeat on several occasions, proffered the following advice.[15] Marion should take a white cock; kill it by smothering it under her buttocks or turning it around fast; take its testicles; put them into a feather pillow slept on by Hainsselin; leave them for eight or nine days; remove the testicles from the pillow; burn them until they were powder; and put the ashes into the food and wine of her beloved. This spell would not only render Marion irresistible to Hainsselin, so that, in Margot's words, "he would not be able to have enough of her," but would also ensure that his love was eternal. Marion did as she had been instructed. She noticed that Hainsselin loved her as much as ever but no more.[16] Margot's most drastic remedy was to construct two wreaths from certain herbs purchased on the vigil of the feast of Saint John the Baptist—an auspicious day for the harvesting of magical herbs.[17] Marion was to take the wreaths to the newly made couple's nuptial dance and drop them surreptitiously so that Hainsselin and Agnesot would trample on them. The desired results would be not only that Hainsselin's love would be a match for Marion's, but also that he would be incapable of making love to his own wife, Agnesot. Marion did as she was told.[18]

Early returns on the spell were hardly encouraging: the following day in the course of a day trip, some female companions told Marion that "the said Hainsselin had had sex with his wife a very great number and amount of times." But this inauspicious rumor (at least from Marion's perspective) seemed to have been a false alarm. When she returned to Paris she instead heard that, since their nuptials, both spouses had been very ill and that Hainsselin had been unable to consummate the marriage.[19] Marion immediately consulted Margot who said, with apparent satisfaction, "that it was good that they couldn't have sex, and this was the way of the wreaths," adding, somewhat wryly, that now "the wife had plenty of time to be sick."[20]

Marion's efforts to manipulate Hainsselin's affection progress from the age-old use of menstrual blood as a love potion (something that had been cautioned against since early penitential literature) to the more complicated spell with a rooster. These first two spells, which it was hoped would unite the powers of love retention with the properties of an aphrodisiac, could be construed as relatively harmless.[21] But the episode with the wreaths is different, in fact inverting what Margot initially attempted to depict as part of a curative regime. Instead, it was a deliberate move into the malevolent realm of *maleficia,* in that the practitioner intended to inflict active harm. In this case, the desired effect was to render Hainsselin impotent with his wife in order to undermine the marriage. By the later Middle Ages, such activity was perceived as unequivocally diabolical. In one of his quodlibetical questions, for instance, Saint Thomas Aquinas describes the devil as stronger than matrimony, insofar as he could effect impotence before the marriage was consummated, leading to its dissolution.[22] Later works, such as the fifteenth-century *Formicarium* of John Nider or, more spectacularly, the *Malleus maleficarum* will expatiate at length on how women in particular, spurred on by jealousy and malice, were wont to frustrate their erstwhile lovers' attempts at marriage by diabolically induced impotence.[23]

In keeping with this context of diabolism, Margot's final spell for promoting Marion's happiness represented a transition from natural magic to demonic magic, which required the explicit invocation of the devil.[24] In the course of her testimony, Marion had merely reported that Margot muttered certain inaudible words over the wreaths. But Margot, undone by torture and the evidence of her friend Marion's betrayal, whose denunciations the court had made Margot witness in person twice, was eventually prepared to tell her examiners what they wished to hear.[25] She admitted that she had, in fact, invoked the devil in the following manner: "Enemy I conjure you in the name of the father, son, and holy spirit that you come to me here."[26] Repeating these words three times without stopping, she proffered the wreaths. She also made another little wreath from leftover herbs, which she threw in a bin near herself and Marion. Then Satan appeared, looking the same as he does in the Passion plays, though without the horns. When he asked what she wanted, she told him that the wreath in the bin was for him and that he should ensure that no one could help Hainsselin and his wife until the wrongs they had perpetrated against Marion had been righted. Satan took the wreath from the bin, leaving via the window. His departure was accompanied by a great noise, sounding "like a terrific wind."[27]

What I interpret as Margot's unpersuasive but deeply pathetic efforts to meet her examiners' expectations, culminating in a devil resembling the one in the Passion plays, should not eclipse the fact that her attempted interventions were not simply hostile to this marriage, but sprang from a *modus vivendi* that was entirely antithetical to the institution generally. Part of this ethos may have stemmed from society's construal of the prostitute as *fille commune,* or "common woman"—common to all, hence discouraged from devoting her attentions to one. In line with this perception, various regulations forbade a prostitute to have a lover or to refuse a customer, while some law codes denied that a prostitute could be raped.[28]

It is impossible to pronounce upon the extent to which the so-called "common women" internalized this negative description. And yet, clearly many would recognize themselves as permanently estranged from marriage.[29] Bereft of the kind of institutional support that marriage would have garnered from church and state (even if this support was often only symbolic), these women were at the mercy of male affection in all its variability and mutability—a situation that required stabilization by whatever means were available, in this instance, recourse to magic. Masculine unreliability ensured that these "daughters of sin" would ultimately rely on other women. Indeed, if men had their love, women had their trust. Bound by secrecy, women would provide each other with both moral and magical support.

Margot herself is a case in point. Some forty-four years before the trial, while still in her youth, she had been taken from her home in Beaune by her lover: "she did his will with her body and was abandoned to all his good friends who wished to do their pleasure and will in all the different cities of the realm where she was led." Thereafter, she lived for many years "with other women in a life of sin."[30] Her exemplary loyalty to other women is apparent throughout her testimony. During her first interrogation, when Margot was still claiming that she had been attempting to cure Agnesot, true to the promises that she exchanged with Marion in the women's prison, she scrupulously avoided mentioning Marion or any other living person.[31] She accordingly attributed her lore to her "hearth mother."[32] In her subsequent confession, Margot claimed to have learned the spell with the cock and the invocation of the devil from a Flemish girl, "another girl of sin, like herself," some twenty-four years earlier in the field below Montmartre. The girl's name was long forgotten.[33]

Margot's decision to help Marion seems to have been based primarily on friendship. According to Margot's account, Marion came to her house angry and grieving, having just learned of Hainsselin's engagement and claiming that she could "barely live for the love of him."[34] She was literally tearing her dress and her hair. Seeing her friend so distraught, Margot promised to help—provided that Marion would swear never to testify against her.

Marion's very love for Hainsselin would, in turn, render her ever more dependent on female community and magic. Moreover, for all her depth of emotion, she never seems to have required, or at least expected, its regularization in marriage.[35] Perhaps she had achieved a semipermanent status as

Hainsselin's mistress, which might be inferred from their sleeping arrangements. For instance, Marion managed to secret the rooster's testicles into Hainsselin's pillow, which he slept on for two or three nights. Careful not to touch his pillow, in compliance with Margot's instructions, Marion would move her own pillow when she wished to kiss him, thus avoiding his.[36] She may also have been financially supported by Hainsselin. According to Margot's confession, Marion exclaimed on a number of occasions that she would be driven "out of her senses" if Hainsselin persisted with his plans for marriage. She continued, however, that "it would seem better to be a crazy woman [fole feme] at his maintenance and countenance than any other kind."[37] In fact, in using the term *fole feme*—a common euphemism for whore—Marion seems to be making a grim pun on her state of mind and her station in life.[38] Perhaps she was only a prostitute who fell in love with a regular client. It is even possible that Hainsselin was Marion's pimp as well as her lover. This would be one way of interpreting Marion's threat to Hainsselin when they parted company: that within a year he would realize that no other woman could bring him as many "goods" (biens) as she could.[39] Alternatively, Marion repeatedly represents herself as a respectable woman in court. In fact, she made a sufficiently good impression on her judges that several wished to spare her the death penalty.[40] Marion's characterization of herself as a *fole feme* could be a tacit recognition, and possible internalization, of society's tendency to stigmatize the heterosexually active single woman by conflating her with a prostitute—a conflation that has been analyzed by Ruth Karras.[41] From this perspective, it is interesting to ponder whatever verbal play might underlie the apparent coincidence of the term for the independent businesswoman, *feme sole,* and *feme fole.*[42] Both categories presented undeniable challenges to masculine authority.

One might assume that women like Margot and Marion understood their wayward lives as undercutting any plausible candidacy for married life. But there may also be a sense in which the very intensity of Marion's passion registered as incompatible with the institution of marriage.[43] For, as conceived in the Middle Ages, marriage was an inappropriate arena for the indulgence of extreme sexual passion. Saints Jerome and Augustine had both maintained that certain sexual excesses that were disgusting enough in a prostitute were even more to be censured in a wife, and their comments were reiterated by authorities such as Gratian and Peter Lombard.[44] One variant of Augustinian counsel actually encouraged the wife to send her husband to a prostitute rather than herself suffer the excesses of untamed passion and "unnatural" sex. This Augustinian-inflected sentiment does surface in surprising places, such as, for example, in Andreas Capellanus's argument in favor of extramarital affairs on the basis of the fact that passionate love was the more damnable in marriage. Turning our analytical lens only a fraction, we can hear the spirited voice of Héloïse—not only proudly preferring to be Abelard's whore than Augustus's wife, but, more to the point, attempting to dissuade her beloved Abelard from ever marrying her.[45]

In short, these women's shared trepidation about marriage may be seen not only as self-abnegation, but also as a form of critique. In this case, the critique centers upon what marriage excludes, what passions and activities are expelled in the process of its constitution as a sacramentally sanctioned institution. Active at the fringes of the marriage of Hainsselin and Agnesot is a self-selected band of ill-wishers: women—situated in unauthorized but interstitial social locations—who pool unofficial knowledge and unsanctioned experience into a cluster of counterinstitutional practices. The result is a resolute social solidarity that only torture and the full weight of the judicial system can undo.[46]

Les Liaisons Dangereuses

Coexisting with the perception of marriage as a hallowed institution that shuns excessive or inappropriate passion and carnality is the contrary view of the marital bond as so overly implicated in the flesh that it conflicts with a rigorous level of spirituality. This perspective was ostensibly supported by Saint Paul's recommendation that married couples separate temporarily for prayer (1 Corinthians 7:5)—counsel that would create ever-widening ripples in posterity's reflexive pool of ascetical practices. It was generally understood that sexual activity was especially antithetical to heightened spiritual states, forestalling, for example, the possibility of mystical rapture or impeding the spirit of prophecy.[47]

I would like to bear this set of complexities in mind when engaging with another case that occurred in Paris some eighty years before the burning of Margot and Marion—the trial and execution of Marguerite Porete, a mystic from the Low Countries who has frequently been associated with the Beguine movement. Marguerite had several times run afoul of various religious authorities for the dissemination of her mystical work *The Mirror of Simple Souls.* The book had initially been condemned and burned by the bishop of Cambrai at Valenciennes. Unabashed by official censure, Marguerite pursued an itinerant lifestyle, in which she continued to circulate her book, eventually attracting the attention of the French inquisitor, William of Paris. On the basis of a series of incriminating extracts taken out of context, William had the book assessed by a board of twenty-one theologians from the University of Paris, who were unanimous in their somewhat predictable determination that the book was heretical. Marguerite steadfastly refused to cooperate with the Inquisition over the course of her year-and-a-half imprisonment: she would not take an oath, nor would she answer questions. Finally, acting in concert with a team of canonists, William had Marguerite condemned to death on June 1, 1310, and burned at the Place de Grève.[48]

Marguerite, Margot, and Marion had much more in common than a shared execution at the hands of patriarchal authorities. In fact, it was these very areas of convergence that sealed their common fate. According to Maryanne Kowaleski's recent tabulation, single women constituted some 30 to 40 percent of all adult women in the northern European cities of the later Middle Ages.[49] Unmarried and perhaps unmarriageable, each of the three women in question operated within a female community that, for the most part, functioned outside of the sanctioned boundaries of society.[50] Certain social and economic factors had conspired to exacerbate the marginality of both groups in the later Middle Ages. By the fourteenth century, prostitutes constituted some 60 percent of the victims of violent crimes in Paris.[51] Moreover, the prostitute suffered intensely from the urban pauperization that occurred over the course of the fourteenth century.[52] As members of a larger constituency of female celibates in an urban setting, women like the Beguines would also be implicated in these increasing liabilities.[53] Occupying an ambiguous position between lay and religious worlds, such women were further bereft of the protections available to each. Barred by Lateran IV's ruling against the creation of new orders, the Beguines and parallel groups lacked not only a rule but also the stability of traditional monastic vows.[54] An individual Beguine's vow of chastity, for example, was temporary—existing only so long as she was a member of any given Beguinage. Moreover, owing to their mixed status, such loosely affiliated pious women were treated with hostility by various religious authorities—particularly members of the mendicant orders, who regarded groups like the Beguines as rivals.[55]

This precarious position, exacerbated by persecutions in the late thirteenth century, was further undermined in the fourteenth century as

Beguinages became progressively impoverished and the members of their communities increasingly exposed.[56] In 1304, only six years before Marguerite's trial, the continuator for the chronicle of Guillaume of Nangis reports how a Beguine, a "pseudo mulier" of Metz, deceived the French royal court with her false (and politically pro-Flemish) revelations. Her imposition on the royal family culminated in the *maleficia* she administered to poison the king's brother, a crime to which she finally confessed under torture.[57] Historians have recently speculated that the trial of Marguerite Porete (also labeled a "pseudo mulier" by the same chronicler) reflects the anti-Beguine sentiment being further fueled by the fracas surrounding the contemporaneous Templar trial.[58]

But in addition to the marginality common to prostitutes and Beguines alike, the three women in question were further united by what might be described as "criminous love," eventuating in illicit contact with the supernatural, whether through *maleficia* on the one hand or tainted mysticism on the other. We have already seen this at work in the trials of Margot and Marion: the passionate excesses of the latter enlisted the merciful, but irreligious and antisocial, magic of the former. They owed all their magical knowledge to women from Flanders. Marguerite Porete, a woman from Flanders who originated in Hainault, would be incriminated by the reckless and disturbing imagery in which she couched her mystical love of God.[59]

The Mirror of Simple Souls drew on the language of *fine amor,* a literary convention celebrated for its dazzling manipulation of the boundaries between sacred and profane love.[60] But these boundaries had never been discreet in the theological tradition. The bride of the Song of Songs, ever sick with love, suffered from the spiritual wounds inflicted by her celestial bridegroom. Theologians, from Origen to Richard of Saint Victor and beyond, had meticulously demonstrated the close correlation between carnal and spiritual lovesickness.[61] Aquinas, following Augustine, argued that love was the originary passion (or, as we would be more inclined to say, emotion) from which all others ultimately derived.[62] The passions, though symptoms of human frailty and described by Augustine as diseases or disorders of the soul, are nevertheless deemed healthy if their objects are healthy.[63] Love of God was in no way exempt from the sway of the passions. Indeed, Aquinas will even note that certain authorities insist that passionate *amor* is more God-like than mere *dilectio,* as the former implies a certain passion in the sensual appetite, while *dilectio* is restrained by reason. An individual can, accordingly, make his or her way to God more swiftly when drawn passively through the power of *amor*.[64] Moreover, extreme carnal love was believed to induce a complete abstraction from the senses—symptomatic of the famous lovesickness of the Middle Ages. This love-induced stupor was superficially identical to the effects of mystical rapture, by which the soul is commonly understood to be seized by divine love.[65]

Thus Jacques Lacan's flamboyant diagnosis of Gian Lorenzo Bernini's *The Rapture of Saint Teresa* as orgasmic would surprise few medieval theologians, since they were fully apprised of the shared essence of divine and human love.[66] But they might resist Lacan's tendency to elide the distinct *telos* of each, immediately recognizing his inability to discern between different types of ecstasy as an error. Indeed, it was precisely such a breakdown in discernment of which Marguerite was suspected in her own lifetime. According to *The Mirror,* the path to union with God required not only that the Soul bid farewell to the virtues, but even a metaphoric descent into sin preceding the ultimate ascent toward divine union.[67] In the context of apophatic (or negative) theology à la Dionysius the Pseudo-Areopagite, such startling analogies are comprehensible; in the context of an inquisitional tribunal for heresy they are not. The main focus of the Parisian theologians' objections to Marguerite's work was the assertion "[t]hat the annihilated soul takes leave of the virtues, nor is it any longer in their servitude."[68] This startling principle received the following treatment in an account of Marguerite's execution by the continuator of Guillaume de Nangis's chronicle: "that the soul annihilated in love of the creator is able and ought to concede to nature whatever it seeks and desires without reproach of conscience or remorse."[69] Predictably, this mystical proposition was interpreted by the religious authorities as lending itself to antinomianism and sexual abandon, as the subsequent persecution of the Beguines so poignantly attests.

The boundaries between the kinds of love at issue in *The Mirror* are eroded still further over time. Jean Gerson, the chancellor of the University of Paris in the early fifteenth century, who is famous for his attacks on female mystics,[70] argued that while the passions as experienced in brute animals were good, all human passions were corrupt and deserving of contempt. He was additionally apprised of the fact that love (*amor*) or desire (*libido*) was at the root of all passions, as well as of the incumbent potential for slippage between different categories of love.[71] Hence Gerson's *On the Distinction between True and False Revelations* of 1402 indicates the dangers of confusing the true gold of divine love with its carnal counterfeit—an error to which ignorant women were especially prone. In corroboration of his sense of danger, he relates how "a certain devout woman wrote that she suspected nothing so much as love, even more than the devil, and even when it was turned to God and to persons of proven sanctity."[72] Through a maneuver akin to the psychoanalytic concept of "splitting," by which a subject attempts to control his or her environment by dividing it into good and bad forces, Gerson's commendation of a good woman's wariness toward love ushers in a bad woman's dangerous lack of discrimination in love.[73] Thus, evidence for an unsavory love afoot amid the Beguines and Beghards is adduced from "a certain little book written by a woman with unbelievable cleverness. Her name is Marie of Valenciennes." Robert Lerner was the first to identify Gerson's Marie as Marguerite Porete, observing that Valenciennes was the place where Marguerite's book was initially condemned and burned.[74]

But any doubts remaining about Marie's identity are soon dispelled by the actual characterization of her beliefs. According to Gerson's account, her contentions regarding the peculiar privileges of spiritual love were supported through the application of the Augustinian dictum "Have charity, and do what you want."[75] Mistakenly ascribing the prerogatives of the liberated soul in heaven to the soul still fettered to the body, "in her intellectual pride, combined with passionate love, she fell into error. And so she thought she would always enjoy God while this powerful passion for him grew in her soul, however far she was from following God's precepts."[76]

Central to Marguerite's entire spiritual program was the view that the soul could be annihilated and become one with God—a daring aspiration that was, to Gerson's mind, a particularly objectionable trend in contemporary mystical thought and one that he expressly associated with groups like the Beguines and Beghards. He accordingly reviles the various manifestations of what he considers to be a pernicious error, often expressed through images of mixed liquids: as when a drop of wine mixes with and becomes indecipherable from a greater amount of water, or when a person partaking of the Eucharist is perceived as becoming God.[77] In fact, Marguerite's conception of annihilation seems to have been modeled on transubstantiation—only the human partaker would become one with the host's divine essence.[78] Just as Christ's martyrdom, or annihilation, is a precondition for the Eucharist, Marguerite likewise describes the union with God in terms of a death or martyrdom—a description that, as Miri Rubin points out, eerily anticipates her own end.[79]

Such quasi-heretical hopes of union convey a feverish desire to dissolve the boundaries of individuated selfhood in order to merge physically with the beloved. I would suggest that a parallel longing is implicit in the sympathetic magic of the age-old love potion that the prostitute Marion first employed. By mixing her menstrual blood with the wine that Hainsselin would, in turn, consume, Marion's form of "mixed liquids" would enable her to become one with her lover. Thus the love frenzy of the so-called *fole feme*, or "crazy woman," could be construed as a concrete and secular rendering of the Eucharistic aspirations of union with the divine that were current among the Beguines. Indeed, after describing his encounter with a contemporary prophetess who claimed that she had experienced the annihilation and then the recreation of her soul in the course of her contemplation of God, Gerson winds up: "a day would not suffice if I wished to enumerate countless women of this sort crazy with love or just plain crazy [insanias amantium immo et amentium]."[80]

As Gerson's condemnations of Marie of Valenciennes and other women of her ilk make clear, women crazy with divine love are well on their way to becoming *foles femes,* since their love, easily corrupted by the passions, will ineluctably descend toward physical consummation. The consummation that Gerson envisages is, not surprisingly, heterosexual—especially since one of his main concerns is the risk that such women invariably present to their clerical advisors. His indictment of Marie of Valenciennes is followed by some exemplary warnings. One concerns a pious man whose spiritual friendship with a nun surreptitiously turned into a carnal attachment, an episode that historians have taken to be autobiographical.[81] Elsewhere, Gerson tells of a woman who preserved her chastity with her husband with remarkable rigor but attached herself to various religious persons without discretion: "nor was she able to be restricted by any warnings to keeping moderation in love; but if those men [viri] whom she loved were not stronger and more virtuous in curbing love, certainly the matter would have had the worst outcome. Not only in the presence of God, but also of men she would have fallen."[82]

Clearly the diagnosis of a spiritual love gone wrong was a powerful interpretative, and heterosexually inflected, model for understanding both Marguerite Porete and the Beguine movement in general. In Marguerite's case, we even have the names of potential *dramatis personae* who could embody the human love interest. At the time of her trial, a certain cleric from Beauvais by the name of Guiard de Cressonessart came to Marguerite's defense and was likewise condemned, although for some reason he was not executed—perhaps owing to his apparent dementia. Calling himself the

Angel of Philadelphia, Guiard believed himself possessed of a special mission to defend the victims of ecclesiastical persecution.[83] Although it is unclear, even doubtful, that Marguerite and Guiard were previously acquainted or that Marguerite was even grateful for his intervention, their one-sided alliance could easily be construed along the lines of the romantic coupling of the contemporary heresiarch Dolcino and his beautiful follower Margherita di Trank, who were burned at the stake in 1307.[84] Moreover, in terms of its imagery, Marguerite Porete's exploration of the language of *fine amor* also fosters a heterosexual telos, which could further be used in support of Gerson's slanderous suppositions.

Marguerite's *Mirror* opens with an exemplum recounting how a maiden, who hears of the noble King Alexander, fixes her love on him, all the time knowing that her chances of attainment are nil. Nevertheless, she comforts herself with a picture of the king that she had painted—a likeness that animates her dreams.[85] Moreover, the Lover at the end of *The Mirror*, who impregnates the Soul with divine seed, is clearly gendered male.[86] Yet any clear heterosexual telos is necessarily derailed by the narration. In the context of a dialogue between Love, Reason, and the Soul, *Lady Love* provides both the focus and stimulant for the female Soul's love yearning, corroborating Barbara Newman's recent assessment of medieval efforts to identify a distinctly female aspect to the Godhead.[87] The "queerness" of this markedly female-identified female configuration could well fit the same-sex erotic imagery ascribed to mystical women by scholars such as Karma Lochrie. The configuration of Marguerite's dialogue could further fit the bill for what Judith Bennett has recently described as a "lesbian-like" formation, or possibly secure Marguerite a place along Adrienne Rich's lesbian continuum. In conjunction with these other factors, one might further conjecture that any mystic, by definition, corresponds with Carolyn Dinshaw's description of Margery Kempe: "her body is an ill-fitting robe for her desiring soul."[88] But, in the context of the other trial discussed, one is additionally struck by the similar roles played by Lady Love and Margot de la Barre. Both female entities attempt to help their respective lovesick friends to the attainment of the particular objects of their passion. Indeed, as in most other love stories, the go-between is the same sex as the lovesick client. Thus, in their common function as facilitator and temporary repository of love yearning, the face of Marguerite's Lady Love and of Margot the bawd collapse into one.[89] Clearly, Marion's trustful reliance on the senior prostitute indicates a solidarity that was grounded in community, shared experience, and friendship. Though little is known of Marguerite Porete's life, one can only speculate that her designation of Love as a lady was salient—not simply driven by the accident that the word for love in the Old French was of the feminine gender.[90] Even if we accept the more compelling reason that Lady Love was a signifier for covert same-sex attraction, I would nevertheless posit that this attraction may have originated in a sense of gender solidarity akin to what we find among the circle of prostitutes.[91]

Love Hurts

Medieval society was psychologically prepared for the ultimate assimilation of the chaste mystic and the multiply violated prostitute in a number of essential ways. Although the traditional lovesickness that loomed so large in the later Middle Ages was thought to be almost exclusively the domain of the male sufferer, and a noble one at that, this assignation was something of an anomaly in the face of woman's otherwise impeccable record of concupiscence.[92] From a biological standpoint, woman was understood to be possessed of a greater degree of lust; her weaker reason would further explain any failure to distinguish between divine and human love.[93] Moreover, despite the growing evidence of female indigence and lack of viable alternatives in urban centers, the prostitute was understood to engage in her profession for personal pleasure—so the prostitute's sordid lot was a teleological representation of the evil propensities latent in female biology, at large. Woman's concupiscible nature was also seen to be at the root of the female propensity toward mysticism. Thus Gerson's *On Mystical Theology: Practica,* when arguing the way in which "souls follow bodies," explains how the soft hearts of women are easily "liquefied" in meditating on the passion owing to their "concupiscible" nature—a physiological disposition that makes them special adepts in the contemplative life.[94] Moreover, on a less theoretical level, the Beguines were victims of slander from their first appearance. And, even as souls were thought to follow bodies, so antifeminist rhetoric moved effortlessly from the presumably infirm female soul to her inevitably frail body. Already by the late thirteenth century, the lascivious Beguine had become something of a stock figure. In Jean de Meun's continuation of the *Romance of the Rose,* the character of Forced Abstinence, dressed as a Beguine, is attended by her compromising companion, the mendicant False Seeming. This famous example was but the merest tip of the iceberg.[95]

The distance between mystic and prostitute was considerably lessened by two important interrelated factors that have been widely discussed by scholars such as André Vauchez. First, there is the medieval tendency to invert binaries in accordance with the scriptural enigma that the last shall be first in the order of salvation (Luke 14:10). This principle admitted not only the possibility of the socially humble outranking the elite, but even floated the anomalous premise that the most sinful, if truly penitent, could outstrip those who had never sinned in the race for salvation. Their former sin might even serve as a handicap, in the meritorious usage that we occasionally find in sports such as golf.[96] In this context, the example of Mary Magdalene, the most famous of the prostitute saints who was also, significantly, the principal saint of the Beguine movement and who plays a special role in Marguerite's *Mirror,* is especially instructive.[97] Marguerite uses Mary Magdalene to argue that the Soul annihilated by love feels no shame concerning her past sins.[98] As a depraved sinner who brings all the passion of her earlier days to her later life of penitence—thus becoming a contemplative par excellence— Magdalene is transformed from a physical lover of men into a spiritual lover of Christ. Moreover, this idealized model of conversion was constantly reenacted socially by the members of the religious communities founded explicitly for reformed prostitutes.[99]

As women whose actions were, in different ways, determined by their love interests, our three protagonists must invariably be at risk when confronted by contemporary juridical culture. The ecclesiastical courts had been pioneering in their use of the inquisitional procedure. This import from Roman law—also, significantly, introduced at Lateran IV—was adopted for the prosecution of heresy during the pontificate of Gregory IX over the course of the 1230s. Inquisition was dependent on a process of interrogation designed to extract a confession, which by these new standards had become the preferred proof of guilt. The systematic efforts to break down the defendant are juxtaposed with the recommended disassociation and containment of the inquisitor. The influential inquisitor's manual of the Dominican Bernard Gui (d. 1331) explicitly requires the inquisitor to conceal the inner rigor of unmoved justice behind a compassionate face that suppresses any display of indignation or cruelty. Similarly, Clement V's decree before the Council of Vienne in 1312—the same council that was to stigmatize the Beguines for their alleged harboring of the antinomian heresy of the Free Spirit (of which Marguerite Porete was understood to be the heresiarch)— calls for a similar detachment from those prosecuting the heretics: "we decree [that the Office of the Inquisition] be removed from all carnal love, hate, fear, and any temporal affection whatsoever when being exercised so that anyone of the aforesaid [inquisitors] is able to cite without any [feeling], and seize or arrest, and imprison, even placing [an individual] in fetters or iron manacles, if it seems to [the inquisitor] that it ought to be done."[100] This advice was constantly reiterated in a wide variety of inquisitional manuals. Thus at a time when female mystics, like Marguerite, are cultivating a swooning, melting, abandoned love of God, they are being assessed by men who are shaped by an ideology that valued reason and clinical detachment above all else. Nor is it an accident that Marguerite's *Mirror* actually stages the death of Reason so that Love can flourish.

Marion and Margot seem to have fared still worse under French secular law. There is no evidence that Marguerite Porete had been tortured, even though torture was permitted to inquisitors of heresy as of 1252.[101] In a certain sense, her confession was not required as proof of guilt since her continued attempts to circulate her condemned book would already have marked her as a relapsed heretic. The refusal to confess merely signaled her impenitence, the consequence of which was consignment to eternal hellfire. But Margot and Marion did not escape so easily. The French penal system was in the process of assimilating the inquisitional process, with its incumbent reliance on torture.[102] In fact, torture was applied in a full three quarters of the cases discussed in the register of the Châtelet to facilitate a full confession—an extraordinarily high percentage by any standard.[103] And Marion and Margot were not spared.

Moreover, in this climate of suspicion and fear of sorcery, the simplest of love tokens took on the most morbid and incriminating significance. Upon a preliminary search of Marion's room, the sergeants of the Châtelet discovered a box of human hair and a clump of moss locked in her coffer. This immediately triggered the court's suspicion of *maleficia.* Marion was later to explain how, in her unhappy parting with Hainsselin, she grabbed his hood and inadvertently pulled out some of his hair, which she subsequently kept as a token. The moss was a gift from an English squire with whom she had kept company. He had asked her to keep it for love of him, claiming it was taken from a fountain where a virgin was beheaded.[104] One cannot help but linger over this detail. Who was this virgin? Was she a saint? Was she a sinner? Did Marion care into which category she fell? Do we? Should we? Such melancholic reflections must intrude when considering the wistful triangulation of the prostitute who was burned and who kept the relic of an unnamed virgin who was beheaded—kept it, ostensibly, for the love of an unnamed man.[105]

Both prostitution and the Beguine movement, though situated firmly outside of marriage, could nevertheless be construed as tacitly contributing to marriage in essential ways. In line with the Augustinian-inflected tendency to regard prostitution as a necessary evil, it became something of a Scholastic commonplace to liken it to a sewer—a necessary mechanism for siphoning off society's waste.[106] Likewise, the Beguine movement was seen consistently by its supporters as a pious option for unmarriageable women who might otherwise turn to prostitution—thus providing a mechanism for siphoning off a different component of society's waste. A purposeful misreading of Marguerite's text, conditioned by the implicit parallels between the two socially ordained functions of Beguine and prostitute, would ultimately permit the inquisitors to believe that the Beguines had confused and ultimately traded divine love for its debauched human counterpart. An equally willful reading, this time perpetrated by the masters of the Châtelet, would insist that Marion and Margot's pursuit of love required apostasy or a heretical misuse of the sacred.[107] This is the reading that Margot, broken by torture, would eventually confirm in her confession: Satan appeared to her like the devil of the Passion plays, but without the horns.

But it is important to offset the portrayal of these women as consummate victims with the mirror image of these women as consummate agents, since both perspectives contain some truth. For there is also a sense in which our female protagonists chose the uncanny over the homeland from which they were exiled and there attempted to take up residence. Prior to their arrest, Margot and Marion inhabited a world that was diametrically opposed to the ecclesiastically sanctioned love that was contained by marriage—an ostracism that comprehended most other ecclesiastical benefits. For, according to authorities like Jean Gerson, the Church could accept the prostitute's monetary offerings, considering this reception a good deed since it would relieve her troubled heart. Yet the Church could offer the prostitute practically nothing in return. Living in the perpetual state of mortal sin that their profession required, as prostitutes they were even barred from the reception of the sacrament.[108] Perhaps they would have accepted the ecclesiastical consensus that the sorcery they enlisted in pursuit of love was the equivalent of apostasy.[109] A similar disaffection could be evinced from the example of Marguerite Porete. From the heights of her mystical exultation, Marguerite not only bade farewell to the virtues, but also differentiated between "Holy Church the Little," ruled by Reason, and "Holy Church the Great," ruled by Divine Love. She accordingly dispensed with the necessity of the Masses, sermons, fasts, and prayers of the little Church.[110] Condemned for their uncompromising visions of love, the bodies of these women were burned to secure their permanent expulsion from society. And yet, some six centuries later, they still threaten to return. Like all revenants, they are armed with a request, which is nothing less than an implacable demand for interpretative justice.[111]

NOTES

1. Sigmund Freud, "The Uncanny," in *The Standard Edition of the Complete Psychological Works of Sigmund Freud,* ed. James Strachey (London: Hogarth Press, 1955), 17:236.

2. Ibid., 17:220–26.

3. *Oxford English Dictionary,* 2nd ed. (Oxford: Clarendon Press, 1989), 2:837, esp. no. 4.

4. Along with the reduction of prohibited degrees and the concomitant rejection of hearsay evidence regarding consanguinity (canons 50, 52), Lateran IV also sought (unsuccessfully) to outlaw clandestine marriages by forbidding priests to be present at such ceremonies. Canon 51 also required priests publicly to announce upcoming marriages and to conduct an investigation regarding potential impediments (*The Decrees of the Ecumenical Councils,* ed. Norman Tanner [London: Sheed and Ward, 1990], 1:257–59). In addition, the opening statement of faith, intended as a bulwark against heretical dualism, concludes with the assurance that not only virgins but also married individuals shall be saved (canon 1, 1:251). Canon 13 prohibits new religious orders (1:242).

5. See R. I. Moore, *The Formation of a Persecuting Society: Power and Deviance in Western Europe, 950–1250* (Oxford: Basil Blackwell, 1987).

6. On the background and procedure of the Châtelet, see Claude Gauvard, "*De grace especial*": *Crime, état et société en France à la fin du moyen âge* (Paris: Publications de la Sorbonne, 1991), 1:33–45; Bronislaw Geremek, *The Margins of Society in Late Medieval Paris,* trans. Jean Birrell (Cambridge: Cambridge University Press, 1987), 47–53; L. Battifol, "Le Châtelet de Paris vers 1400," *Revue historique* 61 (1896): 225–64; 62 (1896): 225–38; 63 (1897): 42–55, 266–83; Esther Cohen, "Patterns of Crime in Fourteenth-Century Paris," *French Historical Studies* 11 (1980): 308–9, 317n40. For criminality as revealed in the registers of the *parlement* of Paris, see Yvonne Lanhers, "Crimes et criminels au XIVe siècle," *Revue historique* 240 (1968): 325–38. Also see Rodrigue Lavoie's comparison of Parisian systems of justice, as exemplified at the Châtelet, with those in Provence in "Justice, criminalité et peine de mort en France au moyen âge: Essai de typologie et de régionalisation," in *Le Sentiment de la mort au moyen âge,* ed. Claude Sutto (Montreal:

Les Editions Univers, 1979), 31–55. The case, which lasts from July 30, 1390, until the execution of Marion on August 24, is contained within the only surviving register from this period that has been edited, by H. Duplès-Agier, *Le Registre criminel du Châtelet de Paris du 6 septembre 1389 au 18 mai 1392* (Paris: Ch. Lahure, 1861), 1:327–63. Because of its precedential nature, part of this case has been excerpted in Joseph Hansen, ed., *Quellen und Untersuchungen zur Geschichte des Hexenwahns und der Hexenverfolgung im Mittelalter* (Bonn, 1901; Hildesheim: Georg Olms, 1963), 518–20. It is also discussed briefly by Geremek in *The Margins of Society in Late Medieval Paris,* 237–38, 231n115, 81–82; G. W. Coopland, "Crime and Punishment in Paris September 6, 1389, to May 18, 1390," in *Medieval and Middle Eastern Studies in Honor of Aziz Suryal Atiya,* ed. Sami Hanna (Leiden: Brill, 1972), 81–82; Jeffrey Burton Russell, *Witchcraft in the Middle Ages* (Ithaca: Cornell University Press, 1972), 214–15; and Norman Cohn, *Europe's Inner Demons: An Enquiry Inspired by the Great Witch-Hunt* (New York: Basic Books, 1975), 196–97. Women constituted 10 percent of criminals at the Châtelet who were subjected to the extraordinary procedure reserved for second-time thefts, sorcery, murders, and *lèse-majesté.* See Claude Gauvard, "Paroles de femmes: Le Témoignage de la grande criminalité en France pendant le règne de Charles VI," in *La Femme au moyen âge,* ed. Georges Duby, Michel Rouche, and Jean Heuclin (Maubeuge: Jean Touzot, 1990), 328.

7. As we will see, it was some forty-four years since Margot was inveigled into prostitution by her seducer. On freelance prostitutes (i.e., those not engaged in brothels), see Jacques Rossiaud, *Medieval Prostitution,* trans. Lydia Cochrane (Oxford: Basil Blackwell, 1988), 7–8; Geremek, *The Margins of Society in Late Medieval Paris,* 217–21. On the age of prostitutes, see Rossiaud, *Medieval Prostitution,* 32–33, 36–37; Geremek, *The Margins of Society in Late Medieval Paris,* 239.

8. Placing the wreath on her head, Margot then said three Paternosters, three Ave Marias, and made the sign of the cross—invoking the Trinity (*Le Registre criminel du Châtelet,* 1:329). Unless otherwise noted, translations from *Le Registre criminel du Châtelet* and from other works are my own.

9. She gave Hainsselin some herbs in a cloth and told him to keep them in his satchel for eleven days (ibid., 1:329–30).

10. Ibid., 1:330. On the reintroduction of torture in this period, see Edward Peters, *Torture,* expanded ed. (Philadelphia: University of Pennsylvania Press, 1996), 44ff. Also see H. C. Lea, *Superstition and Force: Essays on the Wager of Law—the Wager of Battle—the Ordeal—Torture,* 4th rev. ed. (Philadelphia: Lea Brothers, 1892), 500ff.; Lavoie, "Justice, criminalité et peine de mort en France au moyen âge," 47–48. The type of torture administered, considered mild as far as these things go, involved forcing water down their throats. See L. Batifol, "Le Châtelet," *Revue historique* 63 (1897): 269–97; cf. Cohen, "Patterns of Crime in Fourteenth-Century Paris," 309–10n12.

11. *Le Registre criminel du Châtelet,* 1:336ff. On women and sorcery accusations, see Esther Cohen, *The Crossroads of Justice: Law and Culture in Late Medieval France* (Leiden: Brill, 1993), 94–95. For instances of love magic eventuating in a royal pardon, see Pierre Braun, "La Sorcellerie dans les lettres de rémission du trésor des chartes," *Etudes sur la sensibilité,* Actes du 102e congrès national des Sociétés Savantes, Limoges, 1977 (Paris: Bibliothèque Nationale, 1979), 2:262–63. Note that in the letters of remission it was women who were accused of seeking help through love potions, desperate to hang

onto a man's love. See especially the case in 1355 of Jehann, widow of Michel Fort, who confessed under torture to murdering her late husband. She retracted her confession the next day but acknowledged using a powder to effect a reconciliation with him (262).

12. *Le Registre criminel du Châtelet*, 1:353ff.

13. Ibid., 1:360, 363. As Cohen points out, the formula *et n'avoit aucuns biens,* a corollary to most of the trials at the Châtelet, testifies to the extreme indigence of most of the accused. Only eighteen of the ninety-seven people executed left property ("Patterns of Crime in Fourteenth-Century Paris," 310–11). In accordance with custom, both women were first pilloried at the market square of Les Halles and their offenses read aloud. The swine market was the usual place for execution at the stake. See Esther Cohen, "'To Die a Criminal for the Public Good': The Execution Ritual in Late Medieval Paris," in *Law, Custom, and the Social Fabric in Medieval Europe: Essays in Honor of Bryce Lyon,* ed. Bernard Bachrach and David Nicholas (Kalamazoo, MI: Medieval Institute Publications, 1990), 287. According to Cohen, women were buried alive for theft but burned for treason, sorcery, arson, procuring, and murder ("Patterns of Crime in Fourteenth-Century Paris," 310n13). Female criminals were especially feared, leading to particularly heinous forms of execution ensuring that there was nothing left of their bodies (idem, *The Crossroads of Justice,* 97–99).

14. Her name was Marion la Daynne (*Le Registre criminel du Châtelet*, 1:336). As we will see, the woman who allegedly taught Margot to conjure the devil was from Flanders. According to Rossiaud, in the later Middle Ages many women from war-torn areas of the north, such as Flanders, moved south to take up prostitution (*Medieval Prostitution,* 34). Although Rossiaud is treating a slightly later period, the Hundred Years War was already raging, and such strictures would still pertain. Also note that many of the criminals tried in the Châtelet were from a migrant population (Cohen, "Patterns of Crime in Fourteenth-Century Paris," 311–12). On the human body as preferred material for sorcery, see Braun, "La Sorcellerie dans les lettres de rémission du trésor des chartes," 268. For parallel cases of love magic that attracted the attention of the Inquisition in sixteenth-century Venice, see Guido Ruggerio's *Binding Passions: Tales of Magic, Marriage, and Power at the End of the Renaissance* (New York: Oxford University Press, 1993), 88–129.

15. This standard oath appears many times in the register. Cf. the case of the pimp Raoulin du Pré, in which a prostitute claimed that he swore to marry her (*Le Registre criminel du Châtelet*, 1:151).

16. Ibid., 1:337–38. It was important, however, that Marion never put her own head on the pillow containing the testicles or the spell would have been rendered useless.

17. Ibid., 1:338–39. Marion says that she bought two wreaths of roses in order to adorn herself as other women do on this day as well as a certain herb "aumousnière." She claims that she went to see Margot unaware of the significance of the wreaths, but Margot immediately pointed out that these materials were perfect for bewitching Hainsselin. The editor, Duplès-Agier, suggests that the herb in question could be the "bursa pastoris" or the "pera pastoris" (1:328n1). One of the uses to which this plant seems to have been put was curing toothaches. See G. Henslow, *Medical Works of the Fourteenth Century together with a List of Plants Recorded in Contemporary Writings* (1899; repr. New York: Burt Franklin, 1972), 173. See Bernard of Siena's sermon of 1427 against

witchcraft, which particularly condemns individuals who gather herbs either on this day or the feast of the Ascension (translated in *Medieval Popular Religion, 100–1500: A Reader,* ed. John Shinners [Peterborough, ON: Broadview Press, 1997], 244). Also see Franco Mormando, *The Preacher's Demons: Bernardino of Siena and the Social Underworld of Early Renaissance Italy* (Chicago: University of Chicago Press, 1998), 61.

18. Marion attended the nuptial dance at the Hotel Alençon with the wreaths concealed between her inner and outer garments, tucked into her belt. When the couple, holding hands, were beginning a dance in the round, Marion pretended to retie her shoe, thus letting the wreaths drop (*Le Registre criminel du Châtelet,* 1:341–42).

19. Ibid., 1:342.

20. Ibid., 1:343.

21. Burchard of Worms, for example, assigned five years of penance to the wife who makes parallel use of menstrual blood in order to increase her husband's love (*Decretum* 19.5, *PL,* 140, col. 974). On the different varieties of magic available, see Richard Kieckhefer, "Erotic Magic in Medieval Europe," in *Sex in the Middle Ages: A Book of Essays,* ed. Joyce Salisbury (New York: Garland, 1991), 30–55.

22. Saint Thomas Aquinas, *Quodlibet* 11, q. 9, art. 10, in *Opera omnia* (Parma: Petrus Fiaccadori, 1859), 9:618.

23. John Nider, *Formicarium* 5.5 (Douai: B. Belleri, 1602): 360–65. Heinrich Kramer and James Sprenger claim that one of the main factors drawing women to witchcraft is jealousy of the married. Indeed, certain jilted women cast spells over their erstwhile lovers that create the illusion that their penises have been removed (*Malleus maleficarum* pt. 1, q. 6, pt. 2, q. 1, ch. 7, trans. Montague Summers [London: John Rodker, 1928; repr. New York: Dover, 1971], 45–48, 118–19).

24. On this distinction, see Kieckhefer, "Erotic Magic in Medieval Europe," 36, 39; idem, *Forbidden Rites: A Necromancer's Manual of the Fifteenth Century* (Stroud, Gloucestershire: Sutton Publishing, 1997), 69–70, 73–91. Also see the following love-inducing spells that require conjuration in his edition of the manual in question (ibid., no. 12, 226–68; no. 35, 293–95).

25. *Le Registre criminel du Châtelet,* 1:343–44, 352–53. Margot also requested that Ancel Gohier, her boarder, repeat his testimony in support of her alibi on the day of the wedding (1:350–51).

26. Ibid., 1:355–56. Cf. the parallel conjuration of a spirit named Haussibut in the 1391 trial of Jehenne de Brigue—the only other sorcery trial in the register (ibid., 2:290ff.).

27. Margot was terrified. After the devil left, she said the following spell three times over the wreaths: "'Help me, devils, keep me, and [make it] so Hainsselin cannot have congress [avoire compaignie] with any other than [Marion].' She did this, making the sign of the cross in the name of the different persons of the Trinity" (ibid., 1:356). The spell actually says "me" in the record; but one assumes that Margot is acting as a stand-in for Marion. The latter was present throughout the ritual. She was eventually handed the wreaths.

28. Rossiaud, inexplicably, attempts to soften this harsh ruling, but despite these efforts, the prostitute's lack of parallel recourse for the same offense committed against a matron is still flagrant (*Medieval Prostitution,* 65–66). Cf. Ruth Karras, *Common*

Women: Prostitution and Sexuality in Medieval England (New York: Oxford University Press, 1996), 109. There is one case of the gang rape of a prostitute contained within *Le Registre criminel du Châtelet* (2:505–15). But such crimes were only pursued in exemplary cases (see Cohen, "'To Die a Criminal for the Public Good,'" in *Law, Custom, and the Social Fabric in Medieval Europe*, ed. Bachrach and Nicholas, 285–86). For an overview of the ecclesiastical position on prostitution, see Vern Bullough, "Prostitution in the Late Middle Ages," in *Sexual Practices and the Medieval Church*, ed. Vern Bullough and James Brundage (New York: Prometheus, 1982), 176–86; James Brundage, *Law, Sex, and Christian Society in Medieval Europe* (Chicago: University of Chicago Press, 1987), 389–96.

29. Some prostitutes did, however, marry. Rossiaud argues that this was tolerated by the fifteenth century (*Medieval Prostitution*, 36–37, 70–71; but see also p. 29, which seems to argue in the opposite direction). But frequently these unions turned on the husband continuing to prostitute his wife, as Geremek implies (*The Margins of Society in Late Medieval Paris*, 231–32). Geremek's position, which opines that the chances of a prostitute forming a regular marriage were slight, seems more realistic (ibid., 239; also see note 15, above). Karras also thinks that the respectable marriage of a prostitute was rare, noting the difficulties that a husband had asserting his rights over a wife who was a former prostitute in England (*Common Women*, 81–82).

30. *Le Registre criminel du Châtelet*, 1:328. On pimps, see Geremek, *The Margins of Society in Late Medieval Paris*, 228–39; Rossiaud, *Medieval Prostitution*, 31–32.

31. *Le Registre criminel du Châtelet*, 1:357; cf. 1:351. The prison for women was called "la Griesche." Marion, when produced to repeat her testimony before Margot, said that she regretted "les seremens et promesses" that she and Margot had exchanged since her efforts to keep faith had resulted in torture and decrepitude ("en avoit ses membres moult debilitez et affeibliz" [ibid., 1:353]).

32. Ibid., 1:328.

33. Initially, they spoke about their lovers, but then her Flemish companion offered to teach her how to invoke the devil in the manner described above, a rite that Margot performed then and there in the other woman's presence. She conjured: "Devil aid me, keep me, so that my lover (whom she named by his name at the time) can't have congress with any other than me." Somebody answered her, although she could not see him. But she felt terrible fear and ran into the little room nearby where she would customarily retreat with her customers to have sex with them (ibid., 1:358).

34. Ibid., 1:354. This is corroborated by the boarder Ancel's testimony, which describes the young woman who came to see Margot as very angry (1:348).

35. Geremek refers to Marion as Hainsselin's former fiancée (*The Margins of Society in Late Medieval Paris*, 238). He presumably bases this characterization on the following passage, when Marion hears of Hainsselin's impending marriage: "il vint à sa cognoissance que sondit ami estoit fiancé de nouvel & se vouloit marier" (*Le Registre criminel du Châtelet*, 1:337). I think that "de nouvel" is better interpreted as "recently" as opposed to "again." It is significant that Marion only ever describes Hainsselin as her "ami" and seems content to return to the status quo, when she was his priority. When Margot hears the news of upcoming marriage she cryptically remarks that relationships between two ribalds are a bad idea ("c'estoit mauvaise fiance que d'amour de ribaut et de ribaude" [ibid., 1:337]).

36. Ibid., 1:338. Note, however, that Marion was not able to keep the rooster's testicles in the pillow for the recommended eight or nine nights, which suggests that the couple did not consistently cohabit. Hainsselin clearly continued to sleep with Marion after his engagement was announced, however.

37. Ibid., 1:354.

38. On this usage, see Geremek, *The Margins of Society in Late Medieval Paris,* 215.

39. She claimed that this was the gist of her words: "que avant qu'il feust un an, sondit ami pourroit bien estre courroucie, & que jamais il ne trouveroit femme qui tant de biens li feist comme elle li avoit fait" (*Le Registre criminel du Châtelet,* 1:332).

40. See ibid., 1:334. Geremek, however, interprets such protestations as signifying that Marion belongs to an elite category of courtesan that specializes in the knightly class (*The Margins of Society in Late Medieval Paris,* 238). For the demurrals over Marion's execution, see *Le Registre criminel du Châtelet,* 1:360–63.

41. Ruth Karras, "Sex and the Singlewoman," in *Singlewomen in the European Past, 1250–1800,* ed. Judith Bennett and Amy Froide (Philadelphia: University of Pennsylvania Press, 1999), 130–31.

42. This designation would permit a married woman to act independently of her husband's control with regard to her business. See Martha Howell, *Women, Production, and Patriarchy in Late Medieval Cities* (Chicago: University of Chicago Press, 1986), 15, 20, 29.

43. Cf. Geremek, *The Margins of Society in Late Medieval Paris,* 231.

44. Gratian, C. 32, q. 4, c. 14; C. 32, q. 7, c. 11; Peter Lombard, *Sententiae* bk. 4, dist. 31, 5.2. See Brundage, *Law, Sex, and Christian Society in Medieval Europe,* 240–41.

45. Andreas Capellanus, *The Art of Courtly Love,* trans. John Parry (New York: Columbia University Press, 1960), 7th dialogue, 103; *The Letters of Abelard and Heloise,* trans. Betty Radice, rev. M. T. Clanchy (Harmondsworth, Middlesex: Penguin, 1974, rev. ed., 2003), ep. 1, 114.

46. See Mary Douglas's discussion of the perceived threat of potentially unhappy or interstitial individuals turning to sorcery. Like spiders living in the cracks of an edifice, the kind of power attributed to them signifies their ambiguity and inarticulate status (*Purity and Danger: An Analysis of the Concept of Pollution and Taboo* [London: Routledge and Kegan Paul, 1966], 102).

47. On the tensions between mysticism and sexuality, see Dyan Elliott, "The Physiology of Rapture and Female Spirituality," in *Medieval Theology and the Natural Body,* ed. Peter Biller and A. J. Minnis, York Studies in Medieval Theology 1 (Woodbridge, Suffolk: York Medieval Press, 1997), 147–49; idem, *Spiritual Marriage: Sexual Abstinence in Medieval Wedlock* (Princeton, NJ: Princeton University Press, 1993), 234–45.

48. The documents for the trial of Marguerite and a cleric who attempted to defend her are edited by Paul Verdeyen, "Le Procès d'inquisition contre Marguerite Porete et Guiard de Cressonessart (1309–1310)," *Revue d'histoire ecclésiastique* 81 (1986): 47–94. Verdeyen also includes select chroniclers who discussed the trial. Marguerite's condemnation is also edited by H. C. Lea, *The History of the Inquisition of the Middle Ages* (New York: MacMillan, 1887; repr. 1906), 2:575–78. Also see Lea's discussion in ibid., 2:122–24; Robert Lerner, *The Heresy of the Free Spirit in the Later Middle Ages* (Berkeley: University of California Press, 1972), 71–78; Ernest McDonnell, *The Beguines and Beghards in Me-*

dieval Culture with Special Emphasis on the Belgian Scene (New York: Octagon Books, 1969), 490–96; Bernard McGinn, *The Flowering of Mysticism,* vol. 3 of *The Presence of God: A History of Western Christian Mysticism* (New York: Cross Road, 1998), 244–45. See Miri Rubin's discussion of Marguerite as a type of martyr created by the official Church's indictment of alternative claims to transcendental truth ("Martyrdom in Late Medieval Europe," in *Martyrs and Martyrologies,* ed. Diana Wood, Studies in Church History 30 [Oxford: Basil Blackwell, 1993], 172–77). For a recent treatment of the Beguine movement stressing the daily life of the Beguinage, see Walter Simons, *Cities of Ladies: Beguine Communities in the Medieval Low Countries, 1200–1565* (Philadelphia: University of Pennsylvania Press, 2001). The Place de Grève, though the usual place for pillorying, was not the usual place for burning an individual (see note 13, above). But the document condemning Marguerite is, however, enacted at Grève (Verdeyen, "Le Procès d'inquisition contre Marguerite Porete et Guiard de Cressonessart," 83), while the continuator of William of Nangis says explicitly that she was burned "in communi platea Graviae" (in *Continuatio chronici Guillelmi de Nangiaco* ann. 1310, in *Recueil des historiens des Gaules et de la France,* ed. Danou and Naudet [Paris: Imprimerie Royale, 1840], 20:601; the appropriate passage is excerpted by Verdeyen, "Le Procès d'inquisition contre Marguerite Porete et Guiard de Cressonessart," 89).

49. Maryanne Kowaleski, "Singlewomen in Medieval and Early Modern Europe: The Demographic Perspective," in *Singlewomen in the European Past, 1250–1800,* ed. Bennett and Froide, 49–51.

50. For a discussion of female indigence as reflected in the miracle book for the canonization of Louis IX as well as the formal and informal networks developed to offset these difficulties, see Sharon Farmer, "Down and Out and Female in Thirteenth-Century Paris," *American Historical Review* 103 (1998): 344–72. Farmer is treating a period slightly prior to the various famines and economic and social disasters of the fourteenth century. Also see Farmer's discussion of the anxiety engendered by women living alone, and the efforts to found salubrious communities to forestall this fate ("'It Is Not Good That [Wo]man Should Be Alone': Elite Responses to Singlewomen in High Medieval Paris," in *Singlewomen in the European Past, 1250–1800,* ed. Bennett and Froide, 82–105).

51. Gauvard, "*De grace especial,*" 1:333–34; cf. Karras, *Common Women,* 18, 22.

52. Michel Mollat, *The Poor in the Middle Ages: An Essay in Social History,* trans. Arthur Goldhammer (New Haven, CT: Yale University Press, 1986), 245–46; Rossiaud, *Medieval Prostitution,* 102–3.

53. Gauvard, "*De grace especial,*" 1:336–37. Also see Walter Prevenier's analysis of the rape of the Parisian widow Ysablet des Champions, who was dragged out of the house that she shared with her sick mother to be raped and beaten by four men. Prevenier sees Ysablet's plight as a kind of exemplum for the vulnerability of single, undefended women ("Violence against Women in a Medieval Metropolis: Paris around 1400," in *Law, Custom, and the Social Fabric in Medieval Europe,* ed. Bachrach and Nicholas, 262–84).

54. See Brenda Bolton, "*Mulieres sanctae,*" in *Women in Medieval Society,* ed. Susan Stuard (Philadelphia: University of Pennsylvania Press, 1976), 145–48.

55. See Lerner, *The Heresy of the Free Spirit in the Later Middle Ages,* 37–44.

56. McDonnell, *The Beguines and Beghards in Medieval Culture with Special Emphasis on the Belgian Scene,* 477–78. Farmer shows, however, that even in the thirteenth

century "the Beguinage in Paris did not always provide an adequate social safety net for the women affiliated with it" ("Down and Out and Female in Thirteenth-Century Paris," 360–61).

57. *Continuatio chronici Guillelmi Nangiaco* ann. 1304, in *Recueil des historiens des Gaules et de la France,* ed. Danou and Naudet, 20:590. See Lea, *Superstition and Force,* 494; Lerner, *The Heresy of the Free Spirit in the Later Middle Ages,* 70. The "trials" of the royal house would continue. The entry for 1314 contained the flamboyant adulteries of Queen Margaret of Navarre and her sister-in-law Blanche with two knights, who were brothers. The men, who were senior and had seduced the women when they were still young, admitted that these affairs had persisted for some three years and involved the pollution of many a holy time and place. Both the seducers, and their abettors, suffered grisly deaths (*Continuatio chronici Guillemi Nangiaco,* in *Recueil des historiens des Gaules et de la France,* ed. Danou and Naudet, 20:609–10).

58. Certainly the two cases showed considerable overlap in ecclesiastical personnel, while Philip the Fair may well have seen Marguerite as an opportunity to demonstrate his assiduity in matters of the faith (see Lerner, *The Heresy of the Free Spirit in the Later Middle Ages,* 76; McGinn, *The Flowering of Mysticism,* 245–46). Marguerite's book would continue to act as a lightning rod for still more intense attacks on Beguines, since it was perceived as disseminating the allegedly antinomian heresy of the "Free Spirit" (Lerner, *The Heresy of the Free Spirit in the Later Middle Ages,* 78ff.).

59. Although Marguerite is the first individual that we are certain was burned for a mystical heresy, she may not have been the first. The Flemish mystic Hadewijch, for example, fleetingly refers to a woman who was put to death by the inquisitor, Robert le Bougre, for her "righteous *Minne*" (Lerner, *The Heresy of the Free Spirit in the Later Middle Ages,* 64; McGinn, *The Flowering of Mysticism,* 221). See John Giles Milhaven on the threat presented by Hadewijch and similar thinkers to scholastic theology in *Hadewijch and her Sisters: Other Ways of Loving and Knowing* (Albany, NY: State University of New York Press, 1993).

60. See especially Barbara Newman, *From Virile Woman to WomanChrist: Studies in Medieval Religion and Literature* (Philadelphia: University of Pennsylvania Press, 1995), 137–67, esp. 153–58; Peter Dronke, *Women Writers of the Middle Ages: A Critical Study of Texts from Perpetua (†203) to Marguerite Porete (†1310)* (Cambridge: Cambridge University Press, 1984), 218ff.; McGinn, *The Flowering of Mysticism,* 260.

61. Mary Wack, *Lovesickness in the Middle Ages: The "Viaticum" and Its Commentaries* (Philadelphia: University of Pennsylvania Press, 1990), 22ff.

62. Saint Thomas Aquinas, *Summa theologiae* 1a, 2ae, q. 25, art. 2, resp. (London: Blackfriars, in conjunction with Eyre and Spottiswoode; New York: McGraw-Hill, 1967), 19:48, 49.

63. Ibid. 1a, 2ae, q. 24, arts. 1–2, 19:332–37. See Augustine's discussion of the passions in *The City of God* 9.4–6, trans. Henry Bettenson (Harmondsworth, Middlesex: Penguin, 1976), 345–51. Note that he believes that the passions present certain challenges that automatically provide training in the virtues.

64. Aquinas, *Summa theologiae* 1a, 2ae, q. 26, art. 4, resp. ad 4, 19:70–71.

65. Wack, *Lovesickness in the Middle Ages,* 23–24.

66. See the excerpt from Lacan's *Seminar XX,* in *Feminine Sexuality,* ed. Juliet Mitchell and Jacqueline Rose (New York: Norton, 1982), 147.

67. Marguerite Porete, *Le Mirouer des simples ames* c. 6, 105, ed. Romana Guarnieri, Corpus Christianorum, Continuatio Mediaevalis 69 (Turnhout: Brepols, 1986), 24, 286; idem, *The Mirror of Simple Souls,* trans. Ellen Babinsky (New York: Paulist Press, 1993), 84, 177. See McGinn, *The Flowering of Mysticism,* 254.

68. Verdeyen, "Le Procès d'inquisition contre Marguerite Porete et Guiard de Cressonessart," consultation of April 11, 1309, 51.

69. *Continuatio chronici Guillelmi de Nangiaco* ann. 1310, in *Recueil des historiens des Gaules et de la France,* ed. Danou and Naudet, 20:601. The appropriate passage has also been excerpted by Verdeyen, "Le Procès d'inquisition contre Marguerite Porete et Guiard de Cressonessart," 88.

70. See, for example, Jo Ann McNamara, "The Rhetoric of Orthodoxy: Clerical Authority and Female Innovation in the Struggle with Heresy," in *Maps of Flesh and Light: The Religious Experience of Medieval Women Mystics* (Syracuse, NY: Syracuse University Press, 1993), 24–27; cf. André Vauchez, *La Sainteté en occident aux derniers siècles du moyen âge d'après les procès de canonisation et les documents hagiographiques* (Rome: Ecole française de Rome, 1981), 473–74, and Dyan Elliott, "Seeing Double: John Gerson, the Discernment of Spirits, and Joan of Arc," *American Historical Review* 107 (2002): 26–54. For a painstaking analysis of Gerson's writings in the context of his personal and political commitments, see Brian Patrick McGuire's *Jean Gerson and the Last Medieval Reform* (University Park: Pennsylvania State University Press, 2005).

71. See Gerson's *De passionibus animae* considerationes 5 and 6, in *Oeuvres complètes,* ed. Palémon Glorieux (Paris: Desclée, 1973), 9:5. This work was written in 1408 or 1409.

72. Jean Gerson, *De distinctione verarum revelationum a falsis,* in ibid., ed. Glorieux, 3:51; idem, in *Jean Gerson: Early Works,* trans. Brian Patrick McGuire (New York: Paulist Press, 1998), 356. See McGuire, ibid., 459n53, where it is posited that Gerson is referring to Angela of Foligno's *The Book of Blessed Angela: The Instructions 2,* "The Perils of Spiritual Love," in *Angela of Foligno: Complete Works,* trans. Paul LaChance (New York: Paulist Press, 1993), 221. It is perhaps no surprise that Gerson does not name this work, insofar as he displays considerable antipathy to the circulation of female writings. Elsewhere, he argues that the total absence of writing from women such as Paula or Eustochium is a testimony to their superior discretion (Gerson, *De examinatione doctrinarum,* in *Oeuvres complètes,* ed. Glorieux, 9:467–68).

73. On splitting, see Melanie Klein's, "Notes on Some Schizoid Mechanisms," in *The Selected Melanie Klein,* ed. Juliet Mitchell (New York: Free Press, 1987), 176–200. As is clear from the above discussion of the uncanny, Freud anticipates the patient's development of such a strategy for coping with the world, as is implicit in his analysis of the double. For the strategic deployment of "splitting" by the medieval clergy, see Dyan Elliott, *Fallen Bodies: Pollution, Sexuality, and Demonology in the Middle Ages* (Philadelphia: University of Pennsylvania, 1999), 32, 114–15, 123, 126.

74. See Lerner, *The Heresy of the Free Spirit in the Later Middle Ages,* 165, 166n6. Authors such as Lea had treated Marie as a separate person from Marguerite (*The History of the Inquisition of the Middle Ages,* 2:405).

75. Gerson, *De distinctione verarum revelationum a falsis,* in *Oeuvres complètes,* ed. Glorieux, 3:51; *Early Works,* trans. McGuire, 356. As McGuire points out, Gerson misleadingly ascribes this quotation to Paul rather than to Augustine (see 459–60n57). In a

certain sense, Gerson is correct in characterizing Marguerite's teaching in this way. Her book associates "fear of all kinds of love" with the limited reign of Reason. But Reason, illumined by the light of Faith and the power of Love, "has permission to do all that pleases him, by the witness of Love herself, who says to the Soul: My love, love and do what you will" (Porete, *Le Mirouer des simples ames* c. 13, ll. 36–37, 50–51, ed. Guarnieri, 56; *The Mirror of Simple Souls*, trans. Babinsky, 95). Note that Eckhart, who is thought to have been influenced by Marguerite, was careful to indicate that total freedom was not implied in this text (Lerner, *The Heresy of the Free Spirit in the Later Middle Ages*, 183). Also note the special care that Marguerite took in *The Mirror* to ensure that her book not be open to antinomian interpretations (McGinn, *The Flowering of Mysticism*, 441–42n291).

76. Gerson, *De distinctione verarum revelationum a falsis*, in *Oeuvres complètes*, ed. Glorieux, 3:52; *Early Works*, trans. McGuire, 357.

77. Gerson, *De theologia mystica* consideratio 41, in ibid., ed. Glorieux, 3:286–87; translated in Steven Ozment, *Jean Gerson: Selections from "A deo exivit," "Contra curiositatem studentium" and "De mystica theologia speculativa,"* Textus minores 38 (Leiden: Brill, 1969), 53–55. See Robert Lerner's "The Image of Mixed Liquid in Late Medieval Mystical Thought," *Church History* 40 (1971): 397–411.

78. See Kent Emery's forward to Edmund Colledge's new translation of the *Mirror of Simple Souls* (Notre Dame, IN: University of Notre Dame Press, 1999), ix–xx.

79. Porete, *Le Mirouer des simples ames* c. 131, ll. 130–35, ed. Guarnieri, 388; *The Mirror of Simple Souls*, trans. Babinsky, 224; Rubin, "Martyrdom in Late Medieval Europe," in *Martyrs and Martyrologies*, ed. Wood, 176.

80. This passage occurs in Gerson's second letter to Barthélemy Clantier (ca. 1408) condemning the mystical writings of Ruusbroec. The characterization is prompted by the fact that Gerson rightly diagnosed that Ruusbroec had been influenced by this doctrine of annihilation (*Oeuvres complètes*, ed. Glorieux, 2:102). Although the letter has been translated by McGuire (*Early Works*, 255), I have made my own translation to bring out Gerson's emphasis on gender. Also see Gerson's discussion of how reason becomes distorted by the passions in the lovesick (*De passionibus animae* consideratio 20, in *Oeuvres complètes*, ed. Glorieux, 2:21).

81. Gerson, *De distinctione verarum revelationum a falsis*, in ibid., ed. Glorieux, 3:52; *Early Works*, trans. McGuire, 357. See Brian Patrick McGuire's discussion of this episode, and the way it might have shaped Gerson's attitude toward women, in "Jean Gerson and the End of Spiritual Friendship: Dilemmas of Conscience," in *Friendship in Medieval Europe*, ed. Julian Halsedine (Thrupp, UK: Sutton Publishing, 1999), 236–38. Another instance, relayed to Gerson by a Carthusian friend, concerns a deluded man who actually believed that he was pursuing God in the midst of his fornications (Gerson, *De distinctione verarum revelationum a falsis*, in *Oeuvres complètes*, ed. Glorieux, 3:52; *Early Works*, trans. McGuire, 357).

82. Gerson, *De simplificatione cordis*, in ibid., ed. Glorieux, 8:95. Also see idem, *De examinatione doctrinarum*, in *Oeuvres complètes*, ed. Glorieux, 9:472–73.

83. This clerical effort to intervene is not an isolated event. See Dyan Elliott, *Proving Woman: Female Spirituality and Inquisitional Culture in the Later Middle Ages* (Princeton, NJ: Princeton University Press, 2004), 172–73.

84. Verdeyen, "Le Procès d'inquisition contre Marguerite Porete et Guiard de Cressonessart," 62–63, 65–67; *Continuatio chronici Guillemi Nangiaco* ann. 1318, in *Recueil des historiens des Gaules et de la France,* ed. Danou and Naudet, 20:601. See Robert Lerner, "The 'Angel of Philadelphia' in the Reign of Philip the Fair: The Case of Guiard of Cressonessart," in *Order and Innovation in the Middle Ages: Essays in Honor of Joseph R. Strayer,* ed. William Jordan and Teofilo Ruiz (Princeton, NJ: Princeton University Press, 1972), 343–64, and idem, "Ecstatic Dissent," *Speculum* 67 (1992): 56–57. On Dolcino and Margherita, see Lea, *The History of the Inquisition of the Middle Ages,* 3:112–13, 119. As Lea points out, Dolcino always maintained the innocence of their relations, but few believed him.

85. Porete, *Le Mirouer des simples ames* c. 1, ll. 16–31, ed. Guarnieri, 10–12; *The Mirror of Simple Souls,* trans. Babinsky, 80. Despite this image, Porete's mysticism is relentlessly and starkly iconoclastic, seeking to reach God without images. The nature of this experience enlists intellectual vision alone, the highest form in the Augustinian hierarchy of vision (see Elliott, "The Physiology of Rapture and Female Spirituality," in *Medieval Theology and the Natural Body,* ed. Biller and Minnis, 143–44). An absence of images is symptomatic of Marguerite's aloofness from the predominantly somatic mysticism of late female spirituality, as described in Caroline Walker Bynum's *Holy Feast and Holy Fast: The Religious Significance of Food to Medieval Women* (Berkeley and Los Angeles: University of California Press, 1987). On Marguerite's difference, see Amy Hollywood's "Suffering Transformed: Marguerite Porete, Meister Eckhart, and the Problem of Women's Spirituality," in *Meister Eckhart and the Beguine Mystics* (New York: Continuum, 1994), 87–113; cf. idem, *The Soul as Virgin Wife: Mechtild of Magdeburg, Marguerite Porete, and Meister Eckhart* (Notre Dame, IN: University of Notre Dame Press, 1995), 173–93. Insofar as their freedom from images is concerned, Marguerite's visions, ironically, accorded well with the kind of mysticism Gerson was attempting to promote, which was to be entirely divorced from "phantasms." See particularly his *De mystica theologia practica* consideratio 12, in *Oeuvres complètes,* ed. Glorieux, 8:44; *Early Works,* trans. McGuire, 328; *De meditatione cordis,* in *Oeuvres complètes,* ed. Glorieux, 8:77–84, esp. 83, and *De simplificatione cordis,* in ibid., ed. Glorieux, 8:85–99, esp. 94.

86. Porete, *Le Mirouer des simples ames* c. 122, ll. 139–40, ed. Guarnieri, 346; *The Mirror of Simple Souls,* trans. Babinsky, 201. I refer to the first and original ending of the work as opposed to the string of meditations that Marguerite added later, presumably to make her work more palatable to ecclesiastical authorities.

87. Barbara Newman, *God and the Goddesses: Vision, Poetry, and Belief in the Middle Ages* (Philadelphia: University of Pennsylvania Press, 2003). Amy Hollywood also discusses Porete's feminization of the divine (*The Soul as Virgin Wife,* 7).

88. Karma Lochrie, "Mystical Acts, Queer Tendencies," in *Constructing Medieval Sexuality,* ed. Karma Lochrie et al. (Minneapolis: University of Minnesota Press, 1997), 180–200. (The tendencies Lochrie describes are epitomized in the devotion to the vagina-like wound in Christ's side that appears in late medieval hagiography.) Judith Bennett, "'Lesbian-Like' and the Social History of Lesbianisms," *Journal of History of Sexuality* 9 (2000): 1–24. (Michael Sargent places Marguerite within Rich's lesbian continuum in "The Annihilation of Marguerite Porete," *Viator* 28 [1997]: 268). Carolyn Dinshaw, *Getting Medieval: Sexualities and Communities, Pre- and Postmodern* (Durham, NC, and London: Duke University Press, 1999), 164.

89. At the time of her trial, Margot was living with her daughter, Martinette, accepting permanent boarders as well as selling drinks and renting out rooms to the occasional illicit couple. Geremek introduces Margot into his discussion as an example of a bawd or procuress (*The Margins of Society in Late Medieval Paris,* 237). This, to some extent, accords with Marion's testimony when she confesses that, in return for Margot's help, she promised to keep coming to see Margot frequently and bring as many friends as she could to her hostel and to do her all the good in her power (*Le Registre criminel du Châtelet,* 1:339). There is no evidence that she inveigles young women into the profession or even connects the client with prostitute, however. On the hostility to this class of women generally, see Geremek, *The Margins of Society in Late Medieval Paris,* 234–39.

90. Sargent observes that *amor,* like the German *Minne,* is linguistically gendered female ("The Annihilation of Marguerite Porete," 268).

91. Note, however, that en route to annihilation in what was originally the last chapter of her work, Marguerite notes that the Beguines would think she was in error, along with official religious orders (Porete, *Le Mirouer des simples ames* c. 122, ll. 94ff., 344; *The Mirror of Simple Souls,* trans. Babinsky, 222).

92. Wack, *Lovesickness in the Middle Ages,* xi.

93. See Elliott, *Fallen Bodies,* 41ff.

94. Gerson, *De mystica theologia practica* consideratio 2, in *Oeuvres complètes,* ed. Glorieux, 8:21–22. See Elliott, "The Physiology of Rapture and Female Spirituality," in *Medieval Theology and the Natural Body,* ed. Biller and Minnis, 157ff. Also see Newman's citation of the thirteenth-century Lamprecht of Regensburg, who likewise speaks of woman's special susceptibility to desiring God because of their soft hearts (*From Virile Woman to WomanChrist,* 138).

95. See Renate Blumenfeld Kosinski's "Satirical Views of the Beguines in Northern France," in *New Trends in Feminine Spirituality: The Holy Women of Liège and Their Impact,* ed. Juliette Dor et al. (Turnhout: Brepols, 1999), 237–49.

96. André Vauchez, *Les Laïcs au moyen âge: Pratiques et expériences religieuses* (Paris: Editions du Cerf, 1987), 254. Cf. McGinn's discussion of Marguerite's "Binary Dynamics," in *The Flowering of Mysticism,* 253–57.

97. On Magadalene's cult, see Katherine Jansen, *The Making of the Magdalen: Preaching and Popular Devotion in the Later Middle Ages* (Princeton, NJ: Princeton University Press, 1999), esp. 258–59 (on Magdalene as a model of conversion) and 32–35, 168–77 (for Madgalene's identification as a prostitute). On prostitute saints, generally, see Ruth Karras, "Holy Harlots: Prostitute Saints in Medieval Legend," *Journal of the History of Sexuality* 1 (1990): 3–32; idem, *Common Women,* 120–22; Rossiaud, *Medieval Prostitution,* 140–42. For a discussion of how these currents are revealed on an iconographic level in the cathedral of Chartres, see Marie Madeleine Gauthier and Colette Deremble, "Les Saintes protitutuées, legende et imagerie mediévales," in *La Femme au moyen âge,* ed. Duby, Rouche, and Heuclin, 219–40. For Mary Magdalene's special prominence among the Beguines, see Newman, *From Virile Woman to WomanChrist,* 141, 172; Jansen, *The Making of the Magdalen,* 273–74.

98. Porete, *Le Mirouer des simples ames* c. 76, ed. Guarnieri, 210–12; *The Mirror of Simple Souls,* trans. Babinsky, 150.

99. On communities for repentant prostitutes, see Leah Otis, "Prostitution and Repentance in Late Medieval Perpignan," in *Women of the Medieval World*, ed. Julius Kirshner and Suzanne Wemple (Oxford: Basil Blackwell, 1985), 137–60; Jansen, *The Making of the Magdalen*, 177–84. On Parisian houses, see Farmer, "'It Is Not Good That [Wo]man Should Be Alone,'" in *Singlewomen in the European Past, 1250–1800*, ed. Bennett and Froide, 93; Geremek, *The Margins of Society in Late Medieval Paris*, 212. Rossiaud suggests that many retire from active service around the age of thirty to become "abbesses" in brothels or bathhouses, while others retire into the penitential communities founded for reformed prostitutes (*Medieval Prostitution*, 36).

100. Bernard Gui, *Practica inquisitionis hereticae* 4.4, ed. Célestin Douais (Paris: Alphonse Picard, 1886), 233; *Corpus documentorum inquisitionis haereticae pravitatis Neerlandicae*, ed. Paul Fredericq (Ghent: J. Vuylsteke; The Hague: Martinus Nijhoff, 1896), 1:167–69, no. 171. On the inquisitional procedure and its impact on female spirituality, see Elliott, *Proving Woman*.

101. This was permitted by Innocent IV's bull *Ad extirpanda*. See Peters, *Torture*, 65.

102. Gauvard, "*De grace especial*," 1:145–51.

103. Ibid., 1:37.

104. *Le Registre criminel du Châtelet*, 1:332.

105. These distinctions may not have been salient ones for a majority of medieval individuals either. Even as the official Church of the high and later Middle Ages was reluctant to declare contemporary martyrs as saints, the laity was increasingly prepared to honor those who died unjustly as saints. See Rubin, "Martyrdom in Late Medieval Europe," in *Martyrs and Martyrologies*, ed. Wood, 162; Elliott, *Proving Woman*, 59–60, 174–79. My colleague Mary Jo Weaver has suggested that the unnamed virgin was the Welsh St. Winefride, who was beheaded by an unsuccessful suitor. A fountain was said to have sprung up where her head fell.

106. See Rossiaud, *Medieval Prostitution*, 80–81; Bullough, "Prostitution in the Later Middle Ages," in *Sexual Practices and the Medieval Church*, ed. Bullough and Brundage, 176.

107. By this period, all witchcraft was considered to be heretical, involving either a tacit or expressed pact with the devil (Russell, *Witchcraft in the Middle Ages*, 18–19; 144, 147; see Cohn, *Europe's Inner Demons*, 175–76).

108. Gerson discusses these matters in his vernacular work *Contre la luxure* of 1402, where he raises the question: "Ces foles femmes sont elles en estat de salut? Je di que non; et ne doivent point estre receues au sacramens. Doit point l'eglise recevoir leurs offrandes? Je dy que oy, s'elles ne font rapines ou fraudes" (*Oeuvres complètes*, ed. Glorieux, 7, pt. 2:818). See Gratian, C. 32, q. 4, c. 11. Cf. Thomas of Chobham, who states that prostitutes must abstain from the Eucharist, unless they repent (*Summa confessorum* art. 7, dist. 2, q. 6, c. 2, ed. F. Broomfield [Louvain and Paris: Béatrice-Nauwelaerts, 1968], 348). Also see ibid. art. 7, dist. 2, q. 6, c. 3, on the penance of prostitutes, where Thomas requires that the priest absolve them as if they were excommunicated ("tanquam excommunicate debent absolvi," 350).

109. The register's only other sorcery trial similarly ended at the stake. The case likewise arose from the milieu of the prostitute and involved the retention of the love of a man. In this instance, the sorceress learned her trade from a woman who never washed

her hands on Sunday, would say neither a Paternoster nor a Benedicte, nor would she make the sign of the cross (*Le Registre criminel du Châtelet,* 2:280–81). Geremek further points out that, as with Margot and Marion, the sorceress was old and her client was young (*The Margins of Society in Late Medieval Paris,* 307–8; cf. Cohn, *Europe's Inner Demons,* 196–97, and Russell, *Witchcraft in the Middle Ages,* 214–15). See Geremek's breakdown of the types of crimes (*The Margins of Society in Late Medieval Paris,* 50, table 2) and the various types of executions accorded (53, table 5).

110. Porete, *Le Mirouer des simples ames* c. 19, ll. 10–14; c. 16, ll. 20–21, ed. Guarnieri, 74, 66; *The Mirror of Simple Souls,* trans. Babinsky, 101, 99. On the Soul taking leave of the Virtues and Love's justification to Reason for this leave-taking, see Porete, *Le Mirouer des simples ames* c. 6, 21, ed. Guarnieri, 24, 78–82; *The Mirror of Simple Souls,* trans. Babinsky, 84, 103–4.

111. On ghosts and their demands, see Jean-Claude Schmitt, *Ghosts in the Middle Ages: The Living and the Dead in Medieval Society,* trans. Teresa Lavender Fagan (Chicago: University of Chicago Press, 1998), 6, 40, 63, 69, 75. Also see Jacques Derrida's compelling analysis of the episode with Hamlet's father in his *Specters of Marx: The State of the Debt, the Work of Mourning, and the New International,* trans. Peggy Kamuf (New York: Routledge, 1994), 3–48.

Chapter 4

Gendering the Disenfranchised

Down, Out, and Female in Early Modern Spain

ANNE J. CRUZ

The history of a tolerant Spain where diverse minority cultures lived peaceably and harmoniously with the Christian majority has long been cherished by many scholars, in particular by medievalists who ascribe this feature, known in Spanish as "convivencia," to their period.[1] Indeed, during the Middle Ages, Spain's three religious groups—Jewish, Islamic, and Christian—maintained relatively stable relations until 1492, when the Catholic monarchs, Isabel of Castile and Ferdinand of Aragon, gave orders to expel non-converted Jews and Granada, Spain's last Islamic stronghold, fell to the Christians.[2] The social upheavals at the end of the medieval period imposed increasing hardships on Spain's minority groups, who were persecuted for religious heterodoxy, despite their varying levels of assimilation.

For the Muslims especially, conversion to Christianity did not guarantee that they would safeguard their customs, as had been promised in the *capitulaciones,* or accords, signed by the Catholic monarchs. Nor did it assure them of their place within the community. Internal migrations, their forced dispersal from the Alpujarras Mountains in the 1570s, and, in Valencia principally, their skills as agricultural workers ensured that the majority of Moriscos, as the converted Muslims were called, remained geographically as well as culturally isolated until their final expulsion from Spain between 1609 and 1614.³ Following Islamic law, Moriscas led even more reclusive lives than the men. Women identified strongly with their religion and customs through material and corporeal means. Although circumcision was an exclusively masculine sign of difference for both Jews and Muslims, Moriscas clung to such practices as dying their hair and bodies with henna, wearing their distinctive clothing, and covering their faces with a veil.

That the Moriscos rightfully claimed Spain as their country did not keep the Christian majority from viewing them as outsiders. Often marginalized by their religion, language, and customs, Moriscos, as I explain later in this essay, formed part of the disenfranchised "other" that, despite the pressures to assimilate, faced constant oppression from and rejection by the majority. Yet, as a social group, they were not alone in their difference. While the Moriscos are only now coming out "from the shadows," as Mary Elizabeth Perry describes in her recent book *The Handless Maiden,* another marginalized group, that of the Gypsies, has perhaps been mythologized too much.⁴ Gypsies have become almost ubiquitous with Spanish culture, thanks in part to the exotic legends that have grown around them from the early modern period on.⁵ Despite the many cultural differences between the two, Moriscas and Gypsy women assumed female stereotypes that are still prevalent in Spain today. In this essay, I compare these two groups of women to shed light on the phenomenon of gendered otherness as it was shaped by early modern Spanish fiction and by contemporary historical documents, such as legal decrees and economic treatises.

The first fictionalized version of Gypsy life in early modern Spain to have a lasting impact on our perception of the group is a short story by Miguel de Cervantes. Beginning with the stereotype already set in place in the sixteenth century, his exemplary novel *La gitanilla* (*The Little Gipsy Girl*), while it contributes to the Gypsies' notoriety, also speaks to the women's marginality and difference:

> Gipsies seem to have been born into the world for the sole purpose of being thieves: they are born of thieving parents, they are brought up with thieves, they study in order to be thieves, and they end up as past masters in the art of thieving. Thieving and the taste for thieving are inseparable from their existence, and they never abandon them till they reach the grave. One of this tribe, an old gipsy who might have graduated from the school of Cacus, brought up as her granddaughter a

girl whom she called Preciosa and to whom she taught all her gipsy arts and frauds and thieving tricks. (*The Little Gipsy Girl*)[6]

As seen through the eyes of the majority, the Gypsy women, like the Moriscas, comprise a gendered "other" that exemplifies the worst evils of their social group.[7] In Cervantes's fanciful tale, Preciosa, seemingly a member of Spain's scorned minority, is in reality the daughter of a noble family, stolen in infancy by an old Gypsy. The novella dwells on the implausible love between the beautiful but disreputable girl and a young aristocrat, who is impelled to survive a two-year trial period with her tribe before she will consent to marry him. In the final scene, Preciosa—a name that connotes not only the young girl's physical beauty, but also her social value and moral virtue—is recognized by her biological mother through a birthmark on her breast and the unique distinction of two conjoined toes. As one would expect from a tale that springs from romance, Preciosa's unveiling as a young woman of noble birth solves the mystery of her social identity and happily wraps up the plot.[8]

Yet, like Preciosa's toes, which can be counted as either one or two, the author's intention in narrating a history (or story) of the Gypsies may be accounted for in several ways. In a recent materialist study of Cervantes's works, Carroll B. Johnson neatly divides the novel's critics according to their ideological stance: those who take the narrator's words as the author's; and those who believe that Cervantes has "some surprise egalitarian message up his sleeve."[9] The narrative itself complicates matters, since the novella's exemplarity moves beyond the fictional romance genre to combine Cervantes's flair for literary allusion with his penetrating investigations of gender relations and economic exchange among early modern social groups. At one point, Preciosa even assumes the same characteristics attributed to poetry by the poet-page don Sancho: "a maiden of great beauty, chaste, pure, discreet, shrewd, modest, and extremely circumspect" (*The Little Gipsy Girl*, 43). However, just as the plot is no mere foil for the author's interest in narrative poetics, neither is it restricted to prescribed notions of gender or economic systems.[10] Preciosa's return to her aristocratic origins permits Cervantes to examine and represent the Gypsies as an exotic "other" without violating the aesthetic or social decorum of the times.

Seventeenth-century Spanish prose fiction, such as the popular picaresque and courtesan novels, usually addressed the condition of social outcasts in a disguised ethical tone that registered just how low the protagonists

had fallen in order to send readers a moral message. In his own version of
the picaresque, the exemplary novel *El coloquio de los perros* (*The Dogs' Col-
loquy*), Cervantes renders a far darker portrait of Gypsy women. In contrast,
his sympathetic slant on the Gypsies in *The Little Gipsy Girl* implicitly criti-
cizes society for perpetuating the negative stereotypes held of this group,
one marginalized and hated even today.[11] Indeed, as at least one critic has
noted, Cervantes's treatment of the disenfranchised "other" transforms this
novella into much more than an idealized romance based on the observance
of Christian principles, as Alban K. Forcione would have it.[12] Further, by
focusing on Gypsy maidens, Cervantes demonstrates that, for early modern
Spain, this "other" frequently was gendered female, since women—and minority women especially—embodied the many social fears that circulated at
the time.

Still, the novella's denouement too cleanly sidesteps the social taboo
of marriage between different castes, a taboo maintained as strictly by the
Gypsies as by the dominant society. The narrative cleaves to received opinion when describing its Gypsy protagonists' itinerant customs: moving from
place to place in wagons, on mules, and on horseback, the Gypsies, we are
told, camp outside towns, where they sell their wares or steal livestock. The
women make their living by their talents and their tricks; they play the tam-
bourine, sing, dance, read palms, and tell fortunes. The consequences of this
lifestyle for young girls are sagely rendered by the precocious Preciosa, as she
attributes her intelligence and cleverness to her enforced maturation:

> The wits of gipsy girls are different from those of anyone else; they
> are always in advance of their years; you'll never find a stupid man,
> nor a slow woman among the gipsies; for as they depend for their
> livelihood on being alert and shrewd and up to all the tricks, they're
> always sharpening their wits, and never let the grass grow under their
> feet whatever happens. . . . There's not a girl of twelve who doesn't
> know what girls usually know at twenty-five, for they have the devil and
> long habit as their teachers, and from them they learn in an hour what
> you'd expect them to learn in a year. (*The Little Gipsy Girl*, 30–31)

Despite the understanding that Cervantes shows the protagonist, it is
very clear that the Gypsies in the narrative are all thieves. In contrast, the
aristocratic lover, pointedly given the pseudonym Andrés Caballero (Andrés
the Nobleman), never learns how to steal and thus behaves according to
traditional expectations of his lineage. But Cervantes does not condemn the

Gypsies for their errant ways. Instead, he undermines the disparaging view held of the group by correlating their criminal behavior to that of the dominant society. As in another of his novels, *Rinconete y Cortadillo* (*Rinconete and Cortadillo*), Cervantes presents the two opposing social factions—outcasts and "regulars"—symbiotically dependent on each other. Both negotiate their livelihoods by pushing the acceptable limits of each other's transgressions. Indeed, what better way for the Gypsies to save themselves from the hands of the law than by bribing that law? The grandmother understands the similarity between their thievery and the lawyers': "For at the sight of a doubloon with a double face the faces of the attorney and his deadly agents beam with delight—those persecutors of us poor gipsies, who would rather strip and flay us than a highwayman" (*The Little Gipsy Girl*, 41).

The novella nevertheless distinguishes between the act of stealing material goods, which can be easily replaced, and of forfeiting personal honor. This loss is symbolized by the one treasure that Preciosa can ill afford to lose: her virginity. At the sexually ripe age of fifteen, she is well aware that she must protect her purity in order to maintain her worth to the tribe. Like that of aristocratic women, her corporeal integrity emblematizes her social wholeness. Forcione rightly comments that the Gypsies' "perverse social order," which banks on women's repression, functions as a mirror image of Spain's social and political establishment.[13] The old Gypsy makes this clear when Preciosa is promised to Andrés during his initiation:

> This girl, who is the cream of all the most beautiful gipsy girls in Spain that we know, we give to you, as wife, or as mistress, because in this matter you can do whatever you best please, for our free and easy life is not subject to finicky ceremonial. . . . Once [a girl] has been chosen, you must not leave her for another, nor must you meddle or interfere with any married woman or unmarried girl. We keep inviolate the law of friendship: no one asks for what belongs to another; we live free from the bitter plague of jealousy. (*The Little Gipsy Girl*, 52)

The stringent mandate becomes even harsher when the group's integrity is perceived to be threatened by the women's violation of its own twisted honor code:

> Among us, although there are many cases of incest, there is never one of adultery; and when adultery does take place with someone's wife, or there is some misdeed on the part of a mistress, we don't go to court

to ask for satisfaction. We are the judges and executioners of our wives and mistresses; we kill them and bury them in the mountains and deserts just as readily as if they were beasts of prey.... We have few things which are not common to us all, except our wives or mistresses, for we want each to have the one destined by fate for him. (*The Little Gipsy Girl*, 52)

Johnson offers this passage as proof that, among other things, Gypsies and the aristocracy concurred in their treatment of women as possessions, thus bringing to light the hidden affinities between these two otherwise distinctly separate groups: "there is an exact correspondence between this ethos and what we see enunciated and acted out as part of the official system of values."[14] But while the Gypsies' gender relations mimicked early modern Spanish nobility, they differed considerably in purpose and outcome. For both groups, woman's worth depended on her virtue as her exchange value, or what she brought to the marriage, which was usually arranged by the parents. Yet Spanish society prized public honor above private agency: women who did not publicly conform to gender roles were usually eliminated from view by hastily being married off or cloistered in a convent, a solution mostly unavailable to—and unwanted by—Gypsy women.[15]

Moreover, Spanish nobles exploited marriage as an effective means to form alliances and create dynasties among exogamous families and also as a means to keep titles and wealth within endogamous family groups. Among Gypsies, endogamy was practiced to conserve the cultural unity of the group. As Angus Fraser points out, purity codes and pollution beliefs serve to safeguard Gypsies from contact with others.[16] Yet despite Fraser's confident view that the Gypsies' behavior stems from their "love of their own distinctive society,"[17] these protective measures seem to signal instead the group's vulnerability to the very real threat of cultural dissolution and extinction.

In Cervantes's novel, an old Gypsy male articulates the Gypsies' mores to apprise Andrés of his responsibilities. While analogous to the dominant social code, the rules are far more overstated in their insistence that Gypsy women be selected, "owned," and controlled by the males. Instead, Cervantes entrusts Preciosa with a will strictly her own that challenges the tribal demands on females. In spite of what is stipulated by the Gypsy code, Preciosa invokes her right to elect her mate: "I have discovered by the law of my will, which is the strongest of all, that I do not wish to belong to you except on the conditions which we agreed between us before you came here" (*The Little*

Gipsy Girl, 54). Yet we should remember that aristocrats rarely harbored desires to assume a Gypsy lifestyle, nor did Gypsies welcome them into their encampments.[18] The differences between the novel's female protagonists, such as Juana Carducha, and their Gypsy counterparts must thus be considered in light of the historical realities of early modern Spain. Preciosa reminds the crowd—and by extension, us as readers—of the hardships brought on by poverty: "Lovers must never say they are poor, because at the outset, it seems to me, poverty is a great enemy of love" (*The Little Gipsy Girl,* 30). She encourages a lieutenant to take bribes, since if he tries to change the customs, he will "die of hunger" (*The Little Gipsy Girl,* 35). Yet when Andrés first offers her one hundred gold crowns, the young girl rebuffs him by responding that not only must they first marry, he must also prove that he is worthy of her and of her tribe.[19] Further, she willingly relinquishes the crowns to her greedy grandmother, exacting from Andrés only the promise that he will never doubt her actions: "you must know that my liberty must never be restricted, or disturbed and burdened by jealousy" (*The Little Gipsy Girl,* 40).

In assigning to the Gypsy girl the qualities of free will and indifference to economic gain, Cervantes paradoxically draws on another, albeit more positive, stereotype of the Gypsy as carefree and independent.[20] As her name confirms, Preciosa assigns her worth within herself and in what she represents to her tribe, a trait that anthropologists associate with modern Gypsies, who perceive their way of life as perpetually in danger of becoming extinct and in need of protection from encroachment by society.[21] In opposition to the stereotype of their salacious nature, Gypsy women in particular are held to especially high standards of sexual conduct.[22] But if the virginal young girl is a fitting match for the noble "caballero" Andrés, she is no less a valued and valuable tribal member, as her exceptional talent for singing and dancing helps to support them all. Since neither the Gypsies nor dominant society has robbed her of her moral or physical integrity, the idealized protagonist lives in both worlds yet transcends them both. Preciosa's contradictory double role as chaste Gypsy and vagabond virgin not only saves her from the typically misogynist expectations that she act according to her kind, it also permits Cervantes to critique the dominant society and more accurately describe the Gypsy lifestyle while respecting the aesthetic decorum of the romance genre.

Preciosa's moral attributes challenge the negative portrayals of Gypsies in contemporary historical documentation. In *The Little Gipsy Girl,*

Cervantes organizes the group under its own laws and focuses on its profitable and even welcome interactions with mainstream society. Inquisition and state documents, however, confirm that the Gypsies, who had arrived in Spain only in the fifteenth century, were soon considered outlaws, and their removal was insistently demanded. They were likened to Jews and Muslims (derogatorily called Moors) for their cultural differences: notably, their language, dress, and their desire to remain unassimilated. Unlike the Jews and the Muslims, however, whose heterodoxy was defined by both their ethnicity and religion, they were not considered heretics. Although the subjects of a royal decree signed in 1499 by the Catholic monarchs ordering that they become sedentary and submit to a master or leave the country, the Gypsies never abandoned the peninsula.[23] Similarly to the demands placed on the Muslims after the fall of Granada, they were ordered to integrate into society, take a job, forego their language and dress, and live in towns.[24] Failure to do so, the pragmatic read, would ensure their deportation in sixty days.[25] Yet, although Charles V reissued the pragmatic on numerous occasions from 1520 to 1556, the Gypsies were not expelled from the peninsula.[26] From as early as the sixteenth century, they began to settle in specific areas of Spain, mainly in Andalusia; the neighborhood of Triana in Seville is still known for its many Gypsy households.[27] Nonetheless, many were frequently condemned for maintaining an itinerant lifestyle. In 1594 the Madrid parliament accused them of being the "most delinquent people in all the Christian republic . . . as it seemed they were a people without laws, because they are not known to respect any, but live a life full of vices . . . . They are a vagabond people, and not one works or keeps a job to support himself, and are publicly known to be thieves and fortune-tellers, predicting over palms and making ignorant people believe that in this way they know and understand what the future will bring."[28]

The Gypsies' worst trait was their seeming lack of religiosity. While their arrival in Spain was supposedly due to their pilgrimage to Santiago de Compostela, Gypsies were taken to be Christians in name only.[29] An Inquisition case in Cuenca accused a Gypsy woman of believing that Gypsy souls did not go either to heaven or to hell but to a beautiful river's edge full of flowers and inhabited by angels and the Virgin Mary.[30] Gypsies were not merely censured for not taking Communion, confessing, or baptizing their infants; they were blamed for committing sacrilegious acts such as fornicating in churches. An anonymous pamphlet accused them of killing a priest and of cooking and eating his head.[31] Since most kept to themselves and lived on open land instead of in the towns, they eluded punishment for their alleged crimes.

Social pressure to expel the Gypsies continued to be strong throughout the sixteenth century and resurfaced in the seventeenth century, as economists known as *arbitristas* again argued for their expulsion. It is not coincidental that in 1609, the year of the first expulsion of the Moriscos, the Gypsies were found to resemble them: "In conclusion, they are such evil people that without having to compare them, they are worse than the Moriscos, because they imitate them in not being Christians and they outdo them in robbing."[32] In 1631, the mayor of Madrid accused Gypsy men of treating women like property:

> Their best intent to marry (if they marry at all) is to the woman who is most sharp and astute in stealing and cheating, without caring if she is a relative or already married. All they need do is to live with her and say she is their woman. Sometimes they buy them from their husbands or win them as pawns.[33]

Apparently shocking society with their wife-swapping ways, Gypsy men were widely accused of incest, polygamy, and divorce. When it served its purposes, Spain's dominant society self-righteously denounced the abusive behavior of Gypsy males toward women. Nevertheless, the mistreatment of women was—and continues to be—a deplorable but real fact in the construction of male and female Gypsy identity. Anthropologists have posited that male abuse of women in Gypsy society stems from a concept of sex/gender relations that privileges the male body. While this notion was prevalent in early modern Spain across both dominant and marginalized groups, it differs from modern sexual relations predicated on gender construction. The Gypsy "way of life" depends on both sexual and gender difference: from childhood, the person's sex determines how he or she is treated by others and how that individual perceives him or herself.[34] In his study of the Hungarian Rom, Michael Stewart describes this bodily difference as "asymmetry of the sexes": "the Romni [Gypsy wife] was a sexually reproductive being and could never get wholly beyond an association with polluting procreation."[35]

But even if they did not hold equal status with men, Gypsy women contributed substantially to their tribe's sustenance by their interactions with the dominant society. If, because of her beauty and virtue, Cervantes's fictional Preciosa may claim noble status, her talents as a Gypsy singer and dancer are no less verisimilar. Indeed, since they had more occasions to interact with mainstream society, Gypsy women posed more of a threat than men. While both genders were accused of thievery, for instance, the Gypsy women were likely to be blamed for more abhorrent thefts, such as stealing small children. The most serious accusations against them involved sorcery or what were called "superstitious practices," a gender-inflected activity, since more women than men were accused of practicing sorcery as well as the considerably more dangerous witchcraft, distinguishable from the "scientific" magic of the Renaissance known mainly to learned men.[36] Although in both cases, women's presumed demonic relations came under attack, the sorceress was believed to form an implicit or explicit pact with the devil, while the witch abandoned Christianity completely to worship him.

Witchcraft thus constituted a case of apostasy, punishable by burning at the stake. Contrary to popular belief, the Inquisition examined these cases cautiously, with the result that Spain participated far less than the rest of Europe in the witch hunts of the early modern period.[37] As was the case with non-Gypsies, the Inquisition most often prosecuted Gypsy women for sorcery. According to historian María Helena Sánchez Ortega, cases prosecuted by the various tribunals of the Inquisition totaled 115 Gypsy women and 53 Gypsy men.[38] Of these, the highest number of offenses (111) was for sorcery. Sánchez Ortega has catalogued their dealings under four headings: healing arts; fortune-telling; love magic and spells; and searches for hidden treasure.[39] The overwhelming majority of the cases, like those of both "Old" and "New" (the former, early Spanish Christians and the latter, those newly converted from Judaism and Islam) Christian women, have to do with prescribing love potions, reading palms, and telling fortunes. In 1638, the Valencia tribunal prosecuted María de Torres for begging alms from several women after having shocked them by telling their private lives. She told one woman that she had not married for love, although she was now happy, but that someone in "long skirts"—a priest—was in love with her. The Gypsy said she would make the lover's face appear on the surface of a bowl of water. With a silver thimble, she made the sign of the cross on the woman's right hand to protect her from evil tongues and recited several phrases of a prayer to Saint Helen. María de Torres could recite the four prayers required by the Church (the Paternoster, the Ave Maria, the Credo, and the Salve Regina) but knew little Catholic doctrine. She swore that she had tried to dupe the women only in order to make some money. For her trouble, she was condemned to one hundred lashes and three years of exile.[40]

In another Inquisition case, Andrea Bustamante was prosecuted in Toledo in 1623. Asked by two functionaries of the Inquisition for a spell with which to attract two women, she let them into her house, closing all doors and windows. She gave each man a flask with water, told them to lie on the floor, to then get up, and to repeat along with her:

> In the name of the major devil,
> the minor devil,
> and the Lame Devil
> who fell from the heavens,
> and of the star of Caiphas
> and the Lone Soul,
> I conjure you
> so that, just as this flask
> is held tightly in your hands,
> so too will be the hearts of the women
> you men desire.[41]

Placing the flasks in the fire, she shone a candle on them. When the men saw the water boiling, the Gypsy told them to walk around the room. She then asked them for a piece of clothing from each woman to "bind" the couples. Andrea confessed to the tribunal judges that it was all a trick so she could live from the alms the men gave her. Condemned to parade in an *auto de fé* wearing the sign of a sorceress, she received two hundred lashes and six years of exile.

Despite the relatively limited repertoire transcribed in Inquisition documents, Gypsy women were famous throughout Spain for their healing and magical powers. In his study of Inquisition sorcery trials in the New Castile towns of Toledo and Cuenca, Sebastián Cirac Estopañán notes that the tribunals believed the Gypsies to be less sorceresses than tricksters ("embusteras").[42] Several trials involved the theft of articles first asked for by a Gypsy in order to carry out sorcery. The incantations addressed a series of mythical figures, including a noisy devil and the queen of thieves ("reina sardina y la jacarandina"), as well as the more conventional lone soul ("ánima sola"), María de Padilla, and a prayer to the Holy Spirit.[43] Rather than keeping their knowledge a mystery, however, Gypsies were accused of divulging their secrets to other women. In her studies of Inquisition records, Sánchez Ortega was surprised to find very little difference between the incantations utilized by Gypsies and those recited by non-Gypsy women accused of sorcery.[44] Some confessed that they had learned the incantations from Gypsies, a statement difficult to corroborate because Gypsies were notoriously hard to detain. In Cervantes's novella, the frequent forays of the Gypsies into towns and their dependence on the monies obtained by Preciosa's dances and songs reveal the social and symbolic function that Gypsy women occupied in early modern Spain as cultural outlaws who nevertheless interacted continuously with townspeople of various social levels. If the novella makes light of the Gypsy girls' bantering lies, it also warns of the dangers brought on by association with Gypsy women. Along with incantations, fortune-telling, and cures, their knowledge of women's intimate secrets, such as illicit sexual relations and illegitimate births, gave them the power to destroy the honor of the many "decent" women who solicited their help (*The Little Gipsy Girl*, 47).

Inquisition documents demonstrate the abundance of cases, not only against Gypsies, but also against other marginalized women for presenting a threat to society. Like Gypsies, Moriscas were prosecuted by the Inquisition for their supposed magic practices and their healing arts. Unlike Gypsy women, whose survival skills of singing, dancing, and reading fortunes presupposed their circulation among the dominant society, the Arabic-speaking Moriscas often formed a silent minority within a minority that kept very much to itself. The history of the Moriscos is one of increasing oppression by the ruling Christians. Although the pact signed at the surrender of the last Muslim stronghold, Granada, allowed the Moriscos the right to maintain their religion, language, dress, and other customs, there was increasing pressure on them to convert to Catholicism.[45] When the Granada Muslims rebelled, the Catholic monarchs decreed their conversion in 1501, ordering their Arabic names changed to Castilian and all their religious books burned. Those who did not wish to convert voluntarily were to "leave our kingdoms, as we will not allow any infidels in them."[46] An anonymous appeal to the Ottoman Sultan Suleiman, likely dated the same year as the decree, reveals the anxieties sparked by the mass baptisms: "Peace be to you in the name of our previously veiled women, forced to unveil their faces in the midst of barbarians. . . . Peace be to you in the name of our maidens whom the priest drags by their hair to a den of dishonesty . . . . Woe unto us! They have changed the religion of Muhammad for that of Christian dogs, the worst of God's creatures."[47]

Decrees prohibiting Islamic practices were extended in the 1520s to Aragon and Valencia, forcing conversions.[48] Yet Moriscos resisted assimilation and clandestinely continued to practice their customs and religion.[49] The growing conflict with the Ottoman Empire by the middle of the century compelled Philip II to view the Moriscos as an internal danger to Spanish sovereignty. In 1567 he decreed stringent laws banning Muslim customs and the Arabic language. These repressive laws had as their goal the complete disappearance, in three years, of the Hispano-Muslim culture. The Morisco Francisco Núñez Muley wrote to the Granada court complaining that since their customs had already undergone substantial change, they could no longer be considered Muslim. He explained that Moriscas dressed similarly to provincial Castilian women. Since wealthy Moriscas saved their expensive finery for weddings and feasts, it made no sense to have them throw away their clothes and to leave unemployed all the merchants, seamstresses, shoe-makers, and jewelers who dressed them. Poor Moriscas could not afford to purchase a whole new wardrobe. He further stated that Moriscas should be permitted to dye their hair with henna, since this was routinely done for hy-gienic purposes and did not constitute a religious practice. A Morisca should not be forced to remove her veil and show her face, which if beautiful could cause a man to sin or if ugly would keep her from marrying.[50] Núñez also argued that it was unreasonable to prohibit Arabic, the Morisco's native language, since Castilian was difficult to learn and older Moriscos could not be taught it in the three years given them, even if they spent all their time in school.

The internecine struggles among the Granada factions and the monar-chy's intransigence resulted in the Morisco Rebellion of the Alpujarras Mountains near Granada, a war that lasted from 1568 to 1571.[51] A contempo-rary Christian historian reveals his anti-Morisco sentiments in his descrip-tion of the uprising: "It was shocking to see how so many children and adults were still familiar with their damned sect; they prayed to Muhammad, they took part in prayers and processions, with married women baring their breasts and young maidens their heads, and with their hair loose about their shoulders, they danced publicly in the streets, embracing the men."[52] Fearing that the approximately eighty thousand defeated Moriscos would betray the country by siding with the Turks, Philip II decided to disperse them throughout Spain; anywhere from fifty thousand to one hundred thousand Moriscos were displaced from Granada to Extremadura, Western Andalusia, and the two Castiles.[53] Unlike the Moriscos exploited as agricul-tural workers by noble landowners in the northeastern regions of Valencia and Aragon, the impoverished Castilian Moriscos were intensely disliked and feared, since they were thought to spread their infectious religion in a previously unpolluted zone. They were accused of taking part in highway robberies and murders, of lowering the salaries for laborers, and of raising the price of merchandise. For historian Míkel de Epalza, the Church was one of the most important factors in the assimilation or the rejection of the Moriscos in Spanish society, since it created the differences between Old and New Christians.[54]

Since its foundation, the Inquisition was responsible for controlling any kind of religious transgression. Although it prosecuted both men and women, the accusations against Moriscas demonstrate the important role women played in maintaining Morisco beliefs and practices. In Valencia, more than a quarter of the Moriscos tried by the Inquisition for practicing Islam were women. Of these, a significant number were prosecuted for owning illegal texts in Arabic. Among the books owned by Muslims were popular sermons that dealt with moralizing and edifying topics. These sermons were often preached by women to their fellow crypto-Muslims.[55] However, since most Moriscas were illiterate, their resistance to the confiscation of books stems from the symbolic value those books held. Ronald E. Surtz has identified many of the confiscated texts as talismans, or *herçes*: folded pieces of Koranic scripture placed in a small cloth sack and carried in the pockets or around the neck or sewn into clothes.[56] The talisman's magical powers protected the wearer from illness or the devil. While men quickly surrendered the texts and tried to bribe Inquisition officials, women hid these talismans and other books on their person, inside their billowing Morisco *zaragüelles,* or loose pants, and fought off the officials who attempted to search them physically. Surtz perceptively compares the forcible search of the woman's body in her own home to a symbolic rape. For Surtz, both the "feminine-gendered" domestic space and the woman's body were violated by the ruling Catholics. Because the decrees against the Morisco customs ordered them to leave their doors open during the day, we can extend the metaphor to encompass the violation of the Morisco culture as well. As Surtz notes, it was the Morisca who protected and promulgated their culture. Mary Elizabeth Perry documents several cases of Moriscas charged by the Inquisition for "communicating with others" and teaching the "sect of Mohammed." Ironically, several Morisco men defended themselves by confessing they had learned the religion and law of Islam from their mothers or other women.[57] We cannot know, of course, if the men were telling the truth or attempting to save themselves by blaming the women. Certainly, Moriscas maintained Muslim customs within the home, teaching their children their language of *algarabía,* or Arabic, although cultured Arabic, read and written only by educated Moriscos, was taught to boys in clandestine Koranic schools. Marriage among Moriscos followed traditional Islamic customs, with virginity a highly prized commodity and marriages arranged while the couples were very young. Even though Moriscas generally led enclosed lives within their group, some held jobs outside the home: the silk industry employed over one thousand women in Granada, and in Valencia, women also worked in agriculture and the sugar mills. The War of the Alpujarras also contributed significantly to the slave trade: some twenty-five thousand to thirty thousand Moriscos were captured and sold as slaves between 1569 and 1570. Many women who had fought in the war to defend their customs were placed as domestic slaves in Old Christian households. One case of a Morisca is documented in the *aljamiado* writings of the Young Man from Arévalo. He extols the knowledge and wisdom of a ninety-three-year-old woman, the Mora from Úbeda, who was a midwife and Islamic theologian.[58]

The literature of the period reflects the conflicted attitudes toward Moors and Moriscos. Muslims from noble families were idealized in what is called "Maurophile" fiction, such as the tale of *El Abencerraje* (*The Muslim Knight*) included in Jorge de Montemayor's pastoral novel *Los siete libros de la Diana* (*The Seven Books of Diana*) and of Osmín and Daraja in Mateo Alemán's *Guzmán de Alfarache*.[59] Leonard Patrick Harvey questions the veracity of this literature but agrees that at least in some of cases, the voice of the Morisco may be heard. However, Moriscos are also demonized as "other" in texts that attribute to them the same knowledge of magic arts practiced by the Gypsies.[60] Again, Cervantes offers us a literary depiction of Spain's early modern culture: in his novel *El licenciado Vidriera* (*The Glass Graduate*), we read that a certain lady, infatuated with the protagonist Tomás Rodaja, "took the advice of a Moorish woman by giving him one of those things they call love potions, hidden in a Toledo quince, thinking that by this means she would force his will to love her."[61] On eating the quince, Tomás becomes deathly ill; the novel tells us that the woman—and we can be sure, the Morisca—makes herself scarce and is never seen again.

The growing realization that the Moriscos had no desire to assimilate religiously or culturally led Philip III to issue his edict of expulsion in 1609. In *Don Quijote* (*Don Quixote*), Cervantes has Sancho Panza's neighbor, the Morisco Ricote, mouth Christian reasons for their expulsion when he acknowledges to Sancho that the Moriscos had "contemptible and crass intentions" and therefore should not be harbored like a "snake in Spain's bosom."[62]

Yet politics also played a role in the event: because the king wished to placate those opposed to a peace treaty with the Protestants in the Low Countries, he signed the expulsion decree on the same day as the treaty. The controversies surrounding the expulsion, which took place between 1609 and 1614 and left more than three hundred thousand Moriscos homeless or dead, continue to be discussed and debated by historians. Contemporary opinion was strongly divided on the subject: the Valencian and Aragonese nobility, fearing an economic crisis, did not wish to lose their agricultural workers. The Valencian Archbishop Juan de Ribera had struggled for years to convert the Moriscos. Several Valencian bishops and their congregations had long resisted financing eighty rectories mandated by the archbishop in 1573, even when pressured by the king. Finally convinced, on the one hand, that the rectories would never be built and, on the other, that the Moriscos would never consent to conversion, Ribera argued zealously for expulsion. Ironically, the bishops were not so assured, as they urged for continued efforts to evangelize the Morisco population.[63] The Inquisitor General Cardinal Niño de Guevara also shared the belief that once expelled from Spain, Moriscos were certain to lose their souls by living in Islamic countries. Yet, even after leaving the peninsula, Moriscos held fast to their Spanish origins, preferring to be called by place names such as Garnati (from Granada); Balansi (from Valencia); and Zagri (from the Catalan-Valencian border). Beyond their point of entry at Oran, they were viewed as foreigners by the local Arabs, who frequently attacked and robbed them.

The Morisco expulsion was based as much on the cultural as on the religious and political anxieties of the majority. Viewing the Moriscos as an alienating "other" culture, Old Christians feared the destruction of the social order by their sexual practices. Mary Elizabeth Perry affirms that Christians transformed "Moriscos into a deviant group by inscribing the body through a process of sexualization"; they sought to discredit minorities "by associating them with sexual perversions."[64] The Koran had come under attack for allowing "great license so that a man can have many women, young ones and as many as he can take in battle and can maintain, and not only single women, but even those belonging to others."[65] Among Moriscos who could afford two wives, the ceremonies were officiated by a Catholic priest and by the local *alfaquí* respectively, with only the Catholic ceremony acknowledged as legitimate.[66] Although polygamy was not a frequent practice, Moriscas were perceived as dangerous to Christian society for their ability to reproduce. In 1598, the physician and economist Cristóbal Pérez de Herrera insisted that, along with the poor unwilling to work, minorities such as the Moriscos and the Gypsies represented a serious threat to society:

> I believe that if [poverty] is not remedied rapidly, in twenty or thirty years, the major part of these kingdoms (save for some wealthy people of quality) will belong to beggars and French migrants, since so many are [French], Moriscos, and Gypsies, and they are constantly reproducing and growing, while we are decreasing swiftly through wars and religion.[67]

As the economic effects of the Morisco expulsion were increasingly felt throughout Spain, attitudes toward minority groups changed. The very same year the expulsion began, a decree was promulgated expelling Gypsies from Spain if they did not abandon their traffic in merchandise and instead take up agricultural jobs: "[The Gypsies] should not work as merchants, trade in any kind of merchandise, or own dry-goods shops or [shops] of any other kind, but instead all should dedicate themselves to the said planting and fieldwork, under penalty of serving the kingdom in the galleys for six years."[68] In 1611 the Council of State again insisted it would uphold all laws obligating Gypsies to work as agricultural laborers.[69]

A decade after the expulsion, the depopulation of Spain's kingdoms began to seriously preoccupy the economists. Pedro Fernández de Navarrete, for instance, blamed the decrease in population on what he termed "the many and numerous expulsions of Moors and Jews," but he could not help adding to his complaint that they were the "enemies of our Holy Catholic faith."[70] Although the Gypsies' irreligiosity frequently came under fire, what most bothered *arbitristas* was their moral behavior, leading Sancho de Moncada to call Gypsy women "common whores," since he believed they were "shared by all the Gypsy men."[71] Nonetheless, despite the many calls by *arbitristas* for their expulsion, the Gypsies remained in Spain. Pedro Calderón de la Barca's play *Amar después de la muerte* (*Love after Death*), a love story of two Moriscos set during the Rebellion of the Alpujarras Mountains, shows the damages suffered by the dominant society when bent on destroying its cultural "other."[72] Calderón's play was written in 1633, the same year that Philip IV promulgated a decree prohibiting any intent to expel the Gypsies:

> It does not seem convenient to expel [the Gypsies,] because the lack of population in which these kingdoms find themselves after the

Moriscos' departure and that caused by current deprivations cannot withstand even the smallest evacuaton, especially by this group, which is not Gypsy by nature, but by cunning and wickedness, and [if] reformed, can live like all the rest.[73]

Philip IV's hope in the Gypsies' reformation springs from the same notion held by modern anthropologists that Gypsies do not reflect a particular ethnicity and therefore cannot be attributed essential characteristics. Their anticipated rehabilitation, along with the acceptance of the return of the Moriscos and *conversos* to Spain at midcentury, reveals the extent to which minority groups were reassessed as possible solutions to the country's economic woes. Philip IV's government, led by the Count-Duke of Olivares, thus contradicted its original accusation that blamed the Gypsies and the Moriscos as "others" for those same woes that had served to justify their expulsion.

In early modern Spain, women of all social groups functioned as *pharmakos* figures: if their sexuality threatened the moral fabric of the nation, they made up for it through their gender, since all women could potentially render their procreative and recreational services to both the minority and the dominant male hierarchies. For this reason, although segregated within their communities, neither Gypsies nor Moriscas should be considered entirely marginalized. As we have seen, Gypsy women in particular depended for their livelihood on their interactions with dominant society. While women's social value varied according to each group, their beauty and youth were qualities prized by all, and Gypsy women, such as Cervantes's fictional Preciosa, were esteemed for their greater instinct for survival in a hostile environment. Similarly, Moriscas were valued for their knowledge of feminine arts such as cooking, midwifery, healing, and sorcery. Procreation was an important factor for all, since it ensured each group's continued existence; it was most likely the reason that Moriscos and Gypsy men cohabited with more than one mate. Yet, since the sexual recreation afforded men by women also served a social and moral purpose, Gypsies and Moriscas maintained a contradictory relationship with the dominant culture of Spain. Although condemned for their perceived immorality, Gypsies and Moriscas were sexually stereotyped by their literary representations that insistently invoked their licentiousness and libidinality.

Feminist scholars are rightly reassessing the degree to which women at all cultural and social levels could be controlled by patriarchal structures of power. Not only did women attempt to subvert or resist these systems, they often colluded with and appropriated those same systems. Indeed, just as we no longer accept the abundant normative writings of the period as historical proof of the control of women by their male counterparts, we no longer assume that women in early modern Spain submitted passively to the dominant patriarchal structures. We must not forget, however, that regardless of their social standing and whether they succeeded in overriding the system, as early modern women themselves have written, they were still considered morally and physically inferior by society. Early modern history teaches us that, although Gypsy women often scorned and tricked non-Gypsy men, they did not escape the ire of their own fathers, brothers, husbands, and lovers. Islamic women were in the main kept illiterate and as servants within their homes. Women in minority groups were thus doubly disenfranchised in early modern Spain: by the dominant society, which disparaged them for belonging to these marginalized groups, and by the male members of the minority groups, who frequently profited from and victimized them because of their gender.

NOTES

1. The classic study of relations among the three religions is by Américo Castro, *España en su historia: Cristianos, moros y judíos* (Buenos Aires: Losada, 1942); see also María Rosa Menocal, *The Ornament of the World: How Muslims, Jews, and Christians Created a Culture of Tolerance in Medieval Spain* (Boston: Little, Brown, 2002).

2. Although the first *capitulaciones,* or accords, took place with the Granada Muslims in 1492, forced baptisms did not begin until 1501.

3. While numerous Muslim leaders of Granada became willing converts to Catholicism and took Spanish names, most were less accepted socially and remained only marginally assimilated. Those from all other areas in Castile were native speakers of Castilian and highly assimilated by the time of their conversion. The Muslims of Catalonia, Valencia, and Aragon were not forced to convert until 1523–26; Valencia, especially, had a large community of Moriscos who remained unassimilated. See Leonard Patrick Harvey, *Muslims in Spain, 1500 to 1614* (Chicago: University of Chicago Press, 2005), 92–99.

4. Perry selects the folk legend of Carcayona, the handless maiden, as a metaphor for the Moriscos' suffering and mistreatment by a cruel ruler. Mary Elizabeth Perry, *The Handless Maiden: Moriscos and the Politics of Religion in Early Modern Spain* (Princeton, NJ: Princeton University Press, 2005), 21.

5. See Lou Charnon-Deutsch, *The Spanish Gypsy: The History of a European Obsession* (University Park, PA: Pennsylvania State University Press, 2004).

6. In Miguel de Cervantes, *Exemplary Stories,* trans. C. A. Jones (New York: Viking Penguin, 1972; repr. 1984), 19.

7. According to Leblon, the Indian origins of the Gypsies were corroborated in the eighteenth century through linguistic comparison. Although they probably left India in the tenth century, it is uncertain whether they formed a homogenous population or became so by reason of their language and customs. Bernard Leblon, *Les Gitans d'Espagne: Le Prix de la différence,* (Paris: Presses Universitaires de France, 1985), 9–10. The first mention in Spain of Gypsies is of a "count" Tomás de Egipto, who received twenty-three florins in 1435 from Blanche of Navarra (25). The Spanish term "Gypsy" evolved from the archaic Spanish "Egiptano," from the Gypsies' early references to "little Egypt," a Turkish town named Izmit (or Isnikmid) near the Peloponessus (10–11). For more on the origins of the Gypsies in Spain, see Angus Fraser, *The Gypsies* (Oxford and Cambridge, MA: Blackwell, 1992; repr. 1994); Antonio Domínguez Ortíz, "Documentos sobre los gitanos españoles en el s. XVII," in *Homenaje a Julio Caro Baroja,* ed. Antonio Carreira et al. (Madrid: Centro de Investigaciones Sociológicas, 1978), 319–26; and María Helena Sánchez Ortega, *Los gitanos españoles: El período borbónico* (Madrid: Castellote Editor, 1977).

8. Cervantes also takes up the mistaken identity plot in *Pedro de Urdemalas,* which, like his other interludes, echoes his other works and embellishes the genre, this time, by having the king attracted to the young girl, who turns out to be the queen's niece. Miguel de Cervantes, *El rufián dichoso; Pedro de Urdemalas,* ed. Jenaro Talens and Nicholas Spadaccini (Madrid: Cátedra, 1986).

9. Carroll B. Johnson, *Cervantes and the Material World* (Urbana, IL: University of Illinois Press, 2000), 20.

10. Alban K. Forcione, *Cervantes and the Humanist Vision: A Study of Four "Exemplary Novels"* (Princeton, NJ: Princeton University Press, 1982), 118–19. Forcione suggests an artistic corollary between Preciosa and her author. Diana de Armas Wilson offers a rhetorical reading of Preciosa's role as poetic allegory in "Defending 'Poor Poetry': Sidney, Cervantes, and the Prestige of Epic," in *Ingeniosa invención: Essays on Golden Age Spanish Literature for Geoffrey L. Stagg,* ed. Ellen M. Anderson and Amy R. Williamsen (Newark, DE: Juan de la Cuesta, 1999), 29–34. For illuminating social and economic interpretations of this novella, see Alban K. Forcione, "Afterword," in *Cervantes's "Exemplary Novels" and the Adventures of Writing,* ed. Michael Nerlich and Nicholas Spadaccini (Minneapolis: The Prisma Institute, 1989), 331–52; Alison Weber, "Pentimento: The Parodic Text of *La Gitanilla,*" *Hispanic Review* 62 (1994): 59–75; Joan Manuel Resina, "Laissez-faire y reflexividad erótica en la *Gitanilla,*" *MLN* 106 (1991): 257–78; William Clamurro, "Value and Identity in *La Gitanilla,*" *Journal of Hispanic Philology* 14.1 (Autumn 1989): 43–60. Carroll B. Johnson profitably critiques and expands these views in his "De economías y linajes en *La Gitanilla,*" *Mester* 25.1 (Spring 1996): 31–48; and *Cervantes and the Material World.*

11. In stating this, I side with the readers who see Cervantes as "out of tune with the official values," as Carroll Johnson explains the critical divide (*Cervantes and the Material World,* 95). However, I do not mean merely to extol Cervantes's sympathetic treatment of Gypsy society, but also to investigate his equally ambivalent attitude toward the group.

12. E. Michael Gerli, *Refiguring Authority: Reading, Writing, and Rewriting in Cervantes,* Studies in Romance Languages 39 (Lexington, KY: University Press of Kentucky, 1995), 26.

13. Forcione, "Afterword," in *Cervantes's "Exemplary Novels" and the Adventures of Writing,* ed. Nerlich and Spadaccini, 331–52.

14. Johnson, *Cervantes and the Material World,* 103.

15. The compulsion to keep dishonor from being made public forms the crux of the wife-murder plays, such as Calderón's *El médico de su honra* (*The Physician of His Honor*), *El pintor de su deshonra* (*The Painter of His Dishonor*), and the aptly titled *A secreto agravio, secreta venganza* (*Secret Vengeance for Secret Insult*), with the woman, guilty or not, murdered as a means of defending male honor. Most often, however, adulterous women were conveniently removed from the occasion of sin by being dispatched to a convent; unmarried women caught "fornicating" were also given dowries to ensure that they married quickly and were reincorporated into society.

16. Fraser, *The Gypsies,* 246–47.

17. Ibid., 211.

18. According to Bernard Leblon, Cervantes invokes both the story of a man named Maldonado who became a Gypsy for the love of a young woman and his aunt's love affair with don Martín de Mendoza, the illegitimate son of Diego de Mendoza, the Grand Duke of Infantado, and the Gypsy María Cabrera (*Les Gitans d'Espagne,* 2). While the myth of the beautiful Gypsy seductress of aristocrats is very much at play in Cervantes's novella, it was—and still is—far easier for Gypsies to be absorbed into society than the reverse. For the novella to ring true—or for a Neoplatonic interpretation that assuages skeptical readers—Cervantes resorts to Preciosa's beauty: "Here is Andrés, a noble and intelligent young man, brought up all his life at court and spoiled by his rich parents, and all of a sudden he's changed to the point of deceiving his servants and friends, disappointing the hopes which his parents had for him . . . and throwing himself at the feet of a girl, to be her lackey—a girl who, beautiful as she was, was a gipsy after all. Oh, the privilege of beauty, which rides rough-shod over and drags even the most francy-free along the ground by the hair!" (*The Little Gipsy Girl,* 17).

19. I disagree with Johnson's reading of this passage, which he interprets as Preciosa's ruse to place an even higher market price on herself by not giving in unless Andrés marries her: "She refuses to sell [her virginity] for 'promesas y dádivas' [promises and gifts] but that doesn't mean it isn't for sale. It means simply that the price will be higher: the price tag on this particular joya [jewel] is 'the ties and bonds of matrimony'" (Johnson, *Cervantes and the Material World,* 105).

20. That these qualities are also attributed to his most idealized and idealistic protagonists—Don Quixote chief among them—perhaps reveals Cervantes's disbelief in their attainment.

21. Paloma Gay y Blasco, *Gypsies in Madrid: Sex, Gender and the Performance of Identity* (Oxford and New York: Berg, 1999), 175.

22. Gypsy scruples have apparently changed little since the seventeenth century. According to Gay y Blasco, while both Gypsy men and women hold themselves to a rigid code of behavior, the code for women stresses in particular their sexual conduct: "the Gitanos distinguish themselves from the Payos [non-Gypsies] because Gitano women

behave modestly, as good, decent women should do, and because Gitano men are generous, righteous, and courageous, as good men should be" (*Gypsies in Madrid,* 63).

23. Along with numerous *pragmáticas* (pragmatics), the *real cédula* (royal decree) was reissued in 1539: "The Gypsies should settle and learn a trade or leave the kingdom" (los egipcianos tomen oficio y se asienten o salgan del reino); Archivo Histórico Nacional (hereafter AHN), ca. 1529, 2nda parte; my translation.

24. Antonio Domínguez Ortíz, *El Antiguo Régimen: Los Reyes Católicos y los Austrias,* vol. 3 of *Historia de España,* ed. Miguel Artola (Madrid: Alianza, 1988), 212.

25. "We order the Egyptians who wander in our Kingdoms and Lands together with their women and children that, from this day, when this law is announced and promulgated in our Court and in the villages, places, and county seats, until the next sixty days, each [Gypsy] live by the trades for which they are known and that they agree to stay in their current location or with their masters whom they serve and who will give them what they need and that they do not go on the road together travelling throughout our Kingdoms as they now do or else, that within those sixty days they leave our Kingdoms and never return in any way, under penalty, the first time, . . . of one hundred whippings and eternal expulsion from these Kingdoms; for the second time, that their ears be severed and they be chained for sixty days, and expelled as stated; and for the third time, that they be turned over to whomever takes them as captives" (Mandamos a los egipcianos que andan vagando por nuestros Reinos y Señoríos que con sus mujeres e hijos, que el día en que esta ley fuera notificada y pregonada en nuestra corte y en las villas, lugares y ciudades que son cabeza de partido, hasta los sesenta días siguientes, cada uno de ellos vivan por oficios conocidos y mejor supieren aprovecharse estando de estadía en los lugares donde acordaren asentar o tomar vivienda de señores a quien sirvan y les den lo que hubiere menester y no anden vías juntos viajando por nuestros Reinos como lo hacen o dentro de otros sesenta días primeros salgan de nuestros Reinos y no vuelvan a ellos de manera alguna, so pena de que sin ellos fueren hallados o tomados, sin oficio, sin señores, juntos, pasados los dichos días den a cada uno cien azotes por la primera vez y los destierren perpetuamente de estos Reinos; y por la segunda vez, que los corten las orejas y estén sesenta días en la cadena y los tornen a desterrar como dicho es; y por tercera vez, que sean cautivos de que los tomare). *Título XVI del libro XII, Novísima Recopilación.* Quoted in Leblon, *Les Gitans d'Espagne,* 28; my translation. See also Fraser, *The Gypsies,* 100.

26. The pragmatics were reissued due to "the serious damages provoked by the Gypsies on the public wealth, committing murders, robberies, and thefts, and other noxious crimes to the public cause, all harmful to and in detriment of the King's subjects, who receive [the Gypsies'] bad example" (por los graves daños que los gitanos ocasionan al bien público, cometiendo muertes, robos y hurtos, y otros delitos nocivos a la causa pública, todo ello en daño y perjuicio de los súbditos del Reino, que reciben mal ejemplo). Quoted in Leblon, *Les Gitans d'Espagne,* 36; my translation.

27. George Borrow's romanticized depiction of the Gypsies' arrival in southern Spain is worth citing for its many stereotypes, which the author has helped perpetuate: "[B]ut far, far more [suitable], Andalusia, with its three kingdoms, Jaen, Granada, and Seville, one of which was still possessed by the swarthy Moor,—Andalusia, the land of the proud steed and the stubborn mule, the land of the savage sierra and the fruitful and

cultivated plain: to Andalusia they hied, in bands of thirties and sixties; the hoofs of their asses might be heard clattering in the passes of the stony hills; the girls might be seen bounding in lascivious dance in the streets of many a town, and the beldames standing beneath the eaves telling the 'buena ventura' [fortune] to many a credulous female dupe; the men the while chaffered in the fair and market-place with the labourers and chalanes, casting significant glances on each other, or exchanging a word or two in Rommany, whilst they placed some uncouth animal in a particular posture which served to conceal its ugliness from the eyes of the chapman." George Borrow, *The Zincali: An Account of the Gypsies of Spain,* 4th ed. (London: J. M. Dent; New York: E. P. Dutton, n.d.), 40.

28. "D. Gerónimo de Salamanca y D. Martín de Porras dixeron que en estos reynos anda un género de gente que se nombran gitanos cuya vida y trato es la más perdida que hay en toda la república cristiana . . . que parece que son gente sin ley, porque no se save que guarden ninguna, sino que del todo viven llenos de vicios . . . . Son gente vagabunda, sin que jamas se halle ninguno que trabaje ni tenga oficio con que sustentarse, son publicamente ladrones, embuidores echando juicios por las manos haziendo entender a la gente ignorante que por alli alcanzan y entienden lo que ha de suceder." *Actas de las Cortes de Castilla,* 53 vols. (Madrid, 1877–1939), 13:220. Quoted in María Helena Sánchez Ortega, *La Inquisición y los gitanos* (Madrid: Taurus, 1988), 14; my translation.

29. Sánchez Ortega, *La Inquisición y los gitanos,* 15.

30. Ibid., 72.

31. Pedro Villalobos, *Discurso jurídico político en razón de que a los gitanos bandoleros de estos reinos no les vale la Iglesia para inmunidad* (Salamanca, 1644); and *Relación verdadera de las crueldades y robos grandes que hacían en Sierra Morena unos gitanos salteadores, los quales mataron un Religioso y le comieron la cabeza cozida, y de la justicia y castigos que dellos se hizo en la villa de Madrid* (Lisboa, 1617). Cited by Sánchez Ortega, *La Inquisición y los gitanos,* 21.

32. "En resolución, es tan mala gente que sin comparación exceden a los moriscos, porque en no ser cristianos les imitan y en los robos les ganan." *Actas de las Cortes de Castilla,* 26:163. Quoted in Sánchez Ortega, *La Inquisición y los gitanos,* 15; my translation.

33. "La mejor información que hazen para casarse (si es que se casan) es de la muger mas diestra y astute en hurtar y engañar, sin reparar en que sea parienta o casada: porque no han menester mas que juntarse con ella, y dezir que es su muger. Algunas vezes las compran a sus maridos, o las reciben empeñadas." Juan Quiñónes, *Discurso contra los gitanos* (1631). Quoted in Sánchez Ortega, *La Inquisición y los gitanos,* 17–18; my translation.

34. Gay y Blasco stresses that the Gypsies' particular understanding about what persons are, and what they should be, is a gendered one: "the perpetuation of 'the Gitanos' as 'a kind of people' (*clase de gente*) depends on the ongoing enactment of the Gitano morality by each Gitano man and woman" (*Gypsies in Madrid,* 14–15). Elsewhere, she notes the difference between sex and gender: "In their understandings the distinction between women and men is portrayed as given, fixed and unquestionable, and it is linked to the genital endowment of individuals: *mujeres* are the ones with *chochos* (female genitalia . . .) and *hombres* are the ones with *pijas* (penises)" (*Gypsies in Madrid,* 69).

35. Michael Stewart, *The Time of the Gypsies* (Boulder, CO: Westview Press, 1997), 227–28. "Gypsy women's ties to the natural world through their bodily functions also serve to distinguish them from non-Rom women, whom the Gypsy men view as shameless, and good only for sex, but not procreation" (*The Time of the Gypsies,* 226).

36. See Wayne Shumaker, *The Occult Sciences in the Renaissance: A Study in Intellectual Patterns* (Berkeley: University of California Press, 1972).

37. For witchcraft in Spain, see María Tausiet, *Ponzoña en los ojos: Brujería y superstición en Aragón en el siglo XVI.* (Madrid: Turner, 2004). For witchcraft persecution in early modern Europe, see Bengt Ankarloo and Gustav Henningsen, eds., *Early Modern European Witchcraft: Centres and Peripheries* (Oxford: Clarendon Press, 1993); Wolfgang Behringer, *Witches and Witch-Hunts* (Cambridge, UK: Polity, 2004); H.C. Erik Midelfort, *Witch Hunting in Southwestern Germany, 1562–1684* (Stanford: Stanford University Press, 1972); Lyndal Roper, *Witch Craze* (New Haven, CT: Yale University Press, 2004); Walter Stephens, *Demon Lovers: Witchcraft, Sex, and the Crisis of Belief* (Chicago and London: University of Chicago Press, 2002); and Deborah Willis, *Malevolent Nurture. Witch-Hunting and Maternal Power in Early Modern England* (Ithaca, NY, and London: Cornell University Press, 1995); among others. Recently, the misogynist singling out of women in such treatises as the *Malleus maleficarum* has been attributed to the religious crises in the Renaissance: just as skeptical Protestants called the sacraments into question because their efficacy could not be scientifically proven, so Catholic persecutors argued for the existence of the supernatural by attacking illiterate witches, whose sexual interactions with demons were perceived as a passive means of gathering knowledge (Stephens, *Demon Lovers,* 182–90).

38. The tribunals are those of Granada, Sevilla, Córdoba, Barcelona, Valencia, Murcia, Llerena, Toledo, Cuenca, Valladolid, Zaragoza, Logroño, the Canary Islands, and Mallorca (Sánchez Ortega, *La Inquisición y los gitanos,* 399–402).

39. Ibid., 265.

40. AHN, Inquisición, lib. 941, fol. 39. Cited in Sánchez Ortega, *La Inquisición y los gitanos,* 272.

41. "En el nombre del Diablo mayor / y del diablo menor / y del Diablo Cojuelo / que cayó del Cielo / y de la estrella Caifás / y del ánima más sola / te conjuro / para que así como esta redoma / está apretada en la mano / así estén los corazones de las mujeres / que estos hombres pretenden." AHN, Inquisición, leg. 3732, no. 24. Quoted in Sánchez Ortega, *La Inquisición y los gitanos,* 275; my translation.

42. Sebastián Cirac Estopañán, *Los procesos de hechicerías en la Inquisición de Castilla la Nueva (Tribunales de Toledo y Cuenca)* (Madrid: Consejo Superior de Investigaciones Científicas, 1942).

43. Ibid., 206.

44. Sánchez Ortega, *La Inquisición y los gitanos,* 265.

45. Henry Charles Lea, *The Moriscos of Spain: Their Conversion and Expulsion* (London: Bernard Quaritch, 1901), 20–21.

46. "Y sy al fin no se quisyesen convertir de su voluntad podeysles desir que han de yr fuera de nuestros Reynos porque no avremos de dar lugar que en ellos aya ynfieles" Royal *cédula* dated September 23, 1501. Quoted in Pascual Boronat y Barrachina, *Los moriscos españoles y su expulsión: Estudio histórico-crítico,* 2 vols. (Valencia: Francisco Vives y Mora, 1901), 1:113; my translation.

47. "13. La paz sea contigo en nombre de unos rostros obligados a descubrirse en el seno de barbaros tras haber permanecido velados. 14. La paz sea contigo en nombre de unas doncellas a quienes el cura arrastra por los cabellos al lecho del deshonor. . . . 56. Ay! pues nos cambiaron la religión de Muhammad por la de los perros cristianos, las peores de las criaturas." Mercedes García Arenal, *Los moriscos,* facsimile ed. (Granada: Universidad de Granada, 1996), 34–37; my translation.

48. Leonard Patrick Harvey, *Islamic Spain: 1250 to 1500* (Chicago: University of Chicago Press, 1990), 334–35.

49. Míkel de Epalza, *Los moriscos antes y después de la expulsión,* 2nd ed. (Madrid: Mapfre, 1994), 80, 89.

50. García Arenal, *Los moriscos,* 54.

51. Ferdinand Braudel, *The Mediterranean and the Mediterranean World in the Age of Philip II,* trans. Siân Reynolds (New York: Harper, 1972–73), 2:790.

52. García Arenal, *Los moriscos,* 64; my translation.

53. Antonio Domínguez Ortíz and Bernard Vincent, *Historia de los Moriscos: Vida y tragedia de una minoría* (Madrid: Alianza Editorial, 1984), 35.

54. Epalza, *Los moriscos antes y después de la expulsión,* 92.

55. Harvey, *Muslims in Spain,* 151.

56. Ronald E. Surtz, "Morisco Women, Written Texts, and the Valencia Inquisition," *Sixteenth Century Journal* 32 (2001): 424.

57. Mary Elizabeth Perry, "Behind the Veil: Moriscas and the Politics of Resistance and Survival," in *Spanish Women in the Golden Age: Images and Realities,* ed. Magdalena S. Sánchez and Alain Saint-Saëns (Westport, CT, and London: Greenwood, 1996), 44.

58. The Morisca's name was Nuzaya Calderán, or possibly María la Calderera; she was "wise woman" in Arabic, which is still *curandera,* a "practitioner of popular and especially herbal medicine." What is most unusual about her is her learning; she knew Arabic "very well" and interpreted the Koran (Harvey, *Muslims in Spain,* 189–92).

59. For literary examples of Maurophilia, see María Soledad Carrasco-Urgoiti, *El moro de Granada en la literatura (del siglo XV al XX)* (Madrid: Revista de Occidente, 1956).

60. In Vicente Espinel's *Vida del escudero Marcos de Obregón,* for instance, we read "I felt hurt, like all the others, because I could not aspire to honors or to appointment as a magistrate or higher dignities, and because I realized that such deprivation of honor (*infamia*) would be everlasting, and that being a Christian, whether in outer appearance or inner truth, would never be enough." Quoted in Harvey, *Muslims in Spain,* 200; his translation.

61. Cervantes, *Exemplary Stories,* 128.

62. Miguel de Cervantes, *Don Quijote,* ed. Diana de Armas Wilson, trans. Burton Raffel (New York: Norton, 1999), 2:450–51.

63. Epalza, *Los moriscos antes y después de la expulsión,* 122.

64. Mary Elizabeth Perry, "The Politics of Race, Ethnicity, and Gender in the Making of the Spanish State," in *Culture and the State of Spain, 1550–1850,* ed. Tom Lewis and Francisco J. Sánchez, Hispanic Issues 20 (New York and London: Garland, 1999), 39.

65. Ricoldo de Montecrucio, *Reprobación del Alcorán* (n.p.: n.d.). Quoted in Perry, "The Politics of Race, Ethnicity, and Gender in the Making of the Spanish State," in *Culture and the State of Spain,* ed. Lewis and Sánchez, 50n13.

66. Raphael Carrasco and Bernard Vincent, "Amours et mariage chez les morisques au XVIe siècle," in *Amours légitimes, amours illégitimes en Éspagne (XVIe–XVIIe siècles)*, ed. Augustin Redondo (Paris: Publications de la Sorbonne, 1985), 138.

67. "Porque pienso cierto que, si no se remedia esto con brevedad, dentro de veinte o treinta años, ha de ser la mayor parte destos reinos (fuera de alguna gente de calidad y rica) de mendigantes y gascones, por ser gran parte dellos desta nación, moriscos y gitanos, porque éstos van creciendo y multiplicándose mucho, y nosotros disminuyéndonos muy apriesa en guerras y religiones." Cristóbal Pérez de Herrera, *Amparo de pobres*, ed. Michel Cavillac (Madrid: Espasa-Calpe, 1975), 177; my translation.

68. "[Y] no puedan ser trajineros ni acer oficios de mercaderes ni de ningun genero de mercancia ni tengan tiendas de merceria ni de otras cossas sino que todos se ocupen en los dichos oficios de labranza y cultura de la tierra so pena de seis años de seruicio de galera al reino." AHN, Sala de Alcaldes de Casa y Corte, lib. 1200, 1609, fol. 429; my translation.

69. AHN, Sala de Alcaldes de Casa y Corte, lib. 1201, 1511, fol. 185.; my translation.

70. Pedro Fernández de Navarrete, *Conservación de monarquías y discursos políticos*, ed. Michael D. Gordon (Madrid: Instituto de Estudios Fiscales, Ministerio de Hacienda, 1982), 67–68; my translation.

71. Sancho de Moncada, *Restauración política de España* (1619; repr. Madrid, 1779), 206; my translation.

72. Pedro Calderón de la Barca, *Amar después de la muerte* (Madrid: Biblioteca de Autores Españoles, 1945), vol. 12, 681–718. See also my "Making War, Not Love: The Contest of Cultural Difference and the Honor Code in Calderón's *Amar después de la muerte*," in *Calíope, "Con triste canto": Golden Age Studies in Memory of Daniel L. Heiple*, ed. Julián Olivares, 6.1–2 (2000): 27–33.

73. "No parece conveniente expedirlos porque la despoblación en que se hallan estos reinos después que salieron los moriscos y las que causan las necesidades presentes no pueden sufrir ninguna evacuación por ligera que sea, principalmente de esta gente, que no son gitanos por naturaleza, sino por artificio y bellaquería y enmendados se reducirán a la forma de vida de los demás." AHN, Consejos, leg. 7133. Quoted by Domínguez Ortíz, "Documentos sobre los gitanos españoles en el s. XVII," in *Homenaje a Julio Caro Baroja*, ed. Carreira, 320; my translation.

Chapter 5

Sodomy and the Lash

Sexualized Satire in the Renaissance

IAN FREDERICK MOULTON

Living Dangerously: Satire and Sexual Language

By our standards, all of early modern London was living dangerously. Filth was everywhere: open sewers ran through the city center; drainage was inadequate; water was foul. Corpses of dogs and drowned cats lay rotting in ditches. Horse dung and human excrement were in every street. The air in an early modern city would stifle us with its stench. Poor sanitation, of course, led to disease: plague, leprosy, smallpox, and a host of other ailments. Without exception, early modern cities were deadly places to live.

But the phrase "living dangerously" suggests more than just the uncertainties of day-to-day existence; it suggests a choice—a decision to take risks. Someone who lives dangerously is someone who transgresses social norms, who lives outside the conditions of ordinary life. Unlike soldiers, prostitutes, thieves, spies, and heretics, writers often do not live particularly dangerously. But there are exceptions. Some dangerous filth is metaphorical rather than literal. As we shall see, Renaissance satire is marked by disorderly sexuality and aggression—by sodomy and the lash. Satire does not just bring together sex and violence: in satire, sex is violence. Then as now, this is a volatile combination.

As the anthropologist Mary Douglas famously observed, "our idea of dirt is compounded of two things, care for hygiene and respect for conventions."[1] While some conditions actually spread disease, society is often much more concerned with the second concept of dirt—things that are not in their appropriate places: shoes on the table, potting soil on the carpet, a flag on the ground. In these examples the sense of inappropriateness comes, not from any concern for disease, but from a concern for socially appropriate orderly behavior. Shoes should be on the ground, soil in a flowerpot, and flags on flagpoles. Putting things where they "belong"—tidying up—is part of a universal project of creating meaning, of giving order to the disorder of experience. At least since the time of Aristotle, writing, especially literary writing, has been seen as part of the same project: like cleaning a house, telling a story is a means of imposing order, of putting things where they belong, of making sense of confusing and contradictory realities.

But within a given culture, the line between safe and dangerous behavior can be difficult to predict. Things intended as orthodox may appear radical; things intended to be radical may in practice be more orthodox than they seem. The line between acceptable and dangerous writing is especially blurred in satire—writing that uses irony and sarcasm to ridicule foolish or corrupt behavior. More than any other literary genre, satire—whose name comes from the Latin *satura,* meaning "mixture"—takes delight in exploring filth, anatomizing disorder, and focusing on misfits of all kinds. The danger in this sort of writing is that filth—the disorderly subject matter of satire—may contaminate the author.

Though satire as a genre generally promotes "accepted" norms of behavior and traditional social structures, it often uses language and imagery that go well beyond the bounds of good taste or civil discourse. Satire flourished in the contentious intellectual and social world of the sixteenth century. Much Renaissance satire is not elegant—it is furious and savage and foulmouthed. In particular, Renaissance satire employs sexual language in a paradoxical way: the targets of satire are ridiculed as sexually deviant, but in the process, the persona of the satirist himself is sexualized, often with dangerous, unpredictable results.

We often deplore the violence of our own culture, but violence was much more prevalent in daily life in the Renaissance than it is in much of contemporary Western society. The violence of satiric language often matched and mirrored the violence of daily life. Life in Renaissance Italy was famously violent, and if anything, the late sixteenth century saw a rise in banditry and a stubborn persistence of vendetta and private vengeance.[2] Consider the violent lives of the canonical writers of the English Renaissance: Sir Philip Sidney died in battle in the Netherlands; Christopher Marlowe was stabbed to death in a tavern brawl; Ben Jonson killed at least two men; John Donne fought in the raid on Cadiz; Edmund Spenser was involved in the Irish wars; even the young John Milton was proud of his swordsmanship.[3]

What was the role of sexual language in Renaissance satire? In the early modern period the censors feared open political or theological dissent. Sexual deviancy was in many ways considered a symptom or a symbol of the more serious threats of treason or heresy. Study of Renaissance censorship, both that in Catholic and Protestant countries, reveals that the main focus of censorship was always theological and political.[4] It would be wrong to suggest that Queen Elizabeth I's bishops or the Council of Trent were primarily concerned with regulating sexually explicit discourse or in prescribing appropriate sexual behaviors. In the early modern period, sexualized discourse is a mode; politics, like theology, is a subject matter. There are many sexually explicit texts in early modern Europe, but there are almost no texts about sex. Satire, in particular, is a genre that uses sex to speak about power. Then as now, sexually explicit language was powerful language—shocking, visceral, and dangerous. It was thus a powerful rhetorical weapon.

This essay examines the relationship between disorderly sexuality and aggression, both in Renaissance satire and in the lives of Renaissance satirists. After addressing some general characteristics of early modern satire and early modern sexuality, it focuses on four sixteenth-century English and Italian satirists who lived dangerously in every sense of the word. Pietro Aretino, known as the "scourge of princes," was stabbed five times and ultimately driven from Rome when his writings angered a papal secretary. Nicolò Franco was tortured and executed for his antipapal writing. Thomas Nashe was forced to flee London when his satiric play *The Isle of Dogs* provoked a two-month closure of the theaters. Ben Jonson, Nashe's collaborator on *The Isle of Dogs,* was imprisoned for his part in its production. Some time later Jonson also had his thumb branded for murdering a fellow actor; but that is another story.[5]

All four of these men—Nashe, Jonson, Aretino, and Franco—assumed the deliberately abusive stance of the Renaissance satirist; all four were punished by the authorities for their writings; all four used sexualized writing to attack their enemies; and all four were accused by their enemies of sexually disorderly behavior. The relation between sodomy and satire, embodied in various ways in these four men's careers, is exemplified in a text by a fifth man—Antonio Vignali, a Sienese intellectual, whose dialogue *La Cazzaria* (*The Book of the Prick*), written in the mid-1520s, goes further than any other sixteenth-century text both in its linkage of sexuality and aggression and in its sexualization of politics.

Sodomy

What were the dangers of being accused of sexually disorderly behavior? And what sexual behavior, precisely, was considered "disorderly" in early modern Europe? Disorderly sexuality is necessarily a vague concept—at times it could be construed as anything beyond vaginal sex between married couples for the purposes of procreation. Much has been written in recent years about the definition of "sodomy" in the Renaissance.[6] It appears that the term was used more generally than now, to refer to various forms of disorderly sexuality, rather than simply to anal sex between men. Whatever the terminology, it is clear that different cultures find different sexual acts particularly repugnant for reasons that go beyond the physical effect of the acts themselves. Our own culture has a particular loathing for sex between children and adults, which in the classical world was often tolerated and even celebrated. The ancient Romans had a horror of oral sex, which was seen as utterly degrading to the person giving pleasure. In early modern Europe, adultery was a far more serious matter than it is now; homosexual relations between men were sometimes harshly punished, sometimes tolerated; and homosexual relations between women seem to have been largely ignored.[7]

In the Renaissance, as in the classical world, sexual behavior was defined largely by the role one took—active and penetrating or passive and penetrated. Object choice was often less important. Masculinity was seen as fundamentally penetrative—and as long as a man engaged in sexual activity in which he penetrated others, he was acting in a masculine fashion. This is not to say that he was necessarily acting well; Christian doctrine and social custom placed relatively strict limits on what forms of sexual behavior were appropriate. In his fourth satire, John Donne does not make a strong moral distinction when "he notes / Who loves whores, who boys, and who goats."[8] All three are acting shamefully, but there is no sense that one is much worse than the other. The butt of Donne's first satire, similarly, is ridiculed in equal measure for enjoying "his plump muddy whore, or prostitute boy."[9]

Nonetheless, sodomy was a crime in early modern Europe, and "acting the sodomite" was certainly a form of living dangerously. Although in England the crime was punishable by death, convictions and executions were extremely rare—and always involved what we would now term "child abuse"—the rape of a minor.[10] In Italy, where sodomitic behavior of various kinds seems to have been relatively prevalent, those convicted of anal sex were frequently sentenced to be burned at the stake.[11] Although certain considerations could lead to a fair amount of leniency in sentencing, prosecutions, convictions, and executions were not uncommon. Accusations of sodomy could thus be not only dangerous, but also deadly.

Traditional Satire and Sexual Invective

Before examining the careers of individual satirists, it is useful to review briefly the social function and generic characteristics of Renaissance satire. Early modern satire is fundamentally conservative, in the sense that it always sees the past as better than the present. Contemporary corruption is contrasted with an imagined golden age of virtue, and the current state of vice and folly is understood as a falling away from earlier perfection. This is a profoundly premodern way of seeing the world. Though we still hear laments about how things were better in "the good old days," few people in postindustrial society truly believe that the world was a better or more comfortable place in the distant past.

Perhaps the most powerful model for Renaissance satire, especially in England, was the Roman writer Juvenal. Juvenal's satires were written at the beginning of the second century AD. The persona of Juvenal's satires is a remarkably consistent figure. He is a wellborn, mature man, who is not particularly wealthy. He complains of having to listen to bad poetry; he hates foreigners and immigrants; he has contempt for hypocrisy and fawning; he despises women; and he sees human ambition as worthless and vain, since suffering and death are the end of all earthly endeavor. All that is worth praying for, he famously says in the tenth satire, is a healthy mind in a healthy body.

Premodern, conservative satire always appeals to notions of good sense and stresses the rightness of traditional social hierarchies. Women should obey men, subjects should obey the monarch, and people should know their place and conform to established norms of behavior. Knowledge of artistic and intellectual tradition is highly prized. Innovation is a dirty word. The perennial targets of such satire include all those who aspire to a place above that given them in the traditional social order: hypocrites, social climbers, learned women, aggressive women—women in general. Also attacked are the members of the elite who, through their degenerate inability to live up to the ideals of their station, forfeit their right to the position they occupy: tyrannical or foolish masters, effeminate men, sensualists, sodomites. Thus, although Renaissance satirists frequently use shocking language and obscene images, this sexual explicitness is not an indication of progressive or libertarian politics; quite the opposite.

Much satiric writing attacks sex as being idiotic—a foolish, irrational, animalistic activity that destroys human dignity. Sexualized invective is one of the most powerful weapons of a conservative writer. Sex in satire is often literally "dirty"—associated with the bodily excrement that, as readers of François Rabelais and Jonathan Swift are well aware, constitutes the other primary image of human degradation in the satiric tradition. Sodomy, especially in its primary connotation of anal sex, is a perfect image to link sexuality and excrement in a profoundly negative view of the physicality of human existence. This linkage of sex and shit goes back to the roots of the genre. Juvenal puts it most succinctly: "Do you think it's nice and easy," a male prostitute complains, "to ram a normal-sized penis into someone's guts, until you reach yesterday's dinner? The slave who ploughs a field has a lighter task than the one who ploughs its owner."[12] Sex and scatology are used to undermine human dignity, and by extension, to reinforce the need for traditional morals, social hierarchies, and power structures.

A related theme, omnipresent in early modern English satire, is sex as disease. Just as anal sex is presented in satire as a perverse degradation of procreative sexuality, so the (very real) threat of the "pox," or syphilis, turns sex from the celebration of life into a dance of death. Writers focus graphically on the physical effects of the disease—the "burned" genitals, the decaying faces, the corruption, the stink. The seventh satire of John Marston's *Scourge of Villany* describes a gallant who is

> first effeminated by lust, then rots with syphilis:
> Weake meager lust hath now consumed quite,
> And wasted cleane away his martiall spright,
> Infeebling ryot, all vices confluence,
> Hath eaten out that sacred influence

Which made him man.
That divine part is soak'd away in sinne,
In sensuall lust, and midnight bezeling [drinking]
Ranke inundation of luxuriousnes,
Have tainted him with such grosse beastlines,
That now the seat of that celestiall essence
Is all possest with Naples pestilence.[13]

Besides associating sex with disease, this poem is typical of early modern satire in its linkage of sex with emasculation and loss of virility.

In our own culture, effeminacy tends to be associated with homosexual behavior, as if homosexual desire was proof that a man "really" wants to be a woman, but in the early modern period, effeminacy was understood quite differently.[14] A man would become effeminate if he spent too much time associating with women or engaged in "feminine" pursuits, such as dancing or writing love poetry. He would also become effeminate if he expended too much of his masculine seed and energy in sex with women. One of the most succinct formulations of this idea comes from Sidney's *Arcadia*:

> As the love of heaven makes one heavenly, the love of virtue, virtu-
> ous, so doth the love of the world make one become worldly: and this
> effeminate love of a woman doth so womanize a man that, if he yield
> to it, it will not only make him an Amazon, but a launder, a distaff-
> spinner or whatever other vile occupation their idle heads can imag-
> ine and their weak hands perform.[15]

The antidote to effeminacy was for a man to devote himself entirely to the masculine world of the warrior, spending time with comrades rather than courtesans, using his energy fighting rather than fornicating.

Attacks on effeminacy are common in Roman satiric models such as Juvenal, Horace, and Persius, and similar concerns seemed particularly relevant in England in the 1590s, when an aging queen led the nation in its war with Spain. In the Renaissance, as in ancient Rome, social power was largely predicated on the successful performance of masculinity. It is not surprising, then, that fears about effeminacy abounded, nor that the accusation of effeminate behavior was a particularly effective rhetorical strategy.

While effeminacy and sodomy are not identical in early modern think-ing, effeminacy was certainly a sign of disorderly sexuality. Whether it manifested itself in the melancholy lovesickness of the frustrated lover, sensuous dissipation in women's arms, or (perhaps worse) taking the "feminine," passive role in sex with men, effeminacy was a sign of fatal weakness and corruption.

Perhaps the most familiar example of effeminacy in the period is Shakespeare's Mark Anthony, who begins as the most ascetic of Roman soldiers, eating rough berries and drinking horse urine on campaign. But once seduced by foreign luxury, he is soon swapping clothes with Cleopatra, and in the end he cannot even manage to stab himself properly.[16] Shakespeare treats Anthony with sympathy and respect, but similar characters are mocked throughout Renaissance satire.[17]

In early modern culture, gender power tended to be seen as a zero-sum game—if effeminate men gave up their power, rule would be taken up by manly women.[18] Surrender to women implies a surrender to sexual pleasure—itself seen as fundamentally feminine. Premodern satire always involves a degree of misogyny: all the great satirists are known for their severity toward women: Juvenal, Martial, Rabelais, Alexander Pope, Swift, the list goes on and on. The attack on women is at the core of satire's attack on sexuality and sexual pleasure. Women appear in satire as emblems of lust, physicality, irrationality, immorality, fickleness, and "frailty." While this misogyny is evident from the earliest Latin satires, Renaissance satires are also a violent rejection of courtly love and Petrarchan idealizations of the feminine unknown in ancient Rome. "Idealized" in effeminate love lyrics, women must be stripped and whipped in satires.[19] Satiric discourse on women is summed up in a manuscript epigram of the period:

> We men have many faults, women but two
>   No good can they speak, no good can they do.[20]

Satyrs and Cynics

The viciousness of early modern satire comes, in part, from a misreading of the genre's history.[21] In early modern England, the etymology of "satire" (from *satura* or "mixture") was unknown. English rhetoricians believed instead that "satire" came from "satyr." In the sixteenth century, the two terms were often spelled identically. In his *Arte of English Poesie* (1589), George Puttenham claims that satire had its roots in the satyr plays that were performed in ancient Greece as companion pieces to Greek tragedy. In these plays, Puttenham believed, actors would dress up as wild satyrs—half man, half beast—to criticize human vice and folly in crude, open terms.[22] Satire in late sixteenth-century England was vicious—worlds away from the urbane Horatian mode that Jonson would affect in later life and that would characterize the great eighteenth-century satires of Pope. English satirists like Nashe, Marston, Joseph Hall, Thomas Middleton, and William Goddard all presented themselves as raving malcontents. Given their supposedly wild woodland origins, satires should be rough and crude in their diction—full of passion and rage. Satires should snarl like angry dogs.

The canine connection was reinforced by the etymology of the word *cynic,* which is derived from the Greek word for dog. The metaphor was taken up in the titles of several collections of satire: Goddard's *A Mastiff Whelp* (1598), for example, or the *Six Snarling Satires* (1599) attributed to Middleton. The other pervasive image was that of a lash or scourge: Marston's *Scourge of Villanie* (1598), *The Scourge of Folly* (1611) by John Davies of Hereford, and George Wither's *Abuses Stript and Whipt* (1613).

This railing mode is significantly different from classical models. Juvenal's satires are unsurpassed in their anger and aggression, but they are also profoundly Stoic. The dominant tone is one of icy contempt. Though Juvenal's language and imagery are frequently disgusting, he remains aloof from the filth he describes. In the notorious ninth satire, which deals ironically with a male prostitute's ill-treatment at the hands of his patrons, the satirist merely listens indulgently to the prostitute's complaints. As an "innocent" auditor, the satirist is distanced from the harshest observations—like the male prostitute's previously cited remarks about the encounter between his penis and "yesterday's dinner."

Partly because of the false etymology connecting "satire" and "satyr," English satirists were not as careful as Juvenal to keep their hands clean. Puttenham was wrong about more than etymology. Not many specifics are known about Greek satyr plays, but it now seems clear that they were comic and festive rather than fierce and satiric. The false genealogy and etymology linking satires and satyrs ensured that Renaissance English satire was marked by a paradox not found in its Roman models. In the English satire of the 1590s, a snarling, cynical satirist full of passionate rage denounced other people's inordinate passion. The paradox of the railing satirist produced some powerful rhetoric but left satirists like Thomas Nashe and Ben Jonson open to charges of immorality. Emulating Juvenal's savage indignation, but dropping his stoic persona for that of a wild satyr, English satirists often seemed like the hypocrites who are the subject of Juvenal's second satire. "How can you lash corruption," Juvenal asks ironically, "when you have the best known butt-crack of all the Socratic buggers?"[23] Although Juvenal sees satire as a lash whipping criminals, he seldom uses the metaphor of the biting dog—his punishments, however harsh, are presented as being rational and judicial, not bestial.

Jonson and Nashe: *The Isle of Dogs* and Beyond

By using sexualized images, early modern satirists risked appearing sexually disorderly themselves. How do they know so much about "perverse" sexual practices? How is it that those filthy words are so at home in their mouths? The remainder of this essay will address several prominent examples of how the dangerous contradiction between filthy language and alleged moral purpose worked itself out in the actual lives of satirists, both from England and from Italy. As we will see, in Italy satire was more explicitly—and crudely—sexual, and the punishments for transgression were correspondingly harsher.

Thanks largely to the image of himself he put forth in poems such as the "Ode to Himself" and "To Penshurst," Ben Jonson is often thought of as a serene Horatian moralist, not a Juvenalian railer. His early career, however, was quite different. In 1597, while Shakespeare was exploring the nature of ideal kingship in the *Henry IV* plays, two of his young rivals, Jonson and Thomas Nashe, collaborated on a play called *The Isle of Dogs*. The details of their collaboration are unclear. In the disastrous aftermath, Nashe claimed to have written only the first act and to have had nothing to do with the rest of the play, although given his reputation this seems unlikely.

The play was performed, probably at the Rose Theatre, in the summer of 1597 and provoked a spectacular reaction. On July 28, 1597, at the request of the lord mayor of London, the Privy Council ordered that all theaters be closed until the beginning of November.[24] By August 15, the actors who performed the play were imprisoned, as was Jonson. They were held in the Marshalsea prison for almost two months. Nashe seems to have escaped prison, though he was obliged to spend several months hiding in the provincial town of Great Yarmouth. In his absence, his London rooms were searched for seditious material by an order of the Privy Council.

We do not know what was so dangerous about *The Isle of Dogs*. No copy of the play has survived. Then as now, the Isle of Dogs refers to an area of

London—the marshy flatlands across the Thames from Greenwich. Today the area is graced by the corporate towers of Canary Wharf, but in Nashe's day Queen Elizabeth was said to keep her hunting dogs there. Perhaps *The Isle of Dogs* saw the fetid swamp as an analogy for the larger island of England. Perhaps it used the royal kennels to symbolize a sycophantic royal court.

Given both its title and its authors, it is probable that *The Isle of Dogs* was largely satiric. "Railing" satire was very popular in England in the late 1590s, and Nashe in particular had gone to a fair amount of effort to create an image for himself as a "snarling satirist." For several years, he had deliberately provoked a pointless literary quarrel with Gabriel Harvey, a Cambridge don, whose brother Richard had insulted Nashe in a pamphlet. Nashe and Gabriel Harvey wrote several books against each other in an escalating war of words that ended only when a 1599 order by the bishops of London and Canterbury decreed "that all Nasshes bookes and Doctor Harvyes bookes be taken wheresoever they maye be found and that none of theire bookes bee ever printed hereafter."[25] Though he was an accomplished scholar, Harvey was not particularly skilled at the witty rhetoric required by this sort of public conflict. Nashe, who had spent many years writing for the popular press, had no trouble getting the better of Harvey.[26]

Nashe attacked Harvey for being a foolish, clumsy, stuffy, incompetent old man who had risen above his station. Harvey attacked Nashe for being a dissolute young man who was abusing his intellect in displays of bawdy and disorderly writing. In the early 1590s, partly to get the attention of Lord Strange, a potential patron, Nashe had written a lengthy narrative poem known as "Nashe's Dildo," which recounted a foolish young man's inability to satisfy the whore he has hired for sex. She rejects him in favor of her "little dildo" and then kicks him out of doors. "Nashe's Dildo," now known by its more polite title "Choice of Valentines," was not only sexually explicit, but also described the fragility of masculine identity.[27] If Nashe wrote it as a comic attempt to get Strange's patronage, he miscalculated badly. Strange seems to have paid it little attention. Harvey, on the other hand, attacked Nashe for writing an "unprinted packet of bawdye, and filthy Rymes in the nastiest kind." At a time of national crisis, when all energies were needed to combat foreign threats, there were, Harvey said, no "bawdy howers for the songes of Priapus, or the rymes of Nashe"—"[t]he date of idle vanities is expired."[28]

Nashe's "Dildo" was not printed in the period, though it circulated fairly widely in manuscript. It was attacked not only by Harvey, but also by John Davies of Hereford, who claimed that good men tore the poem to pieces in their rage.[29] Writing an erotic poem that stresses male weakness left Nashe open to accusations of effeminacy himself. A woodcut published after the *Isle of Dogs* debacle shows Nashe not only chained as a prisoner, but also with the beardless face of an effeminate man and the unbuttoned doublet of a dissolute lover.[30]

The 1599 bishops' order that banned Nashe's books was one of the most overt efforts at press censorship in the Elizabethan period, but whatever its motives, it was not part of a systematic attempt to regulate printed material. Instead, it is clearly a scattershot reaction against material perceived as undesirable for a variety of undefined reasons. It is especially concerned to regulate the printing of political materials, satires, and histories in particular.

Though it proved largely ineffective, the bishops' order is a good indication of the sorts of material the authorities found threatening and the types of discourse they wished to control. Several volumes of satires and epigrams are explicitly named, including works by John Marston, Sir John Davies, and Joseph Hall. The order specifies "that noe Satyres or Epigrams be printed hereafter"; "[t]hat noe Englishe historyes be printed excepte they bee allowed by some of her majesties privie Counsell"; and "[t]hat noe playes be printed excepte they bee allowed by suche as have authorytie."[31] Cyndia Clegg has argued convincingly that the bishops' primary concern in this order was to protect their ally, the Earl of Essex,[32] but whatever their motive, the broad terms in which the order is worded make clear the bishops' desire for extensive control of printed materials, even if such sweeping commands were difficult to implement in practice.

It is unclear what effect the bishops' order actually had on Nashe: his last pamphlet, *Nashe's Lenten Stuff* (1599), makes excuses for *The Isle of Dogs* and promises a further response to his enemies.[33] But by 1601 Nashe was dead, possibly of plague, though the circumstances and date of his death are unknown.

Nashe's collaborator Jonson returned to writing satire almost immediately. *Every Man out of His Humor,* a long, almost unactable, satiric play was a flop in the playhouse but a great success as a printed book.[34] The foolish cast of *Every Man out of His Humor* contains several sodomitic characters, most prominently the fat railer Carlo Buffone, who is ultimately punished by having his mouth sealed with wax. Shortly after *Every Man out of His Humor,* as if emulating Nashe's quarrel with Harvey, Jonson engaged in a protracted dispute with his fellow dramatists Marston and Thomas Dekker. Just as Nashe's enemies tried to portray him as effeminate and sexually disorderly, Jonson's rivals characterized him as a "hermaphrodite" and sodomite, who "screw[s] and wriggle[s] himself into great men's familiarity."[35] And they repeatedly compared him with Buffone, his own caricature of a sodomitic satirist.

Indeed the confusions of *Every Man out of His Humor* come largely from Jonson's inability to separate his railing satirist hero, who appears variously as Asper (whose name means "bitter") and as Macilente ("biting"), from the various fools, knaves, and degenerates he attacks. By the end of the play, he seems just as driven by his "humors" and passions as any of the others.

While Jonson continued to write satire throughout his career, he came to reject the railing Juvenalian mode in favor of a more rational, sober, and detached style, modeled on Horace. His shift in persona from an angry young railer to a cool, dispassionate critic was enormously successful and marks a crucial step in the evolution of the figure of the author in English culture. The calm authority of Jonson's later poetry—especially his epigrams and verse epistles—helped establish him as a classic figure whose works deserved the same reverence and respect as their Roman models. His status as a great author was insured by his publication of a folio collection of his works in 1616 that gave pride of place to his Horatian epigrams. Thus Jonson found ways to exploit successfully the dangers and attractions of disorderly sexuality in his texts, while projecting a rational, authoritative persona that protected him from accusations of personal disorder and misconduct.[36]

Italian Models: Aretino and Franco

As in many literary genres, from epic to pastoral, English satirists looked to contemporary Italy as well as ancient Rome for models of practice. Especially attractive to writers like Nashe and Jonson was the tradition of pasquinades associated with Pietro Aretino. Pasquinades were anonymous satiric poems attached to a battered statue known as Pasquino near Piazza Navona in Rome.[37] The poems were highly critical of the papal authorities and often extremely crude in their language and sentiments. Begun in the early 1520s as a reaction to the unpopular election of the foreign Pope Adrian VI, they quickly became a Roman tradition that persists, in residual form, to this day.

Pasquinades spared no one. They commented publicly on the private meetings of the Conclave of Cardinals. They mocked the local Roman oligarchy and powerful Italian families like the Medici, as well as the king of France, the Holy Roman Emperor, and the pope. Throughout sixteenth-century Europe, Pasquino became an emblem of the plain speaking subject who dared openly to criticize his rulers. Although there was no English tradition of posting poems on a particular statue, Pasquino appears in the title of several English satiric pamphlets, from Sir Thomas Elyot's *Pasquil the playne* (1533) to *Pasquil's Return to England* (1589), an anti-Martinist pamphlet sometimes attributed to Nashe.

Italian authors like Pietro Aretino were admired by English satirists like Nashe and Jonson both because of their outspoken honesty and their financial success. Aretino was quite possibly the most financially successful man of letters of the sixteenth century.[38] He began his career as a courtier and satirist in the Rome of Leo X, but quarrels with Leo's successors led to his flight from Rome in 1525, after one of the papal secretaries attempted to have him assassinated. After a period of wandering, Aretino settled in Venice in 1527. At that time Venice was the greatest printing center in Europe, and access to the Venetian press, coupled with the relative political freedom he enjoyed there, made Aretino extremely successful. He wrote satiric plays and bawdy dialogues; he published his letters to influential patrons; and he churned out popular devotional works, such as the *Vita de Maria Vergine* (*Life of the Virgin Mary*) (1539). He supported the Venetian state and acted as business agent for his friend Titian.[39] Aretino's power to shape opinion ensured that he was widely feared and respected. He cultivated a reputation as the "scourge of princes," and his motto was "Veritas odium parit"—"the truth brings forth hatred."[40]

Despite the opulent comfort of his years in Venice, Aretino's life is a case study of dangerous living in the sixteenth century. Before being driven from Rome, he not only wrote pasquinades against the pope, he also wrote the famous *sonetti lussuriosi* (lustful sonnets) accompanying the erotic prints of his friend Marcantonio Raimondi[41] and played a prominent role in public festivals of misrule. Once safely in Venice, he became, if anything, more outspoken. His sexually explicit *Dialoghi* (*Dialogues*) (1534) open with the scandalous depiction of a convent in which monks and nuns engage in minutely described orgies of masturbation and anal sex.[42]

Not only did Aretino use accusations of sodomitic conduct to attack his enemies, he was himself a sodomite. He lived a life of bisexual promiscuity, filling his house with courtesans and male secretaries. Although in later life he had hopes of being made a cardinal, he was rumored to be an atheist.

Jonson, who knew Aretino's works well, used him as a model for Volpone.[43] In fact, Jonson's entire career as a satirist can be seen as an attempt to appropriate the subversive energy of Aretino's writing, while at the same time distancing himself from the taint of sodomy linked with the Italian writer.

Even in Venice, Aretino was not completely safe. In 1538 he was faced with unspecified accusations of blasphemy and sodomy and had to flee the city until the Duke of Urbino could sort things out for him.[44] Nothing came of the accusations, but sodomy in Venice was a crime punishable by burning, and the accusations demonstrate how hazardous it was to play the sort of literary game at which Aretino made his living.

The charges against Aretino were probably provoked by Nicolò Franco, one of Aretino's secretaries. Franco's career provides a useful contrast to that of his master. Like Aretino, he came from a humble background, and he built his career on his wit and his willingness to shock.[45] He arrived in Venice in 1536 and for a time seems to have been Aretino's protégé. Rightly or wrongly, Aretino blamed Franco for the charges brought against him, and shortly after his return to Venice he threw Franco out of his house. In 1540 Franco left Venice and soon afterward wrote a book of obscene sonnets called *La Priapea*.[46] One after another, in graphic detail, Franco's poems describe Aretino's alleged sodomitic desires and practices. In their rage and sexual explicitness these poems go far beyond anything published in Renaissance England. An introductory poem is addressed to "Pietro Aretino, Scourge of Cocks." In it Franco apologizes to Aretino for presenting him with so many cocks in his poems. But, he concludes, "Your big ass will be satisfied by them, finding here its accustomed food." The volume continues in a similar vein, and many poems attack the pope, as well as Aretino: "what do popes do," sonnet 35 asks, "except eat, drink, and bugger?"[47]

Denied access to the Venetian press by his quarrel with Aretino, Franco had difficulty finding patrons and establishing himself as a man of letters. In 1559, after Aretino's death (from natural causes) Franco finally found favor at the papal court and was elected to the Accademia Romana. After the death of Pope Pius IV, however, Franco's position quickly became precarious, for Pius V, the new pope, was aligned with his enemies. In 1568 Franco was arrested by the Inquisition for his antipapal and obscene writings. After being tortured, he was publicly hanged on March 10, 1570. Officially, Franco was killed for his politics, not his sexuality, but of all the writers we have examined, he was the most explicit and outspoken in his sexualized invective, and he was the most harshly punished.

The social conditions and generic conventions of Italian satire were quite different from those in England. Italian satire was not as dependent on classical models as English satire was; nor was it as conservative in outlook. Aretino in particular had no use for classical precedent and ancient traditions. Alone of the great sixteenth-century satirists, he could not read Latin. Although he remained loyal to the Venetian state and its most powerful families, he had little bias in favor of aristocracy as a class. He is in many ways a remarkably modern figure and tends to champion clever servants over stupid masters, like some sixteenth-century forerunner of Pierre-Augustin Caron de Beaumarchais. But while Aretino was not a cultural conservative, he was no revolutionary either. He could be brutally critical of contemporary corruption, but he seldom looked back to a lost golden age. He was quick to point out problems, but he had few solutions.

The sexuality of his writings, too, has something modern about it. Sex in Aretino may be wonderful or horrid, but—in the tradition of Giovanni Boccaccio's *Decameron*—it is always presented as a central fact of human existence, not as a shameful sin to be lamented or a guilty pleasure to be repented. What is shameful is the hypocrisy of those who, like the monks and nuns in the *Dialogues,* immerse themselves in sexual pleasure while pretending to be above it. For by doing so, they deny their humanity and use their supposed purity as a way of gaining power over others.

Aretino's first major work of erotic writing, the *sonetti lussoriosi,* are almost unique in the sixteenth century in their celebration of sexual pleasure. They are lyric rather than satiric, and it is their lyricism, coupled with their explicitness, that has led people to think of them as being pornographic. Although their composition and dissemination was part of a campaign by Aretino to embarrass the papal court,[48] the poems themselves attempt to describe what sex feels like rather than using sex as a weapon to attack enemies.

Sonnet 1

[He:] Let's fuck, my love, let's fuck now
Since we were all born to fuck
And if you adore the cock, I love the cunt
And the world wouldn't be worth a fuck without this.

And if it were decent to fuck postmortem
I'd say let's fuck so much we die of it

And then we can fuck Eve and Adam
Who found death so indecent;

[She:] It's really true that if those rogues
Had not eaten that traitorous apple
I know that lovers would satisfy all their desires.

But let's stop this babbling and ram your cock
Into me up to my heart, and do it so that my spirit
Bursts there, on which a cock now is born, and now dies.

       And if it is possible
Don't keep your balls out of my cunt
Witnesses of every fucking pleasure.[49]

La Cazzaria

In Aretino's *sonetti,* sex is a source of mutual pleasure, but in much six-teenth-century satire, the only pleasure expressed is the aggressive pleasure of domination. The view of sexuality underlying this rhetoric is a very old and powerful one, which sees sex purely as masculine pleasure in penetra-tion and domination of an inferior. In this context, even oral sex could be seen, not as the passive taking of pleasure, but as an act of penetration. In classical Latin this formulation is expressed in the word *irrumare,* for which there exists no equivalent in the modern languages—it means "to fuck in the mouth." The locus classicus is Catullus 16:

          I will bugger you and I will fuck your mouths,
Aurelius, you pathic, and you queer, Furius,
who have thought me, from my little verses,
because they are a little delicate, to be not quite straight.
For it is proper for a pious poet to be chaste
himself, but there is no need for his little verses to be so;
which only then have wit and charm,
if they are a little delicate, and not too clean,
and can arouse a lewd itching,
I don't mean in boys, but in those hairy men

who can't move a hard groin.
You, because you have read "many thousands
of kisses," think me not quite a man?
I will bugger you and I will fuck your mouths.[50]

Catullus, attacked for writing effeminate love poems, reaffirms his masculinity by threatening to sodomitically abuse his male critics. In the ancient world, this sort of masculine aggressiveness was relatively unproblematic. Such an act would constitute, not homoeroticism, but rape; not effeminate sensuality, but masculine aggression. By the sixteenth century, however, bragging of sodomitic sex was no longer seen as unambiguously masculine. Though this poem was known in the sixteenth century, I know of no imitations.

But there were those who affirmed the value of sodomy. Nowhere is the association of buggery and power more apparent than in Antonio Vignali's *La Cazzaria,* or *The Book of the Prick.* Vignali's work, written in Siena in 1525, is a dialogue between two men, Arsiccio and Sodo, both members of the Accademia degli Intronati (Academy of the Stunned), an elite Sienese literary society. During the course of the dialogue, the older Arsiccio instructs the younger, and suggestively named, Sodo, on various points of sexual knowledge. The second half of the text is given over to an elaborate fable in which Arsiccio describes the origins of human society. In this fable (which is also an allegory of contemporary Sienese politics), Arsiccio sees the human community as the site of a perpetual power struggle for sexual and social dominance. The factions in his imagined republic are body parts: Cocks, Cunts, Balls, and Assholes. The story begins with the seizure of power by the Big Cocks, who disdain their poor relatives, the Little Cocks, and brutally tyrannize the Cunts and Assholes (the Balls, timid traitors, go along for the ride).

Arsiccio's ludicrous (yet serious) fable sees sex as pure domination and intrinsically links sex with political power. The Big Cocks are eventually overthrown and massacred by a coalition of their foes. But the survivors can come to no solid agreement on how to divide the power they have seized, and the future of the state is uncertain at the fable's end. The body politic, rather than being subordinated to a rational head, is seen as a site of competing and conflicting desires—a body in parts, dismembered.[51]

What is certain is that Arsiccio is using his story of sexual power to seduce Sodo, and as the text ends, it is suggested that his strategy will succeed. Scholars, Arsiccio says early on, make the best lovers, because they know the most: knowledge, power, and sexual potency all go together. This idea ought to be attractive to male elites. Theoretically, Vignali—like Catullus—solved the problem Nashe and Jonson would have with the corruption inherent in sexualized discourse. Sex is only filthy and shameful if it is something done to you—if you do it to other people, it becomes a discourse of domination. *La Cazzaria*, however, was too explicit in its language and too sodomitic in its arguments to be widely disseminated or accepted. In the sixteenth century, unlike in the Rome of Catullus, sexual aggression (sodomy) and moralistic punishment (the lash) had a fundamentally ambivalent relationship.

Although Vignali seems to have intended his outrageous dialogue for manuscript circulation among members of his academy, several printed editions appeared without his consent. Compared to the other writers whose careers we have considered, Vignali got off lightly. As far as we know, he was not punished for writing *La Cazzaria*, although he spent most of his life as an exile from his native city. The reasons for his exile are unclear, though his decision to leave may have been politically motivated. Honored as a noble-man and a scholar, he traveled the courts of Europe and, after a time in the service of Philip II of Spain, he died in Milan in 1559 while in the service of Cardinal Cristofero Madruzzi. Although he was often referred to by his con-temporaries as a man of great literary talent, their memorials seldom men-tion *La Cazzaria*, which was by far his most substantial and significant literary work. Neither hanged like Franco, stabbed like Aretino, imprisoned like Jonson, nor hounded like Nashe, he suffered what perhaps for a writer is a greater indignity. He wrote something so unspeakably filthy that his ad-mirers remained silent about it and his works were forgotten.

NOTES

1. Mary Douglas, *Purity and Danger: An Analysis of the Concepts of Pollution and Taboo* (New York: Routledge, 1991), 7.

2. See Gregory Hanlon, "Violence and Its Control in the Late Renaissance: An Italian Model," in *A Companion to the Worlds of the Renaissance,* ed. Guido Ruggiero (Oxford: Blackwell, 2002), 139–55.

3. John Milton, *The Second Defense of the English People in Complete Poetry and Major Prose,* ed. Merritt Y. Hughes (Upper Saddle River, NJ: Prentice Hall, 1957), 824.

4. Cyndia Clegg, *Press Censorship in Elizabethan England* (New York: Cambridge University Press, 1997); Paul F. Grendler, *Culture and Censorship in Late Renaissance Italy and France* (London: Variorum Reprints, 1981).

5. David Riggs, *Ben Jonson: A Life* (Cambridge, MA: Harvard University Press, 1989), 34–35, 79–80.

6. On definitions of sodomy, see Alan Bray, *Homosexuality in Renaissance England* (London: Gay Men's Press, 1982), 14–16; Gregory W. Bredbeck, *Sodomy and Interpretation: Marlowe to Milton* (Ithaca, NY: Cornell University Press, 1991), 9–23, 89–96; Jonathan Goldberg, *Sodometries: Renaissance Texts, Modern Sexualities* (Stanford: Stanford University Press, 1992), xv–xvi, 19, 120–24.

7. On sodomy laws, see Bruce R. Smith, *Homosexual Desire in Shakespeare's England* (Chicago: University of Chicago Press, 1991), 41–53, and Guido Ruggiero, *The Boundaries of Eros: Sex Crime and Sexuality in Renaissance Venice* (New York: Oxford University Press, 1985), 109–45. On the "invisibility" of lesbian relations, see Valerie Traub, "The (In)significance of Lesbian Desire in Early Modern England," in *Erotic Politics: Desire on the Renaissance Stage*, ed. Susan Zimmerman (New York: Routledge, 1992), 150–69.

8. John Donne, *The Complete Poetry and Selected Prose of John Donne*, ed. Charles M. Coffin (New York: Modern Library, 2001), 106, l. 128.

9. Ibid., 95, l. 40.

10. Smith, *Homosexual Desire in Shakespeare's England*, 53.

11. Ruggiero, *The Boundaries of Eros*, 112; Michael Rocke, *Forbidden Friendships: Homosexuality and Male Culture in Renaissance Florence* (New York: Oxford University Press, 1996), 51–53.

12. Juvenal 9.43–46, in *Juvenal and Persius*, ed. and trans. Susanna Morton Braund, Loeb Classical Library 91 (Cambridge, MA: Harvard University Press, 2004), 354–55; my translation.

13. John Marston, *The Poems of John Marston*, ed. Arnold Davenport (Liverpool University Press, 1961), 140–46, ll. 118–28.

14. Ian Frederick Moulton, *Before Pornography: Erotic Writing in Early Modern England* (New York: Oxford, 2000), 68–109.

15. Sir Philip Sidney, *The Countess of Pembroke's Arcadia* (New York: Penguin, 1977), 134.

16. See William Shakespeare, *Anthony and Cleopatra*, act 1, scene 4, ll. 60–65, and act 2, scene 5, ll. 21–23.

17. Examples abound. See John Donne's first satire (Donne, *The Complete Poetry and Selected Prose*, 94–97), as well as William Goddard, *A Mastiff Whelp* (Dort, Netherlands, 1598), sig. E4r, and Thomas Middleton(?), *Micro-cynicon. Sixe Snarling Satyres* (London, 1599), sig. C4r–C6r.

18. For example, see epigram 74 of John Davies of Hereford's *Scourge of Folly*, in *The Complete Works of John Davies of Hereford*, ed. Alexander Grosart (New York: AMS Press, 1967), 2:16.

19. Juvenal's sixth satire is the urtext of satiric misogyny (see *Juvenal and Persius*, 234–95). Further pertinent examples include: Ben Jonson's epigram 62, in *The Complete Poems* (New York: Penguin, 1988), 53; and the second satire of Everard Guilpen's *Skialethia, or A Shadowe of Truth, in Certaine Epigrams and Satyres*, ed. D. Allen Carrol (Chapel Hill: North Carolina University Press, 1974), 68–72.

20. British Library, MS Add. 10309, fol. 103.

21. Alvin Kernan, *The Cankered Muse: Satire of the English Renaissance* (New Haven, CT: Yale University Press, 1959), 54–63.

22. George Puttenham, *The Arte of English Poesie* (London, 1589), sig. E2v, E4v–F1r.

23. Juvenal 2.9–10, in *Juvenal and Persius,* 64; my translation.

24. Charles Nicholl, *A Cup of News: The Life of Thomas Nashe* (London: Routledge, 1984), 242–49; Riggs, *Ben Jonson,* 32–34.

25. Edward Arber, *A Transcript of the Registers of the Company of Stationers of London,* 3 vols. (London, 1876), 3:677–78.

26. Nicholl, *A Cup of News,* 62–79.

27. Moulton, *Before Pornography,* 168–93.

28. Gabriel Harvey, *Pierce's Supererogation* (London, 1593), sigs. F4v–F6r.

29. John Davies of Hereford, "Paper's Complaint," ll. 65–70, in *The Complete Works of John Davies of Hereford,* vol. 2, ed. Alexander B. Grosart (New York: AMS Press, 1967), 75.

30. Richard Lichfield, *The Trimming of Thomas Nashe* (London, 1597), sig. E2r.

31. Arber, *A Transcript of the Registers of the Company of Stationers of London,* 3:677–78.

32. Clegg, *Press Censorship in Elizabethan England,* 198–217.

33. Thomas Nashe, "Nashe's Lenten Stuff," in *The Works of Thomas Nashe,* ed. Ronald B. McKerrow (Oxford: Blackwell, 1966), 3:153.

34. Riggs, *Ben Jonson,* 67.

35. Thomas Dekker, *Satiromastix: or the Untrussing of the Humorous Poet,* act 5, scene 2, ll. 255–56, in *The Dramatic Works of Thomas Dekker,* vol. 1, ed. Fredson Bowers (Cambridge: Cambridge University Press, 1953), 381.

36. Moulton, *Before Pornography,* 194–219.

37. Over seven hundred pasquinades are collected in Giovanni Aquilecchia et al., eds., *Pasquinate romane del Cinquecento,* 2 vols. (Rome: Salerno, 1983).

38. Moulton, *Before Pornography,* 138, 143. Edward Hutton, *Pietro Aretino: The Scourge of Princes* (London, Constable, 1922), 228.

39. See Luba Freedman, *Titian's Portraits through Aretino's Lens* (University Park: Pennsylvania State University Press, 1995).

40. On "Veritas odium parit," see Raymond B. Waddington, *Aretino's Satyr: Sexuality, Satire, and Self-Projection in Sixteenth-Century Literature and Art* (Toronto: University of Toronto Press, 2004), 93–94, 98–100.

41. See Bette Talvacchia, *Taking Positions: On the Erotic in Renaissance Culture* (Princeton University Press, 1999).

42. Pietro Aretino, *Aretino's Dialogues,* trans. Raymond Rosenthal (New York: Marsilio, 1994), 27–45.

43. Mario Praz, *The Flaming Heart* (New York: Doubleday, 1958), 181–85; Moulton, *Before Pornography,* 206–11.

44. Gian Maria Mazzuchelli, *La vita di Pietro Aretino* (Padua, 1741), in *Lettere sull'arte di Pietro Aretino,* vol. 3, ed. Fidenzio Pertile and Ettore Camesaca (Milan: Edizioni del milione, 1959), 82–83.

45. On Franco, see Giuseppe De Michele, "Niccolò Franco: Biografia con documenti inediti," *Studia della letteratura italiana* 2 (1915): 61–154; and Paul F. Grendler,

Critics of the Italian World, 1530–1560 (Madison: University of Wisconsin Press, 1969), 38–49.

46. Several editions of *La Priapea* seem to have been published in the 1540s, though copies are extremely rare. I refer to an eighteenth-century edition of *La Priapea* currently in the British Library (1079 i9).

47. Niccolò Franco, *La Priapea, Sonetti . . . di N. F.* (n.p.: n.p., [1790]), British Library, 1079i9; my translation.

48. Talvacchia, *Taking Positions*, 3–19.

49. In ibid., 199; my translation. The original Italian as follows:

Sonetto 1

Fottamoci anima mia, fottiamoci presto
Poi che tutti per fotter nati siamo
E se tu il cazzo adori, io la potta amo
E saria il mondo un cazzo senza questo
E se post mortem fotter fuss'honesto
Direi tanto fottiam, che ci moriamo
Per fotter poi de la Eva, et Adamo
Che trovaro il morir si dishonesto
Veramente gli è ver, che s'i furfanti
Non mangiavan quel pomo traditore
Io so che si sfoiavano gli amanti,
Ma lasciamo ir le ciancie, et in sino al core
Ficcami il cazzo, e fa ch'ivi si schianti
L'anima, che'n su'l cazzo hor nasce hor more
       E s' è possibil fore
Non mi tener la potta I coglioni
D'ogni piacer fottuto testimoni.

50. My translation. The original Latin as follows (*Catullus, Tibullus, Pervigilium Veneris,* 2nd ed., ed. G. P. Gould et al., Loeb Classical Library [Cambridge, MA: Harvard University Press, 1988], 22–23):

      Pedicabo ego vos et irrumabo,
Aureli pathice et cinaede Furi,
qui me ex versiculis meis putastis,
quod sunt molliculi, parum pudicum.
nam castum esse decet pium poetam
ipsum, versiculos nihil necesse est;
qui tum denique habent salem ac leporem,
si sunt molliculi ac parum pudici,
et quod pruriat incitare possunt,
non dico pueris, sed his pilosis
qui duros nequeunt movere lumbos.

uos, quod milia multa basiorum
legistis, male me marem putatis?
pedicabo ego uos et irrumabo.

51. See the introduction to Antonio Vignali, *La Cazzaria: The Book of the Prick,* ed. Ian Frederick Moulton (New York: Routledge, 2003).

Chapter 6

The Wind Traders

Speculators and Frauds in Northern Europe, 1650–1720

MARY LINDEMANN

It is curious how often margins and centers intersect, a physical impossibility that is readily apparent in the economic world of the late seventeenth and early eighteenth centuries. Any study of this period of economic history remains unsatisfactory unless it considers the celestial orb of high finance and the crepuscular realm of fishy deals and shady traders. Although the extent to which the two coincided may seem surprising, the overlap characterized the fluid economies of the time, as the career of the Scottish monetary reformer John Law amply demonstrates. Honest brokers and disreputable ones worked cheek by jowl, frequently employed identical economic practices, and often collaborated. In this milieu, speculation could seem very much like fraud, and credit often rested on questionable grounds. Yet both credit and speculation greased the flying wheels of commerce. Those who lived dangerously by speculating or by dealing fast and loose in the burgeoning money markets of pacemaker economies like Amsterdam, Antwerp, and Hamburg, ran the risk of bankruptcy. But not only frauds and speculators went bust; so, too, did reputable firms and prudent businessmen. Moreover, if contemporaries jumped to criticize the dubious economic practices that paved the road to ruin, they just as quickly saw in them threats to the republican heritage these polities shared. While this republicanism remained ill defined (it was certainly not a coherent or well-articulated political phi-losophy), it proved a useful rhetorical device for defining a particular place in the world. By it the good burghers of Amsterdam, Antwerp, and Ham-burg meant something more than a vague concept of *res publica* (in the broad sense of "commonwealth," "public affairs," or "public property"). Such republicanism, as Jonathan Israel has persuasively argued, was "plainly not the ideology of a rural elite, aspiring to dominate a national parliament, but rather of city burghers whose interests were commercial and non-agrarian." It only superficially resembled the "Atlantic" (or rather Anglo-Saxon) re-publicanism that J.G.A. Pocock and others have described and "which is far and way the leading and presiding tradition in post-Renaissance western republicanism as a whole."[1]

Rather, in all these cities, dominated as they were by merchants and bankers (who were, however, not merely economic animals, as Simon Schama reminds us[2]), political and economic virtues tightly entwined, and attacks on suspicious economic actions deployed the same language of disapproval, treachery, and dishonesty that political discourse reserved for traitors and venal officials. But contemporaries only rarely and incompletely separated political virtues and economic ones, and economic practices always bore political implications.

The history of speculation and fraud for Amsterdam, Antwerp, and Hamburg has yet to be written. Although early modernists have been fasci-nated by the great Tulip Craze of 1633–37, beguiled by the career of John Law, and intrigued by the economic maelstrom of the Mississippi Scheme and the South Sea Bubble,[3] they have virtually ignored the equally impor-tant topic of speculation and fraud as part of a political discourse and a civic sensibility that characterized late seventeenth- and early eighteenth-century urban republics. Scholars have acknowledged corruption in more general terms as a central attribute of political discourses and cultures in these centuries and have addressed the unholy trinity of corruption, luxury, and faction/party in tracing the development of an Anglo-Saxon republican moment. While fraud falls easily within the category of corruption, spec-ulation and speculators are more difficult to site, especially in merchant-republics like Amsterdam, Antwerp, and Hamburg, because they nestled so uncomfortably near to established business practices, such as the use of bills of exchange. In commenting on the early forms of speculation in Amster-dam, Schama quite perceptively observes that "moralizing aside ... it was in fact only a more extreme form of the practices which arose naturally in an economy where delivery times were bound to be uncertain and prolonged."[4] Speculators could be frauds, yet the lure of speculation was hard to deny, offering as it did such lovely possibilities of conjuring with pieces of paper. The threads of speculation and even fraud could be difficult to unsnarl because the mercantile ethos, and even the commercial law, of the seventeenth and early eighteenth centuries had not yet decided where legitimate business practice let off and fraud began. Speculation huddled, often hard to discern, in the penumbra cast by the juggernaut of economic change.

Fraud and speculation threatened—or seemed to threaten—the material prosperity, but also the basic political and civic structures, of mercantile republics like Amsterdam, Antwerp, and Hamburg. All three cities were "mercantile" and "republic" in the conviction that a time-tested set of business values and procedures underpinned their governmental form and secured their freedom. Republicanism in seventeenth- and eighteenth-century cities was rooted in the communalism of medieval towns but was not identical to it. Republicanism had little to do with either representation or political rights. Birth, occupation, property, or religion excluded a large number of residents from eligibility for civic office, although many citizens (and perhaps even most) participated in their parish, neighborhood, guild, or militia and felt themselves securely anchored in a cat's cradle of communal networks. Republicanism was, moreover, a state of mind and a rhetorical strategy that cities like Amsterdam and Hamburg (Antwerp was somewhat of an exception) used to distance themselves from other, nonrepublican polities, especially monarchies. These attitudes intersected with very real concerns for their sovereignty vis-à-vis mightier powers (in the case of Amsterdam and Hamburg) and for unfettered control of their internal affairs. All three cities shared one critical republican aspect: they were self-governing. The larger political universe each inhabited was, however, different. Hamburg enjoyed full sovereignty; the city owed no allegiance to a higher authority except a rather loose fealty to the Holy Roman Empire. (Until 1768 Denmark contested—albeit unsuccessfully—Hamburg's autonomy.) Amsterdam, while part of the greater Dutch Republic, was also independent. Yet the creation, economic development, and exploitation of a colonial empire through Amsterdam's two great Indies' companies greatly complicated its relationship with the rest of the world and also opened up scope for economic innovation and financial misdeeds. Although Antwerp's inhabitants generally regarded their city as a republic, it formed an integral part of first the Spanish and then the Austrian Netherlands (after 1713) and thus was repeatedly entangled in the political maneuvering and economic strategies of a larger empire. (S)elected and co-optive city councils governed all three cities (although here Antwerp again formed a special case in that the Spanish or Austrian governor named some important officials and approved the appointment of others).

Since the sixteenth century, each city had followed divergent political and economic paths. Until the Revolt of the Netherlands, Antwerp had been the most affluent city in northern Europe and an economic center *sans pareil.* By the end of the seventeenth century, however, that economic vitality had all but evaporated. Sir Dudley Carleton in 1620 wandered through empty streets never seeing "as many as forty people [together] nor . . . [meeting] a coach or a man on horseback." The peripatetic scandalmonger Karl Ludwig Freiherr von Pöllnitz observed that while Antwerp had once been Europe's "greatest entrepôt," it had "completely decayed" and Amsterdam had risen phoenix-like out of the ruins. Instead of the "thousands" of traders one encountered at the exchanges in London and Amsterdam, the Antwerp Beurs was empty "with hardly thirty people gathering there in the course of an afternoon."[5] While Amsterdam's prosperity did not rest solely on the demise of Antwerp (and was, in truth, of a different character), most early modern observers associated the ascent of Amsterdam directly and immediately with the fall of Antwerp. Most historians still more or less agree that between the 1590s and about 1650 the Dutch (and the Amsterdammers) experienced a golden age that was followed by a period of rather pronounced deterioration. While the whole matter of Dutch economic decline still fuels a fierce debate, little doubt exists that contemporaries considered eighteenth-century Amsterdam extremely prosperous. Pöllnitz, who wrote so slightingly of Antwerp, referred to Amsterdam as "a modern Tyre, the mistress of commerce, and the storehouse of the world [Magasin du Monde]."[6] In the late seventeenth and early eighteenth century, the bases of that affluence had changed: Amsterdam's wealth (and, in particular, the great riches of its *regenten,* that is, the families of the ruling elite) now came from banking and financing and not from active engagement in trade. As Amsterdam waned, however, Hamburg waxed. Although already known in the sixteenth century as the "florentissimum Emporium totius Germaniae," Hamburg in the seventeenth century in no way paced Amsterdam economically. Still, by 1700 Hamburg was fattening itself on the profits of a vigorous Iberian trade and smart mercantile banking. Not until the closing decades of the eighteenth century, however, would it spurt past Amsterdam for good.[7]

Demographic patterns differed as well. Amsterdam grew and grew rapidly. It had 140,000 inhabitants in 1647, 200,000 by 1672, 205,000 in 1700, and 220,000 in 1720. Hamburg's population also expanded vigorously but never became as large, having about 76,200 inhabitants in 1710; not until 1800 did the urban population reach over 100,000. Antwerp, however, stagnated. Of the approximately 100,000 who lived there in 1565, there were only 65,562 left between 1696 and 1705 and just 55,817 at the end of the eighteenth century (1786–95).[8] Despite these sometimes pronounced differences, the same economic innovations, however, disturbed all three in the late seventeenth and early eighteenth centuries.

Speculation, Stockjobbing, and Fraud

With the publication of *The Grumbling Hive* in 1705, Bernard de Mandeville inherited the horns and forked tail once belonging to Thomas Hobbes. Mandeville turned Christian morality on its head in arguing that vice was essential for economic development. For Mandeville, "fraud" and "pride and luxury" were the prerequisites of material progress. His work was, of course, neither primarily nor essentially economic in character but rather "called into question fundamental standards of social behavior."[9]

Mandeville, however, only produced a literate and provocative statement of what others were thinking or doing. By the late seventeenth century, the revision of economic morality and the assimilation of nontraditional business practices were well underway. What had made Mandeville so deeply shocking to his contemporaries was his radical dissociation of private and public virtues and vices. The merchant-republics drew their political legitimacy from a master fiction based on the covalence of the two and that varied the more general theme of a republicanism recently described as "a shared European heritage." Thus, Mandeville became as unpopular in merchant-republics as elsewhere. In these places, the virtuous man and upright citizen was the ethical and successful merchant. All in all he was the person best suited to govern and guide the city as he governed and guided his family and his business. This ideal lay deeply embedded in formal legislation and in the informal rules determining how these societies worked. In such republics, one "glorified the merchant as the republican archetype" in ways that were still difficult in other polities and praised commerce unequivocally as the inestimable school of civic virtue. Commerce was even (as one commentator later argued) a social panacea; its "manly" pursuit had banished poverty and the "corrupting lusts" of leisure, "encouraged benevolence, nurtured common sense, [and] displaced superstition." The merits and faults of the "useful" and "useless" merchants lovingly fabricated by satirists, nonetheless, formed civic credos.[10] (Obviously, these were ideal types, rarely—if ever—to be found as real persons.)

Massive speculation of the kind that swept up the little as well as the mighty had first occurred in the great "Tulip Craze" of 1633–37. After ebbing for a while in the immediate aftermath of the tulip-bulb bust, it rose again in the closing decades of the century and, by the early 1700s, was once more rampant. The economic damage that speculation did was less distressing than the latitude it gave frauds and cheats to deceive the upright or dupe the unsuspecting. It seemed impossible to discern who was and who was not an honest broker. The "great game," as it was most charitably called (there were other, far less savory expressions for it), opened the doors not only to swindlers but to impersonators as well, and all those who entered—or even neared the portals—lived dangerously.

Thus speculation was the bugbear that haunted the economic life of mercantile republics in these decades, and it evoked a series of political and legal measures gauged to curb its destructive effects. The increased deployment of paper instruments in business—bills of exchange, letters of credit, and stocks—inevitably accompanied (and quickened) economic growth but also further distanced business partners and deals from one another, as well as rendering them more anonymous. Stocks offer a good example. The first stocks that could be traded were those of the Dutch East India Company established in 1602. The term *actie,* or stock, apparently came into use in 1606. Very soon thereafter, a major stock-market fraud shook the Amsterdam market. In 1609, Isaac le Maire and others who were trying to found a rival French company achieved a significant decline in prices by spreading rumors detrimental to the Dutch enterprise.[11] The Dutch government in 1610 particularly condemned the custom of what was defined as "wind trading," that is, dealing in East India shares that the seller did not actually possess. (Bona fide owners of shares were, of course, still permitted to sell them.) These edicts did not prevent the "abuses," however, and had to be repeated. The political and military disasters of 1672 spawned a new generation of such measures. Trade in stocks and speculative transactions increased again in the 1680s, provoking a public discussion that mixed political, moral, and economic discourses. A quarrelsome lawyer, Nicolaas Muys van Holy, who spent much of his life litigating against those he termed "frauds, cheats, and enemies of the commonweal," castigated the jobbing of stocks as politically and morally ruinous. For him, no business was "more pernicious for the Fatherland in general." "Citizens as well as foreigners" revealed "vital state and Company secrets" for their own gain. They, moreover, "spread false news and rumors expressly designed to inflate and then to depress" stock prices, thus "demeaning the government . . . and the company itself in the eyes of the people." He placed *actionisten* (stockjobbers) on the same level as traitors.[12]

Scholarly treatment of speculation has focused on the system of John Law, the Mississippi Scheme, and the South Sea Bubble (all in the early 1700s), situating speculation and wildcatting—the Dutch term is "kite flying"—in the history of business, state finance (Law planned to underwrite the French public debt), the Atlantic economy, and fiscal innovation. The "booms" and "busts" of these years generated a flood of writings. The pricking of the South Sea and other bubbles and the dissipation of Law's system in France have greatly influenced how contemporaries and historians have viewed stockjobbing and paper monetarism. Yet here I wish to make a different case, for the criticality of earlier speculative ventures, stockjobbing, and the frauds often associated with them as part of the republican discourse of the late seventeenth and early eighteenth centuries in polities such as Amsterdam, Hamburg, and—if to a lesser extent—Antwerp as well.

This discourse explicitly associated major political crises with new and suspect financial activities. While the tie was only rarely expressed as a causal connection, the transparency of the coupling was crystalline. From the horrible *rampjaar* of 1672—the Year of Disaster—until the signing of the Peace of Utrecht in 1713, Holland was engaged in an international struggle that powerfully affected its internal politics. Antwerp, then part of the Spanish Netherlands, was swept along in this battle of leviathans. Hamburg's turmoil sprung from another source—its problems were primarily internal and so severe that conditions of virtual civil war prevailed from the 1670s until the promulgation of a new constitution in 1712. In both Amsterdam and Hamburg (the evidence is thinner for Antwerp) the discourse of speculation and fraud thus crossed repeatedly with that of republicanism, municipal fiscality, and civic probity. Economic morality and politics were seldom unattached. Speculation formed a convenient whipping boy from about the 1650s until the 1730s, and while condemnation of it would wane by midcentury, it never died out entirely. In the eighteenth century, the economic crime par excellence became "malicious" bankruptcy, meaning bankruptcies that were either planned or caused by unsound business practices, including rash speculation. Earlier, however, contemporaries almost reflexively coupled their angst about speculative practices, the misuse of bills of exchange, and fiscal frauds to a related lack of political scruples. Of course, one must take care here as well to distinguish between rhetoric and reality, without, however, suggesting the irrelevance of the former. Commentators in the second half of the eighteenth century continued to wring their hands over "declining morals" and "rising luxury" at a time when the compromise in favor of material progress and human pleasure had already long been made. In 1702 Christian Wolff—writing before Mandeville's *The Grumbling Hive* appeared—argued that the purpose of society was to encourage the common good and promote the happiness of society, its various groups, and individual members. "After Wolff, most cameralists simply assumed that (especially material) happiness was the main purpose of the state/society."[13] The real triumph of a pleasure ethic did not, of course, dam the flood of criticism, for fraud undermined economic trust and in so doing could subvert an economic prosperity seen as essential to society's greater well-being.

Fraud donned many guises, ranging from a simple diversion of funds to elaborate schemes. Yet, throughout, a necessary and convenient business practice—the use of bills of exchange—continued to be associated with fraudulent practices, or at least was believed to expedite them. Bills of exchange offered scope for fraud and were viewed, for instance, as the bankrupt's favorite method of staving off disaster. Swindles in letters of credit and bills of exchange produced some truly spectacular scandals in these years. Doing business in the seventeenth century, and even more so in the next, and in particular, doing international business, however, was totally dependent on such bills. Bills of exchange had developed in sixteenth-century Antwerp to accelerate the flow of commercial credit and enable trans-European deals. In the seventeenth century, almost all large firms in northern Europe transacted business through bills of exchange, not only to speed their own trade but as a means of making money. The van Colen Company in Antwerp, for example, routinely used bills of exchange for both purposes.[14]

Not only the rich and mighty, however, found bills of exchange expedient. By the end of the seventeenth century, bills circulated so freely that they were frequently lost or stolen. In 1656, for example, in Antwerp Jan la Gat reported that he had "lost or mislaid a particular *obligatie* [valued at] ƒ3000," and in 1705 a similar "Publicatie" informed the public to be on the lookout for "a first-class bill of exchange [in the amount of] 300 Pattacons . . . drawn on Bordeaux . . . by Cornelis Delfgramme on Jacques le Cerff, to the credit of

Joseph Nuñes Pereira, and last endorsed to Alexandre Cocqueel."[15] As these examples indicate, the practices of assignment (in which note bearers transferred the bill to their own creditors for settlement), endorsement (to prevent fraud), and, later, bill discounting multiplied the uses of bills of exchange but also multiplied the deceits in which they could be used—to say nothing of simply forging bills or altering real ones. Bill discounting greatly favored the smoother flow of commercial credit. When a bill was discounted, it became negotiable. At first illegal, discounting had become routine by the second quarter of the seventeenth century, especially in Amsterdam. Some bills changed hands many times.[16]

Such credit was, as John Brewer observes, "everywhere" in the eighteenth century.[17] Economic historians have generally judged the expansion of credit and credit-generating facilities as positive economic developments. Credit, however, also had its shadowy side, and the risks attached to credit in the late seventeenth and eighteenth centuries always made it a somewhat treacherous activity for everyone concerned. Credit was "bound hand and foot to risk-taking and speculation" and was also bound, in the minds of many, to activities that were questionable and marginal—economically and politically—if not downright criminal.[18] All those who engaged in them "lived dangerously," if only for the moment.

Republicanism and Economics

A series of incidents in Amsterdam and Hamburg illustrate how political debate formed around issues of republicanism and economics at the turn of the seventeenth century. One such event involved a man we have already met, Muys van Holy. Muys is not an especially well-known figure; at least modern historians have virtually, probably justifiably, ignored him. Jonathan Israel's massive work on the Dutch Republic does not mention him at all, although elsewhere he devotes a few lines to Muys's involvement in the anti-Orange propagandizing of 1689–90.[19] Muys seems, therefore, political small fry, although he was at times the "mouse that roared." The reigning historical amnesia about Muys, however, obscures the meanings that Muys—and other republicans—drew from speculation and how they associated speculative practices with the decay of republicanism. Speculation, faction, party, and monarchical pretensions were all equally antirepublican in their very nature.

The pamphlet wars surrounding Muys's numerous publications amply demonstrate how his often cross-grained and querulous vendettas against speculators and frauds plucked the chords of republicanism. After he died in 1717, imprisoned and broken, friends buried him in the Nieuw Kerk. Quickly his sympathizers plastered the grave with poems and epitaphs that, among other laurels, panegyrized him as a "Dutch Socrates"; a man who spoke uncomfortable truths and who had literally died for them. "Here lies the corpse of Muys, that noble soul; the Defender of Church and orphans against the knaves. For that crime he rotted long years in prison and was by [these] uncircumcised Turks treated more poorly than a slave."[20]

Muys's writings in the 1680s and 1690s addressed the economic and financial practices that he regarded as destructive of true republicanism. He authored a series of pamphlets condemning the operations of "newfangled" stockjobbing—wind trading—as well as exposing other irregularities in the sale and transfer of East India Company stocks, involving dubious speculative practices.[21] At the same time, he was swept up in a *cause célèbre* that played out on the stage of European power politics. In 1690 a very famous pamphlet appeared, *Spiegel der Waarheyd* (*The Mirror of Truth*). The *Mirror* was probably written by Ericus Walten, a friend of the talented engraver Romeyn de Hooghe, who in 1689 had produced a series of political caricatures (*spotprenten*) that lampooned the French and French politics, but that also vigorously assailed the States Party (the *Staatsgezinden,* or those who opposed the House of Orange) and, in particular, besmirched Amsterdam's *regenten.* Very quickly, supporters of the States Party—the "party of true freedom," as its members called themselves—struck back with an equally virulent *Vindiciae Amstelodamenses, of Contra-Spiegel der Waarheid* (*Contra-Mirror of Truth, or the Vindication of Amsterdam*). The *Contra-Mirror* was a "scandalous chronicle" that vilified *regenten* in other Dutch cities for their slavish acceptance of Orange and especially reviled de Hooghe for his "vulgar and obscene" prints. Muys was widely believed to be the author of the *Contra-Mirror,* supposedly working on the instigation of the powerful Amsterdam *burgemeester* and Orange-opponent, Jan Huydecoper. Whether Muys actually penned the *Contra-Mirror* or not (he always denied authorship) is irrelevant: it accurately reflected his own backing of Amsterdam and the Amsterdam *regenten,* as well as his equally steadfast opposition to the House of Orange. The floodgates opened, and Muys and de Hooghe (and their friends and supporters) loosed waves of verbal arrows. No slander seemed too extreme. De Hooghe, for instance, accused Muys of *lèse-majesté,* of plotting against the life of William III (a completely false charge).[22]

Muys's writings regarded fraudulent practices, speculation, and breach of faith as woven from the single cloth of antirepublicanism. His attacks on speculative practices argued that they subverted both the integrity of the economy and the well-being of the polity. Elsewhere in his writings, he associated other frauds and violations of trust with distressing diminutions of republican sentiment and failures in civic propriety. In 1685 he charged that the *secretaris* (municipal secretary) of Haarlem had embezzled tax monies. Then in 1699 the East India Company's director in Bengal, Arnold Muykens, felt Muys's wrath for his usurious and fraudulent practices (*ontrouw*) while still in office.[23]

More distressing to Muys was the case that developed in 1707 and that ultimately led to his downfall. This incident involved one Jan Gerkens, a Lutheran, who had amassed a great fortune in the Indies. He returned to Amsterdam, married Louise Bleau from a *regenten* family, and died soon afterward, leaving an estate of more than *f*100,000 to his surviving widow on the condition that if she wed or died the estate would be distributed equally between the Lutheran Church and its orphanage. In 1681, Louise remarried but retained the inheritance. Muys, who got wind of this misappropriation rather by accident and in the course of his normal legal duties, embarked on what became almost a holy war on his part to have the monies properly redistributed. This case involved him in yet another exchange of increasingly violent—and probably ill-advised—charges against Bleau's lawyer, Jacob de la Bassecourt, later the city's *pensionaris* (chief legal adviser). This quarrel effectively ended Muys's public career. For the publication of *pasquillen* (libelous pamphlets) and for other libelous acts, he was condemned to the city's Rasphuis prison, where he died. In this, his last public brawl, he sounded again—perhaps more clearly than ever—his battle cry against fraud and raised his voice a final time in calling for the restoration of economic and civic virtues that sustained true republicanism. In his final pamphlet, he argued that his sentence offended the republic's "dearly bought freedom," for "not only is a person permitted to expose monstrous [crimes] and grave transgressions," but it was actually incumbent on each citizen to do so, "in order to preserve the common good [ten gemeenen beste]." Where such "evildoing and deception" (malversatie en falsiteiten) were tolerated, no republic could long stand.[24]

The leitmotif in all these instances was the association of fraud, speculation, and breach of faith. Persons who "lived dangerously" by speculating, defrauding, or misappropriating funds violated the standards of republicanism that men such as Muys held to be the surest guarantors of true freedom. Yet these battles over speculation, fraud, and breach of faith are not merely "texts" whose discourse just needs to be unpacked; they were real events, initiating governmental action and kindling public reactions. Indeed, one might plausibly argue that for most citizens and inhabitants of Amsterdam, Antwerp, and Hamburg, corruption, speculation, and fraud were anything but faceless crimes. In fact, the visages were all too familiar. When people in Amsterdam, Antwerp, and Hamburg spoke of corruption, they certainly did so in the same generalities Gordon Wood has traced for the infant American Republic or J. G. A. Pocock, on a grander scale, has identified in the Anglo-Saxon world.[25] Yet locals most often spoke of corruption specifically: the corruption of a certain *regent;* the financial fiddles of this or that *burgemeester;* the fraudulent bills passed by a particular moneylender, banker, or Jew. The men had names, homes, families, clients, and connections. Everyday discourses and actions that resulted in civil suits or criminal prosecutions turned on individuals who "lived dangerously." They were not the surface manifestations of more deeply seated corruptions but their very essence.

Of course, such discussions were often only the moralists' takes on practices entrenched in and in no way to be rooted out of economic life. Even in the early seventeenth century, speculation formed part and parcel of the economic strategies of extremely reputable firms. One of the most celebrated mercantile clans in Amsterdam was the Trip family, whose stately house today still adorns the Herengracht. The Trips were river traders from Dordrecht, transplanted to Amsterdam in 1614 by Elias Trip. Trip was in at the beginning of the East India Company in 1602 as one of its "chief participants." Like many others involved in the company, he saw it as a way to enhance his own business and profits, in his case cornering the company's market in copper and saltpeter (the greater part of the family's fame and fortune came from the arms trade). Stockjobbing was part of this business, and not only did he deal in the stocks—the *actien*—of the East India Company, he also speculated in its shares; apparently, he was up to his neck in Le Maire's schemes. He, too, was "engaged in the so-called 'blank' trade, i.e. selling ahead, which many considered gambling." His nephew trafficked extensively in shares in the 1660s. Thus, not only fly-by-night investors and shadowy figures speculated and sailed close to the wind; solid firms with large capital assets had also acquired a taste for "innovative" financing and investing. If lesser vessels capsized, crafts of great tonnage, such as the Trips, breasted the waves and grew rich.[26]

Thus we are faced with a conundrum. The use of bills of exchange was, by the end of the seventeenth century, an established business practice without which no urban company could trade successfully outside municipal boundaries. Yet the frequent employment of bills of exchange and, in particular, the very practices that made them so handy—assignment and endorsement—generated opportunities for fraud. Likewise, even though many and perhaps even most businesses of note engaged in some sort of speculative practice, speculation was roundly condemned as a form of gambling, even deceit. The line dividing frauds and speculators quickly blurred, as did the line separating legitimate business practices from impugnable ones. "Insiders" who speculated or played a little fast and loose with bills of exchange lived on the edge and ran the very real risk of tumbling out of respectability and into the netherworld of shady dealers and fishy transactions. Yet those who existed outside the reputable world entirely or hovered on its margins—evanescent entrepreneurs and slick traders—operated in curiously close proximity to plutocrats, estimable citizens, and distinguished gentlemen. Entering the gray world of speculation and sharp business practices was always to embark on a perilous journey. The adventure promised and often delivered huge returns; but just as often it lured onto the rocks of criminality those who heeded its siren song. Throughout the seventeenth and eighteenth centuries, in the exuberant yet treacherous climate of a budding, and then burgeoning, world economy, polities and individuals had to pilot themselves through these shoals carefully to avoid ripping out their keels. No economy—no society—was totally immune, but in the merchant-republics the moral and the political aspects were the most bedeviled and caused the most consternation, as the communal republicanism of the late medieval period felt itself stretched—or rather distended—by practices that seemed to flout old standards and that perhaps heralded the arrival of a new economic morality (or lack of it). The first phase was resistance, or perhaps denial that things had changed at all. Yet compliance or collusion was inevitable, for the very pillars of society and the economy were themselves carried along irresistibly or led the way. Not all, of course, or even most, engaged in criminal practices, but the whole attitude to what was the proper relationship between private and public virtues (as Mandeville had so sharply observed) had to be rethought and reworked. Thus, for many, "living dangerously" was becoming unavoidable or even necessary to insure survival in the rough economic world of raw and thrusting capitalism.

High Finances and Big Swindles

As we have observed with Muys, moralist appraisal of the pernicious effect of speculation on economic morality and even true prosperity was hardly

lacking in the late seventeenth century. In the wake of the Law scandal, however, everyone was hostile. Throughout the nineteenth century, commentators
agreed that "the moral effect" was considerable and that "solid mercantile
practices gave way to . . . a fevered preference for speculating and risk-
taking."[27] Such was hardly the case: speculation and even "gambling" did not
follow merely in the wake of Law schemes. Moreover, Lawism was not an
aberrant variety imported from France but a homegrown weed. Law had
tried his luck in Holland before going to France. Still, by 1720, one would
have been hard-pressed to find a defense of Law, speculation, or any sort of
economic "game of chance" (*hazardspel*). The terms used to excoriate Law
and his system ranged from the appalled to the indignant to the scatological.
The outpouring of anti-Law pamphlets and commentary was immense.[28]
Most critical and most renowned was *Het Groote Tafereel der Dwasheid* (*The
Great Mirror of Folly*), a compendium of anti-Law tracts, plays, and satirical
plates. While the South Sea Bubble and the Mississippi Company sowed
"extensive crops of controversial books and pamphlets" throughout Europe,
nowhere "did there appear such a stout and extravagant piece as this Dutch
volume." Strangely, the speculative fever never spiked as high in Amsterdam
as in the French or English capitals, perhaps because of the earlier symptoms. What received so much negative comment in Holland was the practice of selling against future deliveries, or "selling short." This was the
"windy business" that inflated the value of stocks. In the wake of the excitement, shares in the East India Company rose from ƒ400 to ƒ1200 and in the
less well-subscribed West India Company from ƒ40 to ƒ600 before all col-
lapsed again.[29] Strong emotions produced even stronger language, and no
word, no crime, no perversion seemed too extreme a description for what
wind traders did. Stockjobbers were "crazy" (*gek*), so bereft of their wits that
they properly belonged in a madhouse. Indeed, the need seemed so overwhelming in these years that satirists proposed a special institution for the
incarceration of *actionisten*. These crackbrained speculators would set pre-
miums on anything, including soap bubbles and "whores' turds" (Hoere
Kotten). Such "communal tyrants" (maatschappy Tirannen) must be locked
away to protect society as much as themselves.[30] Madness was the favored
trope, for the mad were by definition incapable of citizenship. Madness,
speculation, and monetary improvidence marched together and not only
metaphorically. Koenraad van Beuningen, a respected Amsterdam diplomat
and erstwhile *burgemeester,* began to lose his wits in his sixties, but "the lu-
nacy that had long smoldered in him, revealed itself suddenly, and first in

financial speculations." In particular, he "began to play" in East India Company stock.[31] Wind trading was a social and political scourge. One response was to associate it with insanity, another with folly. One of Holland's most popular playwrights in the early eighteenth century, Pieter Langendyk, refurbished the stock *commedia dell'arte* buffoon, Harlequin (Arlequyn), as a stockjobber, and the resulting *Arlequyn Actionist* played ten times at the Amsterdam Schouwburg in one month.[32] Law's rise and fall was literally a windfall for Langendyk and his colleagues, who reworked the theme several times. Gijsbert Tijsens took flight with his own set of "wind plays," featuring the *actionisten* "Hopeful-Rich," "Vainglory," "Quarreler," "Daredevil," and "Nutty," all in cahoots with Jewish stock characters named Levi, Judas, and Simon.[33] Another playwright, Hendrik van Halmael, had in the first fifteen years of the century churned out a series of comedies with a half-naive, half-cunning protagonist named Crispyn, who took the stage in multiple roles: "Deceiver," "Account-Book-Falsifier," "Cash-Slasher," "Orphans'-Blight," and "Bloodsucker." Life was grist for the playwright's mill, and writers such as van Halmael had plenty of real material at hand to adapt dramatically.[34]

Comic relief offered one way to deal with frauds; caricature was a more savage response. Many prints in *The Great Mirror of Folly* are grossly obscene. The engraving titled "By veele zit de kei in't hooft om dat men in de wind gelooft" (Many have a stone in the head, so that they believe in wind) showed various wise "doctors" cutting the "stone" out from the foreheads of those suffering from the "windy sickness" or extracting them from their anuses with huge forceps (see fig. 1). "De Windverkopers of Windvangers" (The Wind Sellers or Wind Catchers), while more restrained in its imagery (here several men and women offer paper on the exchange), projected an equally pointed message: everyone engaged in this business is either deceived or a deceiver. Another print placed *actionisten* at a masked ball and thus visually tightened the link between speculation, masquerade, and a court society that itself was the very opposite of a republican community (see fig. 2).

If the blame fell heavily on Law himself, he was not alone in attracting the wrath of his contemporaries. His "system" and those of similar projectors, such as the creators of the South Sea Company in England, were universally branded "hokus-bokus."[35] Although we may now have a greater appreciation for Law's ingenuity and vision, the opinion of the early eighteenth century—after the collapse, of course—was unanimously negative. It was not so much the immediate ruin and actual damage that observers in

FIG. 1.
"By veele zit de kei in 't hooft om dat men in de wind gelooft," in *Het Groote Tafereel der Dwaasheid* (Gedrukt tot waarschouwinge voor de Nakomelingen, in 't noodlottige Jaar, voor veel Zotte en Wyze, 1720). Courtesy of the Koninklijke Bibliotheek, The Hague.

THE WORLD

Here, may the Wand'ring **Eye** with pleasure See
Both **Knaves** and **Fools** in borrow'd shapes agree;
Now Lords and **Ladies** wave their wonted pride,
And walk with **Jilts** and **Bullies**, side by side.
Here, the **Vile Atheist**, to the Worlds surprise,
Puts on a Byshop's Robe for his disguise,
With lude and idle talk profanes the same,
And Nods his Mitre at some fav'rite Dame.
The **Statesman** that Commands his **Princes** Ear,
Descends to Harlekeno's Jacket here,
And tho' at Helm he shares the Mighty Rule,
In Masquerade submits to play the **Fool**.
Here, **Lords** in Footmen's Liv'ries meet the Fair,
And Show us what their real **Father's** were,
Court Highbron Ladies who for change of food,

Can chew coarse Diet if the Sause be good.
Here, Tender Beauty Wedded to an **old**,
Decrepit Fumbler, for the Sake of Gold,
To th' Tavern tempts some vigrous Youth & there,
Displays her Charms in Hopes to steal an Heir,
Here **City Wives**, disguis'd in **Widows Weeds**,
Look out for Sparks to Mend their sev'ral breeds.
These no advantage of their favours make,
Sin not for Gold but Kiss for Kissings Sake.
Here, **Drury Punks** for Maiden Ladies pass,
And dress'd like Nymphs, decoy the Am'rous Al,
He singles out his doe She grants the Prise,
And with venereal Trophies crowns his Joies.
Thus, all the World for Intrest, Love or Fear,
Conceal themselves and in disguise appear

MASQUERADE

...er kan 't Nieuwsgierig oog met Lust en ruymte weyen	Een Jonge schoonheid aan een gryzaard zwak en oud.
...anschouwen 't kleyn begrip van s'waerelds mommereyen.	Geenzins uyt Liefde, maar om schat en geld getrouwd.
...ier Wand'len Schellemen, Vermomd in Narrenschyn.	Tracht hier een jeugdig heer, het wynhuys in te trekken.
Met Narren, die zoo vaak van hun bedroogen zyn;	Om steels voys haar man, een Erve te verwekken.
...ier ziet men de adel van hun achtbaarheyd verlaaten,	Een ryke Pachters Wyf gedost in Weeuws gewaad.
...Het hoer en Heerenwaard, Vermomd, gemeenzaam praaten.	Haakt na een Erfgenaam geteeld uyt hooger staat.
...De Godverzaaker die van Schrift, nog Wetten weet.	Die naamaals om zyn Geest en gaaven hoog gepreesen.
...kt hier zyn vuelen aard in 't heylig Bischops kleed.	Den Jason Steunpylaar des huisgezins mag weesen.
...e Man van Staat, die zelfs zyn vorst schynt te beheeren.	Zy zondigd om geen Goud, zy ruilt geen Geld voor Gunst.
...rlaat zyn Tabbaart hier om Arlequinoos kleeren.	Nog minnegaaven, maar speeld zuyver Kunst om Kunst.
...heen hy 't gebied des Lands als met zyn Koning deeld.	Hier tracht een vuile hoer een Reyne maagd te weesen.
...p dat hy dus vermomd de Grootste Gek verbeeld.	Gedost in zuyver wit als Vestaas rey voordeesen.
...taat Jonkers in Livrey, om duidelyk te verklaaren,	En dus ontsteeke zy 't hart en 't jeugdig heete Bloed.
Vie dat in de Natuur hun rechte Vaders waaren.	Eens jongen Ezels die vast Balki van minnegloed.
...hoo Edle Juffers die het aangenaam gevry.	Tot dat zy om zyn Gunst en mildheid te betaalen.
...chynt te behaagen van een minnaar in Livrey.	Hem met t'veroif besmet van vuile minnekwaalen.
...in oroove of fyne spys geen onderscheyding maaken.	Aldus wil elk door vrees, voordeel, of minnepyn.
Als maar een Lekk're saus de Kost haar wel doed smaaken.	Op s'waerelds Schouwtoneel een Maskerade zyn.

FIG. 2. "Baal, of de waereld in maskerade," in *Het Groote Tafereel der Dwaasheid* (Gedrukt tot waarschouwinge voor de Nakomelingen, in 't noodlottige Jaar, voor veel Zotte en Wyze, 1720). Courtesy of the Koninklijke Bibliotheek, The Hague.

Amsterdam, Antwerp, and Hamburg noted, for all three cities escaped relatively lightly and quickly recovered. Rather, it was the wind traders' purported sinister influence on business morals and the concomitant erosion of republican values that alarmed.

A much-reprinted handbook on commerce signaled the speculative frenzy of the 1720s as a turning point in the economic and political histories of these commercial titans. The discourse of speculation that had developed between 1650 and 1720 became the dominant way of discussing all sorts of faults—political, moral, and mercantile alike—for the rest of the century. Speculators were, in the press of the time, usurers, cheats, evil Jews, and imposters. John Law was a drifter and a visionary but also the minion of kings and nobles, to be placed on the same level with the other great pretenders, adventurers, and scoundrels of the day (see fig. 3). Littler "Laws," men such as the Comte de Floor and Gabriel de Souza Brito were less flashy but equally recognizable characters in northern Europe, making station in Hamburg and Antwerp, Copenhagen and Stockholm, as well as in Amsterdam. Like other malefactors, impersonators, and frauds, the speculators, too, eventually had to flee headlong from their creditors and the law. Speculators were card sharks and the first white-collar criminals. Speculators and their ilk were what good citizens manifestly were not: disguised, showy, migratory. They did business outside normal channels—in Amsterdam not at the 'Change but on Kalverstraat and in the *coffy-huizen* (coffeehouses)—and at the wrong times—coming in the night like "Jewish usurers." They even employed women as middle-"men"! (see fig. 4).

If Law's scheme focused the eyes of the world on speculators and frauds as never before, he was scarcely (as we have seen) the first or only example, or even the most despised. In 1670, the twenty-eight-year-old Theodorus van der Perre was executed in Amsterdam for "repeated forgeries" and especially for "his considerable participation in the making of false debentures." Van der Perre was neither a small-time forger nor did he inhabit the low world of cheap lodgings and cheaper swindles: he was an insider who lived too dangerously. His family descended "from a very prominent lineage in Zealand," and his wife's father was the *burgemeester* Pieter de Vlaming. Van der Perre's life history embodied and at the same time created the social reality of the fraud who played for high stakes using forged or altered papers.[36]

The sentence read on January 16, 1670, condemned van der Perre to death for committing "so many perfidious acts . . . in which he persisted" and that included "the replication and signing of another man's hand to a

M.ᶜ JEAN LAW CON.ᵉʳ DU ROY EN TOUS CES CON.ⁱˡˢ CONTROLEUR GNAL DES FINANCES en 1720.

Sous l'Auguste et Sage Regence   *L'A.ᵛ᷍ᵉ consomme dans l'art de veoir la finance*
D'un Prince aimant la bonne foy: *Trouve l'art d'enrichir les sujets et le Roy.*

FIG. 3. "Jean Law." Courtesy of the Koninklijke Bibliotheek, The Hague.

FIG. 4. Title page/print from Gijsbert Tijsens, *De Bedriegelyke actionist, of de nagthande-laars* (Amsterdam: Hendrik Bosch, 1720). Courtesy of the Koninklijke Bibliotheek, The Hague.

letter of credit in the amount of ƒ60,000," "the suborning of witnesses," and false accusations. The magistrate went on to tick off a series of crimes extending over a period of several years, involving counterfeiting numerous letters of credit, in which he employed a "youth of fourteen years," whose talents in forgery included "the composition of a letter in the name of his [van Perre's] brother" and the fabrication of a "false security" supposedly given by his father. He "exchange[d] all these for ready money." Van der Perre's other swindles included using similarly forged *obligaties* to obtain money from widows; he hauled them to court when they refused to pay or were unable to pay fictitious debts.[37] Of course, forgery was hardly a novelty in the seventeenth century. New was that contemporaries interpreted van der Perre's crimes as rising out of—or at least being abetted by—structural changes in business practices. The fault lay not only in van der Perre's felonious nature, but also in the ways of doing business and in the ease with which paper instruments could be abused. Innovative business practices, if not themselves criminal, nonetheless threatened the political and civil stability of the republic. That the problem lay in structures and not (only) in individual proclivities or weaknesses is reflected in the disapproval voiced about speculation that was, after all, in most of its forms no crime.

More demonstrative of this connection and its growing power as a mode of explanation in the early eighteenth century was the scandal that brewed up around the financier Jean Henry Huguetan in 1711.[38] In the charges and countercharges that flew in this affair, the widow of an Amsterdam merchant, Jean Tourton, not only charged Huguetan with financial misconduct and deceitful practices, but also with a kind of treason in his dealings with France, the French court, and French bankers. It should be recalled that this occurred during the European-wide struggles between the France of Louis XIV and England, Holland, and their allies. In her public accusation, the widow pointed out that Huguetan and his deeds had become "a common subject of gossip [*conversatie*]." The rumor ran that "he had destroyed many honorable families and had plundered millions from his best friends." When he was called to justice, he had to flee in order to elude his fate. "Anyone who knows Jean Henry Huguetan," the pamphlet continued, "knows that he has a grasping nature and that he has always greatly wished to become rich and to seem rich in the eyes of the world." In order to pursue wealth, he left his original occupation as a bookkeeper and became a banker, in which capacity he not only "lent money to the troops of the Allies, but also, as he himself has admitted, to the troops of the enemy, and [all this] during the time he was a citizen and inhabitant of the city of Amsterdam."[39] According to the wife of one of his "victims," he swindled literally millions from friends and business acquaintances, driving many of them into bankruptcy by cunningly manipulating bills of exchange (*wisselbriefe*). The money—the millions that he thus came "to control"—she regarded as "stolen goods." The "most unfortunate" of his many dupes was an old friend and sponsor, Etienne Demeuves, "an honest and aged man," who "after signing bills in the amount of ƒ4,000,000, was forced to declare bankruptcy." The list of those he had ruined was long, for Huguetan's scheming had brought other bankers "who could have maintained themselves and their families in honor and comfort" down into the "greatest need and misery." The widow was hardly alone in her accusations. For example, in 1705 a Genevan banker, Jacques Butiny, accused Huguetan of owing him ƒ155,000 and being in debt to a group of Parisian bankers for more than ƒ1,000,000.[40] The sums of money in one particular deal—or "deceitful transaction"—were considerable; two bills of exchange in 1705 for respectively 624,900 livres and 371,510 livres were drawn on bankers in Milan and Antwerp. They were worthless.[41] The Huguetan case, like that of van der Perre, involved people of substantial reputation and considerable means, with significant political and financial connections that (at least in Huguetan's case) touched most of Europe's money capitals: Paris, Antwerp, Amsterdam, Geneva, and Milan. The truth of the matter is virtually impossible to disentangle from a maze of court records, charges, and countercharges. What remains clear is that terms of the debate and its language vividly displayed all the ambiguities inherent in "living dangerously"—in financial terms—in the seventeenth and eighteenth centuries.

The association of financial malfeasance, or just sharp practices, and political unreliability had a long history in the republics of late seventeenth- and early eighteenth-century Europe. Claims of financial corruption, diversion of funds held in trust, or even simple mismanagement underlay some of the most violent and prolonged political conflicts of these years. In Hamburg, for example, the uprising of burghers against the city council led by Cord Jastram and Hieronymous Snitger from 1682 to 1686 and the virtual civil war of the 1690s derived from a series of "abuses" the city council had allegedly committed. At least one flagrant abuse was judicial; others were financial. The meeting of the Burghers Assembly on May 15, 1698, which deliberated whether or not to accept a compromise proposed by the Imperial Commission set up to end the troubles, raised at least two issues of corruption in financial affairs, specifically asking to have the books of the late secretary of the bank brought before them.[42] Contemporary commentators confidently regarded the bank fraud that the Jewish merchant Meyer Max perpetrated in 1695 as an integral part of the political storm that raged in Hamburg at the end of the seventeenth century. They made the same connections one year later in the scandal surrounding the actions of the Danish agent in Hamburg, August Wygand.[43]

Drawing connections between financial malfeasance and political untrustworthiness—or even espionage—had by then become usual ways of discussing political affairs. Those who engaged in financial double-dealing seemed curiously susceptible to treasonous acts, as if somehow the acid of economic impropriety had corroded their republicanism and their political integrity. They were well on their way to becoming outsiders, to living dangerously, in yet other ways.

NOTES

1. Jonathan Israel, "Monarchy, Orangism, and Republicanism in the Later Dutch Golden Age" (Second Golden Age Lecture, Amsterdams Centrum voor de Studie van de Gouden Eeuw, Universiteit van Amsterdam, March 11, 2004), 5–6. Admittedly, Israel is not interested here in the kind of quotidian practice I want to trace but rather in understanding "the emergence of modern western democratic republicanism" (ibid., 8). See also idem, *The Radical Enlightenment: Philosophy and the Making of Modernity, 1650–1750* (Oxford: Oxford University Press, 2001). On Atlantic republicanism, see J. G. A. Pocock, *The Machiavellian Moment: Florentine Political Thought and the Atlantic Republican Tradition* (Princeton, NJ: Princeton University Press, 1975); Gordon S. Wood, *The Creation of the American Republic, 1776–1787* (Chapel Hill: University of North Carolina Press, 1969); and Martin van Gelderen and Quentin Skinner, eds., *Republicanism: A Shared European Heritage,* 2 vols. (Cambridge: Cambridge University Press, 2002).

2. Simon Schama, *The Embarrassment of Riches: An Interpretation of Dutch Culture in the Golden Age* (New York: Fortuna Press, 1991 [1987]).

3. All of these have attracted much interest among historians. Popular and scholarly works abound. On flower speculations, see E. H. Krelage, *Bloemenspeculatie in Nederland: De tulpomanie van 1636–37 en de hyacintenhandel 1720–36* (Amsterdam: P.N. van Kampen & Zoon, 1942); N. W. Postumus, "The Tulip Mania in Holland in the Years 1636 and 1637," *Journal of Economic and Business History* 114 (August 1929): 434–66. For perspectives on John Law and his system, see Paul Harsin, "La Banque et le système de Law," in *History of the Principal Banks accompanied by Extensive Bibliographies of the History of Banking and Credit in Eleven European Countries,* ed. J. G. van Dillen (The Hague:

Martinus Nijhoff, 1934), 273–300; Lawrence M. Lande, *The Rise and Fall of John Law, 1716–1720* (Montreal: Lawrence Lande Foundation for Canadian Historical Research, McLennan Library, McGill University, 1982); Robert Minton, *John Law: The Father of Paper Money* (New York: Association Press, 1975); Antoin E. Murphy, *John Law: Economic Theorist and Policy Maker* (Oxford: Clarendon Press, 1997). On the impact of Law in Holland, see Jan de Vries and Ad van der Woude, *The First Modern Economy: Success, Failure, and Perseverance of the Dutch Economy, 1500–1815* (Cambridge: Cambridge University Press, 1997), 152–58.

4. Schama, *The Embarrassment of Riches,* 350. See also de Vries and van der Woude, *The First Modern Economy,* 150–51.

5. All quoted in Jan-Albert Goris, *Lof van Antwerpen: Hoe reizigers Antwerpen zagen, van de XVe tot de XXe eeuw* (Brussels: Standard, 1940), 63, 69, 87, 149. One should note here, however, that all these witnesses were Protestants, and either Germans or Englishmen.

6. Karl Ludwig von Pöllnitz, *Lettres et mémoires du baron de Pöllnitz, contenant les observations qu'il a faites dans ses voyages et le caractère des personnes qui composent les principals cours de l'Europe* (Amsterdam: H. G. Löhner, 1744), 3:220.

7. Jonathan I. Israel, *The Dutch Republic: Its Rise, Greatness and Fall, 1477–1806* (Oxford: The Clarendon Press, 1995), 307–27, 610–19, 998–1018; de Vries and van der Woude, *The First Modern Economy,* 665–87; J. L. Price, *Dutch Society, 1588–1713* (London: Longman, 2000), 274–81.

8. On Amsterdam, see Israel, *The Dutch Republic,* 328, 1007; on Hamburg, see Hans Mauersberg, *Wirtschafts- und Sozialgeschichte zentraleuropäischer Städte in neuerer Zeit: Dargestellt an den Beispielen von Basel, Frankfurt a. Main, Hamburg, Hannover und München* (Göttingen: Vandenhoeck & Ruprecht, 1967), 43, 47–48; on Antwerp, see Frans Blockmans, "De bevolkingscijfers," in *Antwerpen in de XVIIIe eeuw: Instellingen—economie—cultuur* (Antwerpen: de Sikkel, 1952), 395–412 and de Vries and van der Woude, *The First Modern Economy,* 52.

9. E. G. Hundert, *The Enlightenment's Fable: Bernard Mandeville and the Discovery of Society* (Cambridge: Cambridge University Press, 1994), 16.

10. Wijnand W. Mijnhardt, "The Dutch Enlightenment: Humanism, Nationalism, and Decline," in *The Dutch Republic in the Eighteenth Century: Decline, Enlightenment, and Revolution,* ed. Margaret C. Jacobs and Wijnand W. Mijnhardt (Ithaca and London: Cornell University Press, 1992), 210; Ernst Baasch, *Holländische Wirtschaftsgeschichte* (Jena: Gustav Fischer, 1927), 232–35; *De Nederlandsche spectator* 218 (1757). The poem and print titled "De nuttige, en nuttelooze koopman" are found in *Het Groote Tafereel der Dwaasheid: Vertoonende de opkomst, voortgang en ondergang der Actie, Bubbel en Windnegotie, in Vrankryk, Engeland, en de Nederlanden, gepleegt in den Jaare MDCCXX. Zynde een Verzameling van alle de Conditien en Projecten van de opgeregte Compagnien van Assuratie, Navigatie, Commercie, &c. in Nederland, zo wel die in gebruik zyn gebragt, als die door de H. Staten van eenige Provintien zyn verworpen; Als meede Konst-Plaaten, Comedien en Gedigten, door verscheide Liefhebben uytgegeeven, tot beschimpinge deezer verfoeijelyke en bedrieglyke Handel, waar door in dit Jaar, verschiede Familien en Persoonen van Hooge en Lage stand zyn geruïneerd, en in haar middelen verdorven, en de opregte Negotie gestremt, zo in Vrankryk, Engeland als Nederland* (Gedrukt tot waarschouwinge

voor de Nakomelingen, in 't noodlottige Jaar, voor veel Zotte en Wyze, 1720); van Gelderen and Skinner, eds., *Republicanism.*

11. J.G. van Dillen, "Isaac le Maire et le commerce des actions de la compagnie des Indes Orientales," *Revue d'histoire moderne,* n.s., 16 (January–February, 1935): 5–21; Dirk Jan Barreveld, *Tegen de Herren van de VOC: Isaac le Maire en de ontdekking van Kaap Hoorn* (The Hague: Sdu Uitgevers, 2002), 18–26.

12. *Middelen en motiven om het kopen en verkopen van Oost- en West-Indische actien, die niet getransporteert werden, mitsgaders ook die de verkoper ten dage van den verkoop niet in eigendom heeft, als mede optie partyen der actien, te beswaren met een Impost ten behoeve van het gemeene Land en de stad Amsterdam* (Amsterdam, 1687) [Knuttel 12611]. The bracketed references signify the pamphlet number assigned by P.C. Knuttel, *Catalogus van de pamflettenversameling berustende in de Koninklijke Bibliotheek,* 9 vols. (The Hague: Algemeene landdrukkerij, 1888–1920); Nicolaas Muys van Holy, quoted in Joseph de la Vega, *Confusions de confusiones . . . 1688: Portions Descriptive of the Amsterdam Stock Exchange,* selected and trans. Hermann Kellenbenz (Boston: Baker Library, 1957), xii–xiii.

13. Isabel V. Hull, *Sexuality, State, and Civil Society in Germany, 1700–1815* (Ithaca and London: Cornell University Press, 1996), 161.

14. R. Baetens, "Een Antwerps handelshuis uit de XVII eeuw: De firma van Colen," *Tijdschrift voor geschiedenis* 73 (1960): 204–6.

15. From July 24, 1656, in Stadsarchief Antwerpen [StA], Privilegien-Kammer [PK], 2847, and from 22 March 1705, StA, PK, 2848. These are only two of many examples.

16. J.A. van Houtte, *An Economic History of the Low Countries, 800–1800* (London: Weidenfeld and Nicolson, Ltd., 1977), 208–18; de Vries and van der Woude, *The First Modern Economy,* 130–31; R. De Roover, *L'Evolution de la lettre de change XIVe–XVIIe siècles* (Paris: Armand Colin, 1953); William Stevenson ["Sometime merchant in Rotterdam"], *A Full and Practical Treatise upon Bills of Exchange: Together with An Account of the Nature of the Bank of Amsterdam, and How Payments are made and received in it, &c* (Edinburgh: John Robertson, 1764). A bill bearer could have a bill discounted "when a third party agreed to purchase a bill before its due date, paying a cash sum which . . . was less than the nominal value of the bill at maturity."

17. John Brewer, *The Sinews of Power: War, Money, and the English State, 1688–1783* (Cambridge, MA: Harvard University Press, 1988), 186.

18. Julian Hoppit, "The Use and Abuse of Credit in Eighteenth Century England," in *Business Life and Public Policy: Essays in Honour of D.C. Coleman,* ed. Neil McKendrick and R.B. Outhwaite (Cambridge: Cambridge University Press, 1986), 65, 78.

19. Jonathan Israel, "The Dutch Role in the Glorious Revolution," in *The Anglo-Dutch Moment: Essays on the Glorious Revolution and Its World Impact,* ed. Jonathan Israel (Cambridge: Cambridge University Press, 1991), 153. "The somewhat weak stream of republican, anti-Orangist pamphlets emanating from opposition writers such as Nicolaas Muys van Holy subsided." There are, however, a series of older works and family histories that treat Muys at greater length. See, for example, the entry (written by M. Roest) in *De Navorscher* 7 (1857): 18–22, 81–85, 150–55, 239–47.

20. See the series of "Gedichten op 't Afsterven & Grafschriften op Mr. Mr. Nikolaas Muys van Holy, Rechtsgeleerde," in Gemeente Archief Amsterdam [GAA], Bibliotheek,

F Muys van Holy, N., Enveloppe 6; quoted in R. B. Evenhuis, *Ook dat was Amsterdam*, 5 vols. (Amsterdam: Ten Have, 1967), 4:246.

21. *Middelen en motiven om het kopen en verkopen van Oost- en West-Indische actien*, . . . [Knuttel 12622]; *Oplossing van de difficulteiten, die by eenige gemaakt werden tegens sekere Memoire behelsende middelen en motiven* (Amsterdam, 1687); *Relaes en Contradictie op de motiven, om het koopen en verkoopen van Oost- en West-Indische actien, te beswaaren met een Impost by de Heer N. M. v. H. Advocaat tot Amsterdam omwetend voorgestelt in [1687]* [Knuttel 12622a]. For a detailed discussion of Muys's arguments and the counterarguments in this debate, see M. F. J. Smith, *Tijd-Affaires in effecten aan de Amsterdamse Beurs* (The Hague: Martinus Nijhoff, 1919), 72–82.

22. *Spiegel der Waarheyd, Ofte t'Samensperkinge tusschen Een Armiaan ende Vroom Patriot, Waar inne krachtig vertoont ende bewesen word, dat door de quade directie ende toeleg van eenige Heerschende Regenten Tot Amsterdam, Ons Land in den voorgaanden, en desen Oorlog Is ingewickelt met Vrankryk* (1690) [Knuttel 13480]; *Vindiciae Amstelodamenses, of Contra-Spiegel der Waarheid. Vertoonende . . . eenige vlekken en gebreken van sommige Hollandsche en andere Provinciaale Bullebakken, welke gewoon zyn de Heeren Regenten van de Staad Amsterdam met leugenen en lasteringen te bekladden* (Amsterdam, 1690) [Knuttel 13484]; C. van de Haar, "Romeyn de Hooghe en de pamflettenstrijd van de jaren 1689 en 1690," *Tijdschrift voor geschiedenis* 69 (1956): 155–71; Ericus Walton, *Vervolgh Op het zeedige Ondersoeck Nae de Reedenen van de teeggenwoordige ongevallen in Englandt, etc. Waer in beweesen wordt, dat er niet alleen in de Provincie van Hollandt menschen woonen, die schuldig zyn aen de onlangs ontdekte Conspiratie in Engeland, tegen haere Majesteyten; maer dat oock heel waaerschijnlijck is, dat het gemelde Complot in dit Landt eerst is gebrowen. . . . Zynde hier by gevoegt eenige Reflectien op de Protestatie, of Verdeediginge des Aerts-Bisschops van Canterbury, en der andere Bisschopen, tegen het zeedig ondersoeck* (1690) [Knuttel 13552]. See also Israel, "Monarchy, Orangism, and Republicanism in the Later Dutch Golden Age."

23. *Memoire Dienende tot bewijs dat de Heer Mr. Dammas Gvldewagen Voor dese geweest Secretaris der Stadt Haerlem gequalificeert tot den ontfang von de 20ste, 40ste ende 80ste Penning, ende altans Raedt en Vroetschap der voorschreven Stadt, . . . de somme van [f]1553.11.8 by hem in syne eerstegeroerde qualityt voor den lande ontfangen, ter quader trouwe heeft verduystert* (n.p.: n.p., 1685) [Knuttel 12247a]; *Missive van Mr. Nicolaes Muys van Holy, advocaet, Aen Den Heere Arnoldo Mykens geweesen Directeur in Bengale, en althans Domheer tot Uitrecht [Utrecht]* (Amsterdam, 1701) [Knuttel 14638].

24. *De Navorscher* 7 (1857): 239–44 describes the case against Bleau (or Blaau) and her second husband. Muys's response to his sentence appeared as *Eisch en Conclusie van . . . Gerbrand Pancras Michielsz. Hooft-Officier der stad Amsterdam, Requirant in cas van Reauditie, tot Arbitraire Correctie van Mr. Nicolaes Muys van Holy, Gerequireerde; Met des zelfs Antwoord daar tegen, . . .* (Amsterdam: H. Bruyn, 1708), 3, 6–7; see also Muys's extensive testimony in GAA, 5061 [Rechterlijk archief], 358.

25. Wood, *The Creation of the American Republic*; Pocock, *The Machiavellian Moment*.

26. P. W. Klein, "The Trip Family in the Seventeenth Century: A Study of the Behaviour of the Entrepreneur on the Dutch Staple Market," *Acta historiae Neerlandica* 1 (1966): 188–95 (195). This is a brief version of his book on the Trip family, *De Trippen in*

de 17e eeuw: Een studie over het ondernemersgedrag op de Hollandse stapelmarkt (Assen: Van Gorcum, 1965).

27. W. Bilderdyk, *Geschiedenis des vaderlands* (Amsterdam: P. Meyer Warnars, 1832–53), 11:58.

28. See, for example, the pamphlets catalogued by Knuttel as numbers 16481–518. This list is by no means exhaustive.

29. Arthur H. Cole, *"The Great Mirror of Folly" ("Het Groote Tafereel der Dwasheid"): An Economic-Bibliographical Study* (Boston: Baker Library, 1949), 3–6.

30. "De Actionisten in 't Dolhuis, of de vereydelde Wind Negotie," in *Het Groote Tafereel der Dwaasheid.*

31. On Beuningen, see Hans Bontemantel, *De Regeringe van Amsterdam: soo in 't civiel als crimineel en militaire (1653–1672)* (The Hague: Nijhoff, 1897), 2:502–3. From the *klinkdicht* (sonnet) titled "Op den Windhandel" in *Het Groote Tafereel der Dwaasheid.*

32. *Vertooningen voor Arlequyn Actionist. Tienmaal verbeeld op den Amsterdamschen Schouwberg, tussen den 28sten October en den 23sten November 1720* in [Pieter Langendyk], *De Gedichten* (Haarlem: J. Bosch, 1721–60), 2:451.

33. Gijsbert Tijsens, *De Windhandel, of bubbles Compagnien, blyspel* ([Quinquenpoix, Amsterdam?]: [Bombario], 1720); idem, *De Bedriegelyke actionist, of de nagthandelaars* (Amsterdam: Hendrik Bosch, 1720).

34. See especially Hendrick van Halmael, *De zeedemeester en kantoorkneght, bedriegers: Blyspel* (Amsterdam: Engelbertus Solmans, 1707); *Crispyn, bedrieger, of de gewaande baron: Blyspel* (Amsterdam: Joannes de Wees, 1705); *Crispyn, boek- en kashouwer, bedrieger: Bly-spel* (Amsterdam: Engelbertus Solmans, 1706); *Crispyn, weezenplaag en bloedverzaaker, zeedenspel* (Amsterdam: Engelbertus Solmans, 1708); *Crispyn en Crispiaan, bedriegers of de gestraffte beurs en kelderplagen* (Amsterdam: Engelbertus Solmans, 1708); and *De Panlikker: Blyspel* (Amsterdam: Jan de Wees, 1704) (Crispyn is a character in this play).

35. Quote on "hokus-bokus" from *Twee Brieven De Eerste aan de Heer N. N. Tot Antwoord op de Brief van de Heer A. Z. En de tweede . . . van de Heer A. Z. aan de Heer N. N. . . .* (Amsterdam: Isaak Stokman, 1720) [Knuttel 16488], 10.

36. As described in Bontemantel, *De Regeringe van Amsterdam,* 2:488; also GAA, 5061, 640i–1.

37. "Eysch en Conclusie van den Heer Gerard Hastelaar Hoofd Officier, deses Stadt R: O:," January 16, 1670, in GAA, 5061, 640i.

38. *Memoire Instructyf, Met de Bylagen, In de zake van de Weduwe Jean Tourton, in zyn leven Koopman tot Amsterdam. Tegens Jean Henry Huguetan, Waer uyt kan gezien, het leven in bedryf van den vermaerden Jean Henry Huguetan, En de deugelykheyt van de pretensie, die de gemelte Weduwe tot zyn laste heeft* (n.p.: n.p., n.d. [1711]); in defense of Huguetan, see *Brief van de Heer T. D. M. aan een van zyn vrienden in 's Gravenhage, geschreven uit Nimweggen den 25 Maart 1711: Over de zaken van de Heer Huguetan, van Odyck, Drossart der Stadt en lande van Vianen, & C. uit 't Frans getranslateert* (The Hague: Gillis van Limburg, 1711); the original French edition of this pamphlet, *Lettre de Mr. T. D. M. à la Haye, écrite de Nimeque, le 25. De Mars 1711: Sur les affaires de Mr. Huguetan, d'Oodyk, Drossart de la Ville e pays de Vianen etc* (The Hague: Gillis van Limburg, 1711) [Knuttel 15979].

39. *Memoire Instructyf,* 1–2.

40. Ibid., 5; *Aanmerkingen op het versoeck, by lettren requisitoriaal van den Geregte van Geneve aan de Heeren van den Geregte der stad Utrecht gedaan, ten eynde het vonnis provisioneel, by denselven geregte, ter instantie van Jacques Butiny koopman etc. tegen Jean Henry Huguetan geweesen, door haar Ed. Achtb. Tegens den zelven Huguetan, zig althans tot Utrecht onthoudende, ter executie mag worden gelegt* (n.p.: n.p., n.d. [1705]) [Knuttel 15419].

41. *Brief van de Heer T. D. M.,* 7, 23; *Aanmerkingen op het versoeck.*

42. *Hamburg: Geschichte der Stadt und ihrer Bewohner,* vol. 1, *Von den Anfängen bis zur Reichsgründung,* ed. Hans-Dieter Loose (Hamburg: Hoffmann und Campe, 1982), 270–87; Hermann Rückleben, *Die Niederwerfung der hamburgischen Ratsgewalt: Kirchliche Bewegungen und bürgerliche Unruhen im ausgehenden 17. Jahrhundert* (Hamburg: Verein für Hamburgische Geschichte, 1970). On the meeting of the Bürgerschaft, see *The Flying Post From Paris and Amsterdam* (London, May 12–14, 1698): 469.

43. *Dero Königl. Majest. Zu Dännemarck Norwegen Gestalten Raths August Wygands Vortrab Der nach und nach von Ihm zu Vertheidigung seiner Ehre und Unschuld heraus zugebenden Schrifften,* . . . (n.p.: n.p., 1696) was the earliest public indication of a battle that went on for years and that played out in public pamphleteering. See the many pamphlets in Staatsarchiv Hamburg, Bibliothek, Sammelband 207 [Acta Hamburgensia, Lochau Sammlung].

Contributors

Anne J. Cruz is professor of Spanish and chair of the Department of Modern Languages and Literatures at the University of Miami. Her publications include *Discourses of Poverty: Social Reform and the Picaresque Novel in Early Modern Spain* (1999) and, as co-editor, *Disciplines on the Line: Feminist Research on Spanish, Latin American, and U.S. Latina Women* (2003). Her current research focuses on women writers of early modern Spain and on the politics of translation in early modern Europe.

Dyan Elliott is John Evans Professor of History at Northwestern University. Her publications include *Proving Woman: Female Spirituality and Inquisitional Culture in the Later Middle Ages* (2004) and *Fallen Bodies: Pollution, Sexuality, and Demonology in the Middle Ages* (1999). Her current research explores the tangible consequences of matrimonial metaphor.

Richard Firth Green is Distinguished Humanities Professor of English at The Ohio State University and director of the Center for Medieval and Renaissance Studies there. He is the author of *A Crisis of Truth: Literature and Law in Ricardian England* (1998) and is currently working on aspects of popular culture in late medieval England.

Anna Grotans is associate professor in the Department of Germanic Languages and Literatures at The Ohio State University. She is the author of *Reading in Medieval St. Gall* (2006). Her current research focuses on language attitudes and linguistic norms in the eastern Frankish Empire.

Barbara A. Hanawalt is The King George III Professor of British History at The Ohio State University. She has written books on medieval English crime, family, childhood, and gender. Her book *Wealth of Wives: Women, Law, and the Economy in Late Medieval London* is forthcoming in 2007. Her future work will be on dispute resolution in medieval London.

Mary Lindemann is professor in the Department of History at the University of Miami. Her most recent book, *Liaisons dangereuses: Sex, Law, and Diplomacy in the Age of Frederick the Great,* appeared in 2006. She is currently writing a comparative history of political culture in three early modern cities: Amsterdam, Antwerp, and Hamburg.

Ian Frederick Moulton is associate professor of English in the Division of Humanities and Arts at Arizona State University. He is the author of *Before Pornography: Erotic Writing in Early Modern England* (2000) and editor and translator of Antonio Vignali's *La Cazzaria,* an erotic political dialogue from Renaissance Italy (2003). His current research is focused on love and the dialogue tradition in sixteenth-century Italy, France, and England.

Vickie Ziegler is professor of German and medieval studies at Pennsylavia State University. Her most recent publication is *Trial by Fire and Battle in Medieval German Literature* (2004). She is currently working on a book on dispute settlement in late medieval German literature.

Index

3 5282 00642 1518